Succeeding with Autism

of related interest

Succeeding in College with Asperger Syndrome
A student guide
John Harpur, Maria Lawlor and Michael Fitzgerald
ISBN 1 84310 201 3

Asperger's Syndrome
A Guide for Parents and Professionals
Tony Attwood
Foreword by Lorna Wing
ISBN 1 85302 577 1

Making Sense of the Unfeasible
My Life Journey with Asperger Syndrome
Marc Fleisher
ISBN 1 84310 165 3

Understanding Autism Spectrum Disorders
Frequently Asked Questions
Diane Yapko
ISBN 1 84310 756 2

Pretending to be Normal
Living with Asperger's Syndrome
Liane Holliday Willey
Foreword by Tony Attwood
ISBN 1 85302 749 9

Freaks, Geeks and Asperger Syndrome
A User Guide to Adolescence
Luke Jackson
Foreword by Tony Attwood
ISBN 1 84310 098 3
Winner of the NASEN & TES Special Educational Needs Children's Book Award 2003

Succeeding with Autism

Hear my Voice

Judith H. Cohen

Foreword by Temple Grandin

Jessica Kingsley Publishers
London and Philadelphia

First published in 2005
by Jessica Kingsley Publishers
116 Pentonville Road
London N1 9JB, UK
and
400 Market Street, Suite 400
Philadelphia, PA 19106, USA

www.jkp.com

Copyright © Judith H. Cohen 2005
Foreword © Temple Grandin 2005

Library of Congress Cataloging in Publication Data
Cohen, Judith H.
  Succeeding with autism : hear my voice / Judith H. Cohen.
    p. cm.
  ISBN-13: 978-1-84310-793-4 (pbk.)
  ISBN-10: 1-84310-793-7 (pbk.)
  1. Autism. 2. Autism--Patients--Biography. I. Title.
  RC553.A88C64 2005
  616.85'882'0092--dc22

                                          2004028472

British Library Cataloguing in Publication Data
A CIP catalogue record for this book is available from the British Library

ISBN-13: 978 1 84310 793 4
ISBN-10: 1 84310 793 7

Printed and Bound in Great Britain by
Athenaeum Press, Gateshead, Tyne and Wear

This book is dedicated to those individuals for whom the term "autism" has profound and personal significance.
I hope that Michael's story will provide others with the belief that an individual with a diagnosis of autism can have a productive and fulfilling life. While Michael is among a select group of individuals who has succeeded so well with autism, I believe that many others will follow in his path.

Contents

Foreword

The story of Michael is a positive story of an autistic boy with a great talent in math, getting a master's degree in math, and starting a career teaching math. This book will provide insights into helping a person with autism make a successful transition from the world of school to the world of work. Michael was brilliant in math and his college professors recognized this. This is why it is so important to develop a child's talent. Too often in special education there is too much emphasis on the deficits and not enough emphasis on the things a person can become good at.

People on the autism spectrum have uneven skills. They may be good at one academic subject and bad at another. In my case I excelled at visual thinking and I used my visual skills in my career designing livestock handling systems. I was terrible at math, and algebra was impossible. One mistake in my math education was not allowing me to try geometry or trigonometry because I could not do algebra. These would have been easier because they are more visual.

The book also talks about professors who mentored Michael and encouraged him. He and I were similar in that we were both sloppy dressers until a mentor who cared about us made us change.

I have observed that there are four factors which help make a bright person with autism or Asperger's successful.

1. Developing talents in the area where the person's skills are strong.

2. Mentors who help nurture talents and provide guidance in social skills.

3.   The individuals who need medication are willing to take it.

4.   To make up for being a social misfit they show a portfolio of their skills. Michael had his high test scores and I showed people my drawings and blueprints. People respect talent and I used my portfolio to get design jobs.

For this foreword I interviewed Michael. He is now employed as a math teacher teaching students aged 12 to 15. He lost his first job because the boss did not like him, but now he has a boss who appreciates him. For a child who did not learn to speak until he was five, he has come a long way.

This book will help parents and teachers help other bright children with autism become successful. I could relate to many of the things that Michael experienced.

Dr. Temple Grandin

Acknowledgements

Although this work focuses on the voice of one individual, Michael, it could not have been accomplished without the voices of many. Michael's family—his mother, father, brother, uncle, and grandparents—all were especially generous in sharing their time, memories, and insights. Reviewing Michael's life was often not easy, because it required revisiting difficult times. However, memories of the difficult times were balanced by very dear thoughts of the many good times.

Michael's mother, with whom I initiated this project, deserves a very special tribute. We both had aspirations that Michael's story would provide information and inspiration to other autistic individuals and their families. Michael's mother contributed detailed information and poignant memories over many, many, interview sessions. Reliving Michael's life was a complex journey for her, but today she takes great satisfaction in seeing her son's successful adult life.

Many professionals have known Michael through the years and all were eager to talk about him and shared vivid recollections. I especially appreciate the administrators, professional staff, and faculty at the preschool, elementary school, and high school that Michael attended. The individuals from these schools who participated in this project take special pleasure in learning about the fine person that Michael is today. His success confirms their enduring belief in him and their expectations that he could succeed admirably. College faculty and administrators, Michael's mentor teachers, and his many friends were also extremely cooperative and helped with information and reflections that provided a full picture of Michael at important times.

Other professionals, especially Michael's psychiatrist, Dr. B., were especially essential contributors, because their expert insights help us more fully understand Michael and the complex life of an autistic individual. My book agent, Kathi Paton, and Jessica Kingsley, Sandra Patruno and other staff have all been supportive in making the idea for this book a reality.

Of course, there are many others to acknowledge. I am blessed with friendships that extend beyond the usual boundaries of helpfulness, and many dear people assisted by providing encouragement and thoughtful feedback. A friend and former student, Jane, read early drafts with a critical and educated eye and her help is greatly appreciated. My husband, Stuart, who is a psychologist, was a very insightful and supportive reader who helped me articulate ideas in a manner that makes them clear and truthful. My son, Robert, is a wonderful editor who helped me stay focused on essentials. And I am grateful for the other members of my family, who are always interested and encouraging!

I want to thank Dr. Temple Grandin, who has graciously contributed to this book by writing the foreword. Dr. Grandin has been widely celebrated for her work in animal behavior and has educated us all about the challenges of autism. With Dr. Grandin's clear voice, insights, and candor she continues to be an inspiration by reminding us of the possibility that all children can succeed.

The final and most important tribute goes to Michael, for whom parts of this process were painful and sad, while other parts consumed us with laughter. Michael's wit and wisdom made this a very enjoyable and productive collaboration. Bagels (always with cream cheese), pizza, and diet soda kept us going over many sessions reliving and reflecting about Michael's extraordinary life. Michael's memory for exact detail was always an inspiration and provided the factual honesty that was essential. Michael gave of his time without reservation and opened all parts of his life to examination. His courage and determination must be applauded! He is a truly remarkable person.

A Note on the Text

In this book the subject, his family, friends, allied professionals, and schools have all been given pseudonyms to meet the subject's desire for anonymity. However, all events, details, and information are fully accurate and truthful based on the recollection of those involved and supporting documentation.

Chapter 1

Meeting Michael

The first meeting

A curious sight struck me. I saw two people standing outside my office. One was a heavy-set young man walking in circles and next to him was a mature woman leaning against the wall. They didn't seem to be communicating with each other, but I assumed that they were a prospective student and his mother who had an appointment with me. The fellow continued to pace in circles with his head down. I thought the behavior of the young man very unusual for a student finishing high school and applying for college. I rushed down the hall, as I hate to be late, and greeted the two. They walked with me into my office and sat across from each other at a small, round, conference table. I obviously didn't know that this first meeting would result in a long and close relationship between all of us, and would also begin a story that would forever change my views about autism.

I vividly remember this first meeting with Michael and his mother. It was a winter day and an especially gloomy late afternoon. At that time Michael was a high school senior who applied for admission into the next year's freshman class of a teacher preparation program that I coordinated. The meeting was arranged because Michael wanted to be a secondary math teacher and needed to be interviewed for this special program. The colleague who usually interviewed students interested in secondary education noticed from Michael's papers that he and I lived in the same community and thought it might be helpful for me to interview a community neighbor. She also asked me to review his credentials carefully, because she was unfamiliar with the high school he attended, but remarked on the very high Scholastic Aptitude Test (SAT) scores that were part of the academic record. (These tests are typically required as part of a college application.) She assumed that his school was a private "prep" school, as it clearly wasn't the public high school that most students in his community attend.

When I reviewed Michael's high school transcript, I immediately recognized that what my colleague thought was a "prep" school was actually a special education high school for students with severe disabilities. In addition to my university position, I'm also a lawyer who works as a child advocate and I have considerable knowledge about special school placements for disabled students. I knew that the community in which Michael and I lived would not have placed a student in this out of district, special education setting, if he could have been educated in the local high school with support services. This led me to believe that Michael had a significant disability, and the unusual behavior I first observed confirmed what I suspected.

While mainstreaming handicapped students into regular school settings was the law when Michael was a child, the impetus to include special education students in the least restrictive environment hadn't really taken full effect. Therefore, it wasn't unusual for some students with special needs to be sent to programs outside the local school district. Most of these students were placed in state supported programs offered by the Board of Cooperative Education Services (BOCES). (BOCES is similar to a school district without boundaries, because it educates students with special needs in a variety of programs all throughout the state.) The fact that Michael did not attend a BOCES school, but instead went to an even more specialized school, sent up a "red flag." This indicated to me that Michael's special needs were different from those customarily seen and required a school setting above and beyond a typical special education program.

Early speculation

After reviewing Michael's academic record on paper I had many questions about him and was eager to meet him and learn more. I speculated about what Michael's disability might be—one that warranted the very special school placement. To be eligible for special education services, students need to go through a rigorous process that results in a decision about whether or not they qualify. The process results in a diagnosis and the disability categories are defined by federal and state law. The vast majority of diagnosed special education students are learning disabled (LD), which in simple terms means that they have more difficulty processing information (organization, storage, and retrieval, etc.) and, among other things, usually have problems with advanced reading and writing skills. Learning disabled people are often highly intelligent and the definition itself precludes the diagnosis from being used with children of less than average ability. But I was also aware that LD students can have a great deal of difficulty performing on standardized tests even with special accommodations. Consequently the very high SAT scores that Michael attained seemed to rule out an LD diagnosis. Also most LD students wouldn't have attended the school that Michael did, because their needs could be met in their local school district with support services.

I suspected that Michael's special education diagnosis might be "emotionally disturbed," but again, many of these students don't achieve at the highest levels on standardized tests and, unlike Michael, often have erratic school performance. This is not because of their lack of ability or their intelligence, but poor school performance is often due to oppositional behavior and inability to maintain the kind of focus needed to get high scores on demanding tests. To be educated in a self-contained special education high school with a diagnosis of emotional disturbance also indicates that the student has a severe behavior problem. Emotionally disturbed students, especially during adolescence, can be aggressive, defiant, and anti-social. They often have trouble with academics.

Another possibility was that Michael might be a "fragile" emotionally disturbed student with a history of severe withdrawal or suicidal tendencies. This is what I supposed was likely to be Michael's profile.

Michael's high school transcript showed that he had very high grades. Being a realist, I know that special education students frequently receive good grades even with less than average performance if they work on their assignments, have good attendance and, especially, if they behave. Consequently, Michael's strong academic record wasn't very compelling, except that he had also attended a science class in a regular public high school and this grade was high. Students who attend Michael's special school often struggle with academics and don't take advanced math and science courses that others take as part of a strong high school program. Given the nature of these students' disabilities, high academic achievement in advanced courses is rarely the norm.

What clearly stood out and surprised me were the very high SAT scores that Michael received. The combined subtest scores in verbal and math achievement were 1390 (630 verbal and 760 math) out of a possible score of 1600, which is very high for any student. Unlike grades from class work these scores on a standardized, objective, test couldn't be the result of just behaving well in class! Regardless of how many criticize the SAT exams and complain about their lack of relevance to actual school curriculum, these tests are an independent barometer of a student's verbal and math achievement. SAT scores can be a more objective and reliable indicator of academic ability than school grades, especially when the local standards of the applicants' high schools aren't known. Grades can also be influenced by behavior, attitude, and teacher bias.

Michael's SAT scores were so high that along with his very strong high school record he was also eligible for the honors college, which required a separate admissions interview with the dean. If Michael were accepted into the honors college, he would receive a substantial scholarship to the university. There was certainly great pressure for Michael to do well in the interview with the dean.

I expected that when I met Michael, he would appear to be a withdrawn, emotionally disturbed, fragile young man, who had superior academic ability, but needed a special setting in order to succeed. I therefore would approach the interview with Michael with a set of questions different from those that I asked others to help determine if he was appropriate for the teacher education program given his special education diagnosis and needs.

Interviews for applicants for this program were conducted while the students were high school seniors and I was accustomed to students being accompanied by either a parent or friend. As new drivers or non-drivers, they often needed assistance getting to the university for a late afternoon or evening appointment. Some parents are especially involved in their child's choice of college and want to be included. The interviews are almost always upbeat. I am always sure to compliment the students on their accomplishments, grades, after-school service, or desire to be a teacher, and tell them if they hadn't been strong candidates, they wouldn't have been called for an interview at all. This usually takes the edge off the meeting. I also assure the students that the interview is really a "getting to know you" session so that I can answer all of their (and often their parents') questions about the program and help them decide if this is the right choice for them. The interviews work well. The students generally feel that all their questions are answered and there is a real person attached to the name of a faculty member at the university they are interested in attending.

The program that Michael applied to enter was a small and competitive five-year combined undergraduate and graduate degree program for students interested in becoming either elementary or secondary teachers. The program required a five-year, full time commitment. Students chose a liberal arts major for their undergraduate education and then completed teacher certification in the fifth year, while they earned a master's degree. All students who applied for the program were interviewed in order to select candidates who had a strong career orientation as well as the academic skills needed for the intense five-year program.

Michael's interview wasn't going to be "business as usual." I doubted whether the program would be compatible with his educational needs or even appropriate for a disabled student, given the very demanding nature of a teaching career. The university also had a program for learning disabled students, who were provided both the academic and the psychological support needed to transition from high school into college. This specialized program worked so well in providing the needed support, that I thought it might be a more appropriate choice for Michael, if he chose to come to our university. I doubted if a special education student, even a very intelligent one, educated in small, sheltered programs, could do well in a moderately sized university without appropriate academic and emotional support.

The interview

During the interview Michael sat to my right and his mother sat to my left at a small, round table in my overcrowded office. Michael rarely made eye contact. He was fidgety, very awkward and looked kind of sloppy with an unstylish haircut and choice of clothes. His shirt wouldn't stay tucked into his pants. His mother was a small woman with reddish hair, who told me that she was a nurse. She was friendly, but was obviously tense and very concerned.

This is not unusual. Parents at these interviews can have a hard time separating from their children and are unsure how much to interject their thoughts and comments into the conversation. Usually, if a student is talkative and strong, the parents take a back seat and only join in with questions about such topics as tuition costs, scholarships, and career options. I've always tried to focus the interview on the students and get them to feel that they are truly the main area of interest. Only in a few cases have I chosen to interview a student without a parent present, when they seemed particularly shy or subdued because of the parent's presence, and sometimes the student decides that the parent should not be present for the whole interview at all.

During our time together, Michael continually blew his nose and made funny noises trying to clear it. I offered him a tissue from a box I always keep handy and he proceeded to take one tissue after another and was on his way towards emptying the box, when I stopped him. I asked Michael, "Besides being OCD [obsessive-compulsive disordered], what's your special education diagnosis?" The conversation stopped. There was silence. Silence continued with looks back and forth between mother and son.

To break the silence I said, "You don't know me, but I want to tell you that besides being a professor I'm also an attorney, who advocates for special education students. Legally, I can't discriminate against you because of a special education diagnosis, and morally I wouldn't do so. But I know that you went to a special education high school, and I need to know what your diagnosis is to see if this program is right for you."

Michael and his mother made eye contact, and finally Michael's mother said to him that it was okay to tell me. Michael said in a soft voice with eyes downcast, "I'm autistic."

I was totally unprepared for this and I frankly couldn't believe what he said. As an educator I thought I knew a great deal about autism and had the same stereotype that most do when the term is used. Autism to me meant a low-functioning, very aberrant individual sitting by him or herself, rocking back and forth, and not relating to others. I also knew about the category of individuals that some have described as being high-functioning autistic and those who have reportedly "outgrown" or been "cured" through intensive efforts and very special and unusual treatment regimens. I've always been skeptical of "miracle" cures, especially with severely impaired children, but know that others have written testimonials about diets and other approaches, including "hug" therapy, that worked for their children. The desperation of parents to "fix" their autistic children is so poignant and understandable. To me, an autistic child was one likely to function at low or borderline levels.

In more recent times there have been accounts of adult autistic individuals who live with their parents or in group homes and struggle to maintain simple jobs and social relationships. I had read a book by a British woman, who claimed to have been autistic, but who married and worked in an office. Her story struck me as a case of misdiagnosis in early childhood rather than as a recovery from autism. I thought that she might have had severe emotional disturbance that mimicked autistic-like symptoms.

I knew of another individual, Temple Grandin, an animal behaviorist with a doctoral degree and a diagnosis of autism, who appeared on television and wrote about herself in several books. Her story was also repeated in a well-known book written by a neurologist, who described individuals with very unusual conditions. Grandin made a strong case that not all autistic individuals are low-functioning or confined to lives as bleak as one might imagine. Temple Grandin is a very unusual individual, who is well-known and distinguished in the field of animal behavior, and says that like cattle she thinks in pictures. She is very candid about the challenges of her autism and even reveals that at times she needs to be enveloped in a special apparatus when she feels over-stimulated by her environment.

Michael was different—an academically successful student with a diagnosis of autism! At that time, I clearly couldn't appreciate just how different Michael is. I was still very skeptical about the accuracy of his diagnosis. I speculated that perhaps Michael had been misdiagnosed. As far as I knew, this young man functioned at unheard of academic levels in both verbal and math skills for an individual with autism.

Many are familiar with the precocity of autistic individuals in mathematics. Dustin Hoffman's portrayal in the movie *Rain Man* created a clear picture of the mathematical "genius" of an autistic person. The character could spontaneously use the most complicated mathematical operations to get astoundingly immediate and correct results to difficult math problems. Ironically, he couldn't perform even the simplest math operations for daily living, such as making change. So Michael's superb math skills didn't challenge the stereotype of autistic individuals with great math ability. However, the verbal skills of autistic individuals are one of their greatest challenges as their ability to relate, converse, and "connect" to others goes to the very center of what autism is all about. I was struck by the unexpectedly high verbal score on the SAT exam, if Michael was truly autistic.

The interview proceeded with a capsule history of Michael's diagnosis of autism in early childhood by specialists at well-recognized hospitals and his education in self-contained special education settings. There was a brief discussion about Michael being given the option of being mainstreamed into a regular school toward the end of his high school years. However, because he had been so successful in the special education setting, his family thought that it wasn't wise to risk a change in placement. The college experience would be the very first time that Michael would be educated in a regular school setting!

Throughout the interview Michael gave brief answers to my questions and rarely elaborated, choosing to stick to the facts when he replied. He told me that he was accepted into the university's honors college, and that his disability had not been recognized during that process. In fact, no one at the university was aware of his special background, including the dean of the honors college. I subsequently found out that of the five colleges that Michael applied to and was accepted at no one was aware that he had always been a special education student. It seems that college faculty or admissions staff are not familiar with special education schools and there would have been no indication of Michael's special learning needs on his high school transcript. Michael sailed through the admissions process without any need to reveal his special education background.

Michael's answer to my question about why he wanted to be a teacher was especially revealing. He told me that teachers had always been his heroes and that he wanted to expose others to the beauty of math. How could any teacher educator resist that answer? Also, as I've learned more about Michael, I've begun to appreciate the attraction that math holds for him. Michael desires certainty in an unpredictable world and he derives great satisfaction from mathematics being exact and something he can always rely on. I've also learned about the importance of schools and teachers in his life. Teachers were the people who recognized him for his strengths and were valued as trusted friends, when he didn't have peers with whom he was comfortable. The world of schools was a place that was dear to him and trustworthy. No wonder he wanted to be a math teacher.

I shared my concern with Michael and his mother that Michael would likely have a great challenge ahead of him adjusting to the college environment, even at a college only about fifteen miles from his home. I also told them that I would not prevent his admission into the teacher education program, but that I was concerned about the appropriateness of his desire to be a secondary math teacher, and wondered if it was realistic. I told him that his entry into this teacher education program would be a two-way decision process: his decision (along with that of his family), as well as the decision of the college faculty. Although Michael's disability wouldn't prevent his acceptance into the program, as with all students his progress would be monitored for continuation into advanced courses.

The interview concluded with some small talk about the coincidence of living only three blocks apart and sharing similar community and cultural experiences. There was also discussion about how Michael would get back and forth to the college. He wasn't able to drive a car and poor public transportation in this suburban area turned a 20-minute car trip into a 1½ to 2-hour trip on two buses concluding with a college shuttle bus or long walk. Michael's mother assured me that transportation was the least of their concerns and that Michael was very successful using public transportation.

Michael was on his way to beginning at our college, and joining the five-year teacher preparation program. Given that he was accepted with a substantial scholarship for the honors college, it seemed likely that this university would be his first choice. His mother also seemed to feel that the atmosphere at this college was friendlier and more accommodating than the others they visited, and she was particularly impressed by the two personal interviews Michael had and the interest taken in him. Michael's mother later told me that she has always believed that someone watches over her son and that it was destined that he and I would meet.

Thus began my relationship with Michael, his mother, and ultimately with his entire family, and the circle of educators and medical professionals who know him. The journey at this college continued through four years of undergraduate education with Michael successfully completing a major in math and minors in computer science and secondary education.

Success, Michael-style

By his own choice, Michael didn't complete the five years of the special program at the university. One January morning during his senior year, Michael woke up and his inner voice told him that he should student teach and graduate instead of waiting to complete the fifth year and the master's degree. He decided to student teach that spring and do his graduate work at another college. Michael told me that he felt that he had "outgrown" this college and wanted a rigorous graduate education with more sophisticated peers, but still wanted to get his teaching certificate as soon as possible, to enter the profession sooner, find employment, and be able to finance graduate school.

This change necessitated a switch from the special five-year program into the traditional four-year program. The faculty cooperated and Michael's schedule for his last semester was changed, although the deadline for student teaching applications was long past. It seems that each educator Michael has known has wanted to help Michael achieve his goals, and this college faculty and staff were no different. One of the most interesting things about Michael is his engaging personality and endearing, seemingly guileless manner. These qualities help people connect with Michael and lead to their support for him.

Michael graduated from the undergraduate program with honors and awards from both the math/computer science and education departments, because of his excellent grades and exemplary service to both departments. At graduation time his academic success story was profiled in a local newspaper, which focused on several students' unique experiences at local colleges. At the time of writing this introduction, Michael is employed full time as a secondary math teacher in a small, private school and has completed a master's degree in math education at a competitive branch of the state university.

I recently told Michael that I was writing about the first time that he and I met, for the first chapter of this book. I asked what he remembered about the interview. I fully expected Michael to relate concern about revealing his autism to me, but this wasn't the case at all. In typical Michael fashion he remembered the month, date, day of the week, and time of day that the interview occurred. He also remembered the weather that day. He denied being nervous about the interview, embarrassed or concerned about discussing his special education diagnosis and school history.

After probing, Michael admitted that he was concerned about entering college, because of the academic challenges he would encounter. He was aware that his high school experience was different from other students entering college. He also knew that the standards in his high school were less demanding and he was concerned about how he would do in college. Subsequently, Michael did say that his freshman year in the honors college was very difficult academically. He learned that his high school curriculum was significantly different from others and he had lots of learning "gaps" to make up. The freshman year in college was different from any of Michael's prior academic experiences, where success came easily and naturally.

I spoke to Michael about fears he might have had fitting into the world of a college student in an environment that was both unfamiliar and far more complex than he was used to. After some thought, Michael replied that fitting in wasn't his worry, because he always felt like an outsider, and this continued in college. He said that he hadn't worried about beginning school, but was concerned once school started, because of the strenuous academic demands of the honors college and because he felt so different from other students.

How can those of us who aren't autistic understand just how different the life of an autistic individual is? The chapters that follow will provide information and insights about Michael's life, his struggles and his successes.

Chapter 2

So this is College—A Regular School with Regular People

Beginning college

The following is taken from a profile of Michael that was part of a feature about college graduates in *Newsday*, a suburban newspaper.

Celebrating New Beginnings

May 20, 2002

When he was 5, Michael couldn't speak. Now 22, he still struggles—sometimes his mouth moves but the words do not come. "It's hard to focus," he said. "Sometimes I say hello to people and I forget to use my voice."

Diagnosed with autism…Michael was never expected to thrive academically and was placed in special education schools from kindergarten to 12th grade. Yesterday, with a 3.69 grade point average and an award for excellence in mathematics, he was among 2,047 graduates [at this] university.

The mathematics major—who told of struggling to make friends and occasional professors who either didn't know or understand his illness—plans to teach high school after receiving his master's degree from [a branch of the] State University of New York. [He chose secondary teaching because] "That's when I think kids change."

The first day in college

The first day that Michael started his college experience was the first time he attended a school where no one knew he was autistic. It was the first time he thought that he could be like everyone else.

What do you remember about starting college?

Michael: I don't really remember that much about the first day at college. A sense of *wow!*—going to the first class—the first day. Because I couldn't drive, my mother would drop me off in the morning and my father would pick me up at the end of the day. I had a three-day schedule so it worked out okay in terms of getting back and forth.

Were you nervous?

Michael: I wasn't nervous at first, but as the semester went on I became nervous. There were lots of gaps—the academics—I was very good in math, but I didn't know lots of the basic things in other subjects.

How about social concerns?

Michael: The first year I was very busy with a lot to focus on—keeping up with school work, working at the drug store part time—it was a lot of work. I worried about academics. It was rough the first year in the honors college; classes were hard. I was very quiet and very focused on the academics. I didn't worry about college until I got there, but once there, at college, I felt on the outside.

Michael was admitted into the university's honors college because of his outstanding high school record, his very high SAT scores, and a favorable interview with the honors college dean. The dean of the honors college interviews many applicants, but he has a distinct memory of the interview with Michael:

Dean G: He was *very* different from others. I would not have guessed autism. But he was clearly wound very tight. If describing him to someone then, I would have said he was physically somewhat stiff. But the thing that leapt out was what I took for a rather high level of anxiety that generated a huge need for order and control. I've never had an applicant who had so many questions and such anxious questions. There was a huge need for specific, detailed information. So I answered all his questions.

I'd take all like him I could find!

Admission into this competitive program meant receiving a scholarship for full tuition for undergraduate studies. Financial concerns were a decisive factor in the choice of colleges for Michael, who had applied to and was accepted by five local colleges. After visiting the schools, Michael found that a couple were too small and at least one seemed too large and it also required a commute into the city.

Michael: Getting into the honors college made me feel sort of smart and after the interview with the honors college dean I decided to choose this school.

According to Shari, Michael's mother, she was convinced that this school was right for Michael and it was only a 20-minute drive from home. People seemed especially interested in him and took the time to meet with him individually. The campus was beautiful and everyone seemed friendly. The large scholarship was an important incentive, because it made it possible to send Michael to a private college without financial hardship for the family. Shari knew that Michael had done well academically in high school, but in the past he had only attended very small, special schools where everyone knew about his disability and treated him with sensitivity and a keen awareness of his special needs.

The college experience was certainly going to be different and she was concerned about how Michael would adjust. She remembered the first day that she sent him to preschool on a minibus with his crying and tantrums. He threw his shoes off and she gave them to the bus driver, who put Michael into his seat and fastened him in. She followed behind the minibus all the way to the school wiping away tears and later hid in the hallway to watch, when he had to be carried into the classroom, because of his refusal to cooperate.

Now he was starting college. When Shari left him at the campus, she realized just how far he had come, but didn't know what problems he'd encounter and how he would handle it all. When he was diagnosed with autism, the doctors had concerns about whether or not Michael would ever talk; who could have predicted that he would be admitted into a college honors program with a large scholarship?

Telling others about being autistic

Tell me about first hiding your diagnosis from others at the college and then why you decided to tell some people—professors and other students—that you are autistic.

Michael: The only reason I was hiding it when I applied to college was that I didn't want to get special services. Before I attended college, I had decided not to tell anyone, because I thought it was kind of unfair to get special accommodations—like untimed tests—that others weren't getting. Normal people don't get special treatment.

I don't mind telling people, but I like to tell people in my own way—I don't want headlines. It's how I am and that's how you are; and I don't play it down—it just *is*. I don't want to bring it up out of the blue; if I tell people, I want it to be relevant to the conversation or they would think it's weird that I'm talking about being autistic. I didn't want to make an announcement wherever I go. If it comes up, it comes up. The only place I'm fussy about not telling people is when I'm going for a job.

You did tell some faculty and students that you are autistic; tell me about it.

Michael: You knew that I was autistic, because we talked about it when you first interviewed me for the teacher education program. You were the only college person who knew that I had a special education background.

As discussed in Chapter 1 Michael's high school was listed on his academic transcript for college admission. I realized that it was a special education high school for students with severe education needs.

Michael: I did discuss being autistic in one biology class about genetics that I took freshman year, because it was relevant to the topic of a book we were required to read. Most of the other students were upper level and they had more background about most things, but I know more about autism than they did. One thing I realized that semester was that there were lots of gaps in my high school education and other students seemed to know about things that I had never heard of.

In Prof. R's class, we were reading a book about an autistic child, *Dibs: In Search of Self*. I think I told him outside of class that being autistic I found that book very interesting and he suggested that I mention it in class. He seemed in some sense to know that I'm autistic and because he said he's very interested in autism, it would be easier for him to notice it in me.

In class, I think I started by just answering a general question and then I took it in the direction of me being autistic. I think that I told the students that being autistic, I could describe some of the characteristics of an autistic person that were listed on a hand-out that was given out by the professor. I picked some of the traits and talked about myself. They were a little surprised.

Did that result in students treating you differently?

Michael: They were mostly older students. I think some might have understood me better, or it provided context for them, but they didn't treat me radically different. Like if someone broke a leg, you'd treat them differently or something. The majority of students were quite disinterested—the ones who never spoke to me before still never spoke to me after.

What was your emotional response to telling people in this class that you're autistic?

Michael: Part of me treated it as fact-based, science-based, and I just said it. I was a little worried about how people perceived it, but not overwhelmingly worried. I didn't let it seriously impact on me and I limited my concern to a fleeting thought, perhaps.

Prof. R, who taught the class: The course that I teach is entitled "Darwin to DNA" and it's a biology course for non-majors. As part of the curriculum we read *Dibs: In Search of Self* and discussed autism as an organic dysfunction. In that context we also did other readings about autism including the Oliver Sacks piece about Temple Grandin, "An Anthropologist on Mars."

In class one day Michael announced that he was autistic. I was interested, but not surprised. I had noticed other things about him before that. In lab class he really could not draw at all; he had good math reasoning, but there was something very different about him. He walked very awkwardly and he especially had a hard time with essay questions. He seemed to understand the material, but couldn't formulate his ideas into a coherent essay.

The students were interested and asked him lots of questions. Many students in the class didn't like him. He spoke in a brash voice and had very poor social skills. Michael did spend lots of time talking about his mother and he and I attributed much of his success in school to his mother's advocacy.

After Michael graduated from college, I arranged for him to meet Temple Grandin at a book signing before a lecture she gave at another local college. I had nominated Michael for an award given in her name to autistic individuals who have succeeded, and he was an award recipient. The meeting and the lecture were one of the first opportunities Michael has had to connect with other autistic people and learn how they manage their lives. He has always believed that there is no one else like him. When he met Dr. Grandin, Michael was in awe of her, knowing her "celebrity" status in the world of autism, and was enthralled by her candor. He deeply appreciated much of what she had to say and identified with the issues she raised.

Rosemarie is a college friend of Michael's, who was also in the honors college and education programs, and took Prof. R's class as well during a different semester.

Rosemarie: I first met Michael when we were both freshmen. I wanted to start an education club for future teachers and he became very interested and contacted me. From that time on we've been good friends. I never met someone like Michael before and he never met someone like me. I come from a very small town and my family is originally from El Salvador. We had many long conversations about culture and religion, and I never had been a friend with someone like him.

We were both freshmen in the honors college, and were both interested in being teachers, so we did have many classes together and had some things in common. It was a new experience for both us. We'd talk endlessly: e-mails, phone calls, after class, and I learned a lot about Michael, but also about myself. I was concerned about whether people would understand my beliefs, and Michael was so interested in me and my background.

I'm also a very serious student and really understood that Michael wanted to learn so much just as I did. I'm in college to study, not party, and I'm an intense person too. I don't understand why others don't value education as I do, especially with the amount of money paid for school. We were both on scholarship so getting high grades was also important to maintain the financial support. My first impression of Michael was that he was very focused, very passionate about learning everything, and especially about getting to know people, but not on a superficial level. He was very meticulous, so tuned into the details of things.

I asked Rosemarie if being a prospective teacher provided any insight about Michael's special education background.

Rosemarie: No, I honestly just noticed his attention to details. He was very unique and he did stand out, but in the beginning I wouldn't classify him, but he was distinctive!

When did you learn that Michael is autistic?

Rosemarie: At the end of my sophomore year I was taking a science course and reading about an autistic child. Michael and I took the same course—Darwin to DNA—at different times. I found the book very interesting and told him about it; and he just told me his story. I gained a greater interest and a more profound respect for him.

I believe that every person has an obstacle in their life and Michael told me about his socialization problem and how he was able to overcome that and go from a small school setting with 8 to 9 students in a class to a college setting with 30 or more students. He was always trying to have people understand him and he was trying to understand people at the same time.

Did you see a pattern of behavior in Michael after learning more about autism and finding out that he is autistic?

Rosemarie: Yes, his gait, the way he walks; very competitive behavior; and he would be so much more focused than everyone else. But all this didn't change my perception of him for any negative reason. I thought even more positively of him and I thought his being autistic was extraordinary.

Do you think your friendship became more than just being friends?

Rosemarie: No, it wasn't a boyfriend–girlfriend relationship, but we were very close friends and still are now and we did spend a lot of time together.

A problem with this friendship developed in the junior year when Michael's behavior began to deteriorate and he became obsessive with Rosemarie. This will be discussed later under social issues at college and his problems in the junior year.

Confronting a special education history

Michael had a painful episode in one education class when the assignment was to have the students write their autobiography, focusing on how their schooling impacted on their views about education.

Rosemarie: In the third year, we both took a class on curriculum and teaching. We were given the assignment of writing an education autobiography and I think it was called a curriculum confession. It was a two-step process. You had to state your philosophy of education and describe your own educational experience to look both at the positives and negatives and then describe how you saw yourself in the education field. It was a very difficult assignment and had to do with lots of soul searching about why you want to be a teacher. You had to pinpoint those key moments in your life to figure out why you want to be a teacher.

I asked Michael why he wanted to be a teacher and he told me it was something that he was used to. I think he meant going to school and he knew he wanted to be a teacher for many years. His school experience was so completely different from most students entering the teaching field and he had to confront his personal history, both positive and negative parts.

Michael, about the assignment: Somehow I think she [the professor] knew ahead of time about me, but I am not sure why. I know I had trouble about the writing of the paper—there were some things I didn't want to look back on and deal with. I have no real memory of the problem with the assignment now.

Why don't you remember?

Michael: There's an element of both not remembering and not wanting to remember—that's a real autistic answer: not wanting to distinguish.

But the assignment made me realize I never had a school experience that the others had. It made me feel more different. I went to a different kind of school. When I went to college it was great—a regular school with regular people and before that time I never looked back and realized that these other people in college did "this and that" and I didn't.

Do you feel that your special ed background is a stigma?

Michael: Somewhat. That's how society is—being a certain color is a stigma, having a certain amount of money is a stigma. I guess in some way I missed those experiences that the other kids had and it was all contained in that.

Do you ever feel inadequate or that there's something wrong with you?

Michael: Yes. I did at that time in that setting.

And now?

Michael: I don't know. I'll always feel that way, but it's not manifest. I'll always have that thought in my mind.

The assignment made me very sad. I had trouble understanding what I was supposed to write and I went to see the professor several times. I handed in the assignment fairly early and she wanted changes. I had trouble making changes in my paper—I just couldn't do it right. I cried in front of her. She tried to convince me that I'm a worthwhile person and not to get really concerned about the assignment.

Did it change your opinion of yourself? I have the impression that you have a strong opinion about yourself.

Michael: Some parts are positive and some are negative. Yeah, I know that I'm intelligent and my morals are correct.

Did the professor respond differently to you once she found out that you're autistic and you had always gone to special education schools?

Michael: No, she interacted with everyone very individually, especially when we were alone in her office. I don't think she got anything in the papers from other students that was abnormal; people tended to put very little into the assignment. People seem surprised when they find out I'm autistic; it compromises what they believe to be true.

Prof. Q, who taught the class: He was reticent about writing autobiographically, even about opening up to me about his history, but then did so privately. We worked it out in a way such that Michael was comfortable revealing what he wished, while still being able to complete the assignment and meaningfully engage in a reflection on his own education and how it shaped his view of education and teaching. He wrote about his values and aspirations, which required him to integrate assumptions and consciously attend to weaknesses and strengths he now carries.

Michael, while adept in the realm of abstract ideas and intellectual questions, I think, was far less skilled in personal domains—talking about himself, sharing what he perceived as his vulnerabilities, inadequacies, weaknesses.

Michael was especially close to two professors in the math and computer science department. One was a senior individual who was shocked to learn of Michael's diagnosis even though they had an especially close relationship. Michael took several classes with this professor and both share a love of mathematics. One day I walked by an almost empty classroom. I noticed that Michael was sitting in the middle of the first row and Prof. M was at the board continuing to write mathematical notes that covered it. Michael sat in front of him, eyes wide open with full attention.

Prof. M of the math dept: You could have knocked me over with a feather when I learned that Michael is autistic. Of course, I have no special acquaintance with autistic children, but I always thought that these people weren't able to function very well in human relationships.

I never had any trouble getting on with Michael. He never seemed uncomfortable or awkward with me. He often spent time with me in my office and, one summer, we got together a few times on a voluntary basis to do some extra-curricular math. Michael smiled a lot. I suppose one might call that childlike, insofar as we adults go around with long faces a certain amount. I cannot believe that often being cheerful should be grounds for classifying someone as having a condition requiring concern. I am at a loss about what makes him classified as autistic.

Prof. M is a kind, gentle and almost stereotypic math professor, who cares little for appearances and dress. On the very cold day that I interviewed him he was wearing two pairs of socks and sneakers. He was not aware of or concerned about differences in Michael's behavior, manner, or dress, but rather focused more on Michael's brilliance in math and sincere desire to learn.

The other professor who was especially close with Michael was a computer science teacher in the math department and coincidentally has a young autistic son. Prof. S traces the roots of his son's disability to characteristics in himself as well as in other men in his family. He was especially tuned into Michael's disability, because of his intense and personal interest in autism.

> *Prof. S:* I first met Michael because of our involvement in a club. I saw him as a pleasant person and a little off the beaten path. He has a few trademark habits that make him stand out, but in computer science, you run into more than your share of people who have their own idiosyncrasies—so I didn't think twice about it. His distinctive characteristics are pauses in speech, being very clumsy (walking in with soda and spilling it over everything), someone who actually chose a seat up front in class, and questions that are so extraordinarily detailed.
>
> I'm not quiet that my son is high-functioning autistic, and one day Michael caught me here late and he came in and told me that he himself is high-functioning autistic. Autistic people know about the category. I know my IQ and we talked about that and I pulled up a Mensa web page. [Mensa is an organization for intellectually gifted individuals.] Michael was answering questions almost as quickly as I was. My son also knows Michael and Michael knows my son; Michael commented several times that my son is similar to the way he was at that age.
>
> With autism it's difficult; what people notice more than other things is the dysfunctions, not the strengths.

I was interested in other faculties' perceptions of Michael and because Michael insists that "math people" are different to begin with I interviewed another mathematician who taught Michael.

> *Prof. R, who taught secondary math education methods:* He's definitely someone who stands out. Initially when you don't know his background you might be put off a bit; but look into his face and listen to what he says and see that clearly he's not trying to manipulate and there's not an ulterior motive as with other students. He doesn't ask questions to waste class time. There's a genuineness that comes across. Yes, a couple of things became apparent right away: focus on very fine levels of detail in a math example and a sort of absoluteness. He had trouble making transitions.
>
> Other students in the class were aware of Michael and knew him from other classes. They anticipated those kinds of behaviors; that he would obsess.

Those faculty members who met Michael when he began college and later saw the kind of person he had become at the end of his undergraduate years, noted remarkable changes. Prof. F, a faculty member who has a low-functioning autistic son, was very involved with Michael when he was a contributor to the college newspaper, because she was the faculty advisor. She commented that even her husband remarked about the changes in Michael over the years, when he saw Michael at a farewell party for Prof. F. that students hosted.

> *Prof. F:* My husband remarked about how much more social Michael had become since he'd last seen him. He was talking to everyone, kind of helping to keep the party going. Who would have thought that Michael would become this more social and interactive young adult, when this awkward adolescent began his college career?

It is apparent that Michael's college experience had a profound impact on his growth and development—socially as well as intellectually.

Academics and extra-curricular activities

> *Prof. R, associate dean of the honors college:* We all wanted him to succeed, not merely because we were conscious of a handicap, but more so because his attitude about learning, his desire to understand, was so sweetly and evidently palpable. I came to like him a lot, and I know he felt that I was on his side.

A substantial part of Michael's sense-of-self revolves around his tremendous success as a student. His love of learning, his ability to teach himself, his talent in mathematics, and his keen ability to focus all had contributed to excellent achievement in high school. The college experience, however, was something that challenged his talents and ability in an environment where for the first time he was being compared with other intelligent and achievement-oriented students in a regular school setting.

An autistic student in the honors college

Michael was admitted to the honors college, which meant that his curriculum was different and more demanding than that of the general student population at the college. At that time, honors college students were given a very substantial scholarship and there was a requirement that they maintain high grade point averages to continue in good standing. Honors college students had smaller classes and got to know each other very well, both academically and socially. There was a separate academic building for most of their classes and a lounge for getting together informally.

The admission to the honors college program had both positive and negative features for Michael. On one hand, he truly reveled in being identified as an "elite" student and enjoyed the positive recognition that went along with this. After all, having been in special education all his life, the "stigma" of being different was now transformed into positive recognition for academic excellence. Small classes, stimulating group interaction, and personal attention from professors were other positives. On the other hand, Michael realized that he would have to work hard to maintain this elite status, and also knew that there were many gaps in his preparation for college. During freshman year he had to work harder than ever before to achieve and he struggled with several courses.

A comment from the associate dean of the honors college and Michael's teacher in two beginning courses:

> *Prof. R*: I remember wondering how he managed to be so upbeat when on essay after essay, though he was trying his best, I rarely gave him more than a C. He kept apologizing for not being good at what he called literature; he was good at math, he kept saying, as if he had to convince me that he was smart enough to be in the honors college. Given that the emphasis of the honors curriculum is not on mathematics, to say the least, I had my doubt about his ability to make it through the program.

Prof. R like all other honors faculty did not know that Michael was autistic, but several faculty sensed that he probably had some kind of learning disability that distinguished him from the other students. Fortunately, Michael had the ability to almost always elicit others' sensitivity and this was true for almost all of the faculty he met. While noting that Michael seemed different from other college students, his sincerity and desire to learn were especially appealing to his teachers and often resulted in their "going the extra mile" for him.

Michael did have difficulty with the social aspects of being a student in the honors college. He quickly became disenchanted with other students who did not take college life as seriously as he did, and frankly, some students lost patience with his incessant questions and continuing debates, which could appear to be argumentative and uncomfortably challenging. Adolescents are not known for their acceptance of those who don't fit the mold. Michael also had difficulty concealing his negative opinions about some of the other students. The directness and bluntness in Michael's language was not diplomatic and did little to obscure what some saw as disdain for them. However, the more typical student response to Michael, especially in class, was acceptance, or at least tolerance.

> *Prof. R of the honors college:* I don't remember any occasion on which his fellow students treated him dismissively or with condescension, and that is surprising considering that his social peculiarities were apparent to them. And yet this is not surprising, because they saw how innocent of guile and aggressiveness, how open, trusting, and good-natured he was.

Another problem Michael faced was a result of the honors students taking many of the same classes together. Consequently, they became very familiar, sometimes too familiar, with each other and cliques formed. At times, this arrangement could be compared with a family, that repeatedly continues to bicker over the same issues. Of course, Michael's social awkwardness continued to plague him, and while he did do well academically, he often felt alone and isolated from other students.

Ironically, there are attributes of being autistic that facilitated Michael's academic work and success in the honors college. At times, when Michael took on a project, this became a totally consuming, central focus for him. An example is the research he did for a senior thesis, which resulted in outstanding work. All honors students are required to complete a thesis to graduate from the program and often delay beginning a project until the end of their senior year. Students who do not complete the thesis can still graduate from the university, but don't get the distinction of having been in the honors college. Michael did his thesis sooner than most, over the summer between his junior and senior year. He realized that his senior schedule was very full and therefore organized his time so that the less hectic summer months would be devoted to this thesis project. His choice of topic logically combined his interest in secondary education with his math talent. It was an exploration of models that could be used for creating students' schedules in high school.

> *Michael:* The aim of this research is to shed light on how to create a schedule which best supports teaching at the high school levels. To achieve this aim, the paper begins with an introduction to traditional, block, and flexible scheduling. Then, a discussion of psychological factors in education leads

to the development of a scheduling model based upon the work of two experts which aims to allow educators to translate learning theory into pedagogical practice.

Michael's thesis was supervised by the new associate dean of the honors college, Prof. D, who comments on his superb work. Michael's love of learning, persistence, and attention to detail were clearly recognized and valued.

> *Prof. D*: Michael is sweet and incredibly motivated to succeed. Great attention to detail and so conscientious. Contrary to reports of lateness during the semester Michael was always on time—never missed an appointment with me as we worked on his thesis which he completed during the summer before his senior year. He was the first to defend [his thesis] in his class; he got an A. He has a mastery of math and especially the logic of quantitative analysis. His insistence on precision and clarity that might have raised issues for him in class were great assets for his research. It was such a pleasure to see Michael succeed in the honors college, which is indeed challenging.

Academic work

It is obvious that one of Michael's strengths is his academic ability, both in terms of his intelligence and desire to learn. College professors clearly noted this, but also commented on unusual attributes of his intellect and learning style. Michael's intensity about school work was both a strength, because he was so focused on learning, and also a weakness, when at times this bordered on obsession. It is especially interesting that those who didn't know that Michael is autistic, or who didn't know a great deal about autism, saw Michael's deficiencies as personality quirks rather than understanding his behavior as an aspect of his disability.

The college that Michael attended also has a program for learning disabled college students. As a result, many faculty were likely to be more sensitive to students' different learning styles and academic needs, and were more tolerant of students' unusual attributes which were attributable to the learning disability. It may be that some of Michael's apparent differences were more readily accepted by faculty in this context. Michael never considered using any of the services of the college learning disability program, because he felt that he did not need academic assistance and did not want to be identified as having learning problems.

Michael: It was not fair to me that some receive special services and others don't, particularly when those services may provide an unfair advantage.

During freshman year I asked Michael what particular challenges he faced academically. He replied with an unexpected remark that professors often didn't give him exact instructions. For example, he related that one professor told the class to go home and think about a topic being discussed in class. This was a dilemma for Michael; he didn't know how long to think about the topic and then couldn't stop thinking about the topic. No doubt few, if any other students, thought the assignment was a problem or frankly even bothered to think about the topic out of class.

On another occasion, Michael told me that a math professor ran after him when he left the room after finishing a math exam. The professor noted that Michael never looked on the reverse side of the exam sheet and didn't see that the exam questions continued. Consequently, Michael had completed only half the test. Michael said that on a prior exam there were no questions on the reverse side of the sheet, so he didn't expect to see any on this test either. What may be obvious to other students often eludes Michael.

Most faculty responded in very positive ways to this unusual student, although Michael does remember some teachers with whom he had difficulties. The typical faculty reaction to Michael was very positive, because they saw him as hard-working and sincere. No doubt this was something that reinforced Michael's love of learning and continued to inspire him to become a teacher. Michael says that he just likes school!

A typical comment about Michael's ability is from a professor in the School of Education.

> *Prof. Q:* He excelled and was an exemplar, outshining his classmates in his careful analysis, critical inquiry and commitment to education. I was quite impressed with Michael's general performance in my classes—especially academically, but behaviorally as well. His anxieties, however, indeed did cause him to need continual reassurance and quite often put him in my office discussing his struggles, the details of assignments, as well as his unique view of things. I found the anxieties to be more often than not unfounded and quite excessive in light of his performance.
>
> Michael is a deep thinker, as evidenced in his queries and course engagement. There was a seriousness and maturity beyond his years, especially beyond the posture of his classmates.

Another professor in Michael's major comments on Michael as a student.

Prof. M of the math dept: Michael has a few interesting mental traits. His ability at conceptual mathematics was better than his symbol manipulation (which was not bad—just that his conceptual understanding was even stronger). Among math majors, it is far more common to run into students who get the symbol stuff very well, but have trouble with advanced concepts.

As a curiosity—Michael had trouble with directions. On one occasion, as we emerged from a classroom, he asked me "Which direction is your office?" When I told him, then he said, "Okay, that means I want to be going this way." That seems like an odd way to navigate to me. In my geometry class he was the only student (in a large class) who got 100 on both midterm and final. I do not know if that means that he has an especially good visual sense or whether he just studied a lot. That would be interesting to know. [Michael has commented that he studied minimally for this class, so evidently his excellent performance was a result of natural talent in geometry.]

Prof. S, who taught a computer science class and is the father of an autistic child: I only taught him in one class. In a group of people—and one of the sharpest groups I had taught in many years—he and one other student were so far above the others that I gave them A+. They were both very bright, but came to it from different places; the other student is driven and studies all the time, but in Michael's case achieving is a force of habit.

I needed a student to work with me on a project regarding a computer program. He was head and shoulders over everyone else. He's very reliable, but Michael got obsessive. He'd ask questions that would drive anyone else up the wall, but I knew where he was coming from, because of my understanding of autism. Michael has a great propensity to fixate on the leaves on the trees and forget the forest. Michael worked on a paper with another student and was especially focused on grammar, but he would lose sight of the big picture.

The way I describe it is that that it's like an itch that you can't scratch enough; he'd sit at the computer screen and sit at the computer screen. He has the intellectual tools to do it, and he'd sit at the screen when others couldn't deal with it anymore; he'd focus on the details about fixing this and that. He had to learn several computer programs by himself by reading tutorial books. This takes someone with great determination.

Another professor of education comments on Michael's willingness to help out when the professor had difficulty mastering an on-line e-mail system that he wanted to use to augment in-class sessions. The system is called "Blackboard."

Prof. S of the School of Education: Blackboard came to dominate my life during that semester. It was the first year that the college used it and there were many problems. Also, students e-mailed in with questions, assignments, etc. at all hours of the day and night. Michael became a lifesaver; he offered to be my unpaid teaching assistant in charge of Blackboard. He posted assignments, responded to queries, and worked diligently to help me master the system. Students also became aware of Michael's academic ability.

Michael was able to use his excellent computer ability, his attention to detail and course requirements, and his need for precision to help other students fulfill course assignments.

Rosemarie, another student in the honors college: We took honors courses together and sat next to each other and often next to the professor. A major problem was getting him to class on time. We would rush in to class late and I would be carrying Michael's breakfast. Michael was far superior to most of the other honors students. He thought with much more depth. He really wanted to learn even if it was a topic very different from mathematics. He had a vested determination to uncover whatever we were reading and partaking in class discussion.

I asked Michael to reflect on the special challenges he faced academically. In typical Michael fashion he responded with a list. The topics Michael listed are given below in what Michael views as their order of importance. Following each topic is discussion resulting from follow-up questions I asked.

Lateness to class

Michael: If I get some place on time, it's almost like it happens by accident. Figuring the whole thing out is a problem—when to get out of bed, being able to get out of bed, and just getting there. Maybe I'm better if it's really important that I get some place on time, like a job, but it's still a problem. If I do get some place on time, sometimes it's by accident.

Time management and organization

Michael: Managing my time has always been a problem and I do better when I have too much to do than when I don't have enough to do.

One day I interviewed Michael in his home, and he showed me the system he used for keeping track of time. Almost an entire wall of his bedroom was covered by a "white board" on which he scheduled his day in half-hour intervals. Next to each time period was the target activity for what he felt he should be doing during that time. I asked him how well it worked. He responded that sometimes it worked, and sometimes it didn't, but it made him feel better to organize his day. He laughed when he told me that when he didn't accomplish the target activity for the time period, at least he knew what he should have done, but didn't accomplish.

Length of class

Maintaining a focus for an entire class was a consistent challenge for Michael, and even harder for him was looking as though he was paying attention. Michael says he thinks best when he doesn't make eye contact and would often stare out the window to help him listen and think. He learned that some faculty assumed that this behavior was a sign of disinterest, so instead of staring out the window he began writing lists. While Michael could be compulsively attentive to detail when he worked individually or at a computer terminal, sustaining attention for two-hour classes was challenging.

Asking too many questions

When I interviewed several of Michael's teachers, they all remarked that any comment they or another student made in class could provoke endless questions from Michael. Michael has difficulty understanding most social situations, and also had difficulty understanding the appropriate "etiquette" of being a college student. Perhaps having been in special education settings for so long, he was used to students behaving in a highly individualistic manner, and he had never been criticized before for asking too many questions.

When Michael started college, he was initially very reserved, and didn't ask many questions, because he didn't want to draw attention to himself. As he became more comfortable with being a college student, his need for clarification became paramount and his behavior changed. He would always sit in the very front of a classroom (a place few college students seek out) and had the constant urge to bombard the teacher with questions. This became tiresome for other students, especially when the questions were raised at the end of the class when all were ready to leave. Michael did learn to modify this behavior to some extent through concerted effort, but often his questioning created barriers between him and other students. Ultimately, Michael learned to stay after class alone with the teacher and also learned to avail himself of a faculty member's office hours instead of taking class time to get his questions answered. Some faculty felt he was annoying and a burden to deal with, but more often faculty enjoyed the time they spent alone with this very interested student.

> *Prof. R of the honors college:* He came to my office very often to talk about the course readings and to get my reaction to his written work as he was working on it. The remarkable thing about these sessions to me was that despite his anxiety and frequent frustration with the difficulties he encountered in grasping the heart of the admittedly complex material required and his trouble organizing and developing his thoughts on paper, the latter in particular, he was also so affable, so cheerful in the face of his difficulties that it was easy to accommodate his needs and answer his sometimes repetitive questions with patience and good humor equal to his.

Asking dumb questions

Michael says that he became aware that the kind of questions he asked in class were different from those other students asked. He also learned that most undergraduates rarely asked questions and did not volunteer to speak in class at all. Along with his many questions were questions that he began to think of as simply "dumb" questions—questions about things that were obvious to others and not to him. Michael's never been sure what's a good question. Many teachers repeat the cliché that there isn't such a thing as a "stupid" question, but in reality, all students and teachers know that there really are stupid questions. In high school, Michael was encouraged to ask as many questions as were needed and teachers saw this as a positive aspect of his classroom learning. The unspoken "rules of the game" changed in college, without Michael's awareness.

> *Prof. R of the School of Education:* He stayed after class almost every session. On some level, he just wanted to get a better handle on some things. He seemed motivated to seek out more information and his questions were never about grades, which is so common today, but he just always had questions about what was discussed.

Michael's need for reassurance also caused him to ask repeatedly about assignment contents, due dates, course material, and the "details" of fulfilling all requirements. He was a stickler for scrupulously reading the course syllabus and was concerned whenever a faculty member deviated from the original course of study. Luckily, Michael chose to attend a college where almost all faculty responded appropriately to this student who had a great need for support and reassurance.

Prof. R of the honors college: Michael came to me frequently for advice about courses and to check obsessively on the number of credits he had yet to complete for honors and so I saw him formally every term of his time at the college.

I asked Michael if he could give me examples of the kind of questions he had asked that he now thinks of as "dumb".

Michael: Sometimes we would be working on a complicated math problem and because I was distracted I would miss something the professor wrote on the board. This might be a simple step needed to solve the problem, and even if it was as simple as something you learn in high school, it was new to me, and I had to ask about it.

Another example would be when we used a calculator with a series of commands that the professor gave us. Sometimes I would miss one or two of these instructions and would fall behind. I needed to get other people to help me, but it's funny that when they told me what to do, I realized that I already knew it, and it was just floating around in my head.

Here's a really weird one. Sometimes I would see a simple word on the blackboard, like "they." And it just wouldn't look right to me. So, I couldn't suppress the need to ask the question about what the word meant. I guess I could have waited a minute or so to see if I figured it out.

If the professor gave the class an oral assignment, it was even harder for me. I remember writing an essay nine pages long to answer an oral question. The professor responded that only the last two sentences I wrote actually answered the question.

I think it takes me longer to hear than it does others, and I can't take notes.

Timed tests / essay tests

Michael: With essay tests you have to start writing right away. That's not the way that I work. I never wrote anything before seventh grade, because I refused to and then I started to write a little so I learned to make corrections, but always on a computer. I never hand wrote—so in an exam book you can't switch paragraphs and edit like you do on a computer. I noticed that others would finish all two to three questions on an exam and I was still on the first. I can't do three questions in fifty minutes. And when I go back to fill in a detail, I'd lose my train of thought.

I asked Michael to explain why he didn't write before seventh grade.

Michael: I just didn't write. No one ever made me write more than a sentence. We used a lot of workbooks and had to fill in the blanks. I remember that the first paragraph I wrote was in seventh grade. I was never a creative person, but my seventh through ninth grade teacher, who I had for all subjects, was very into writing. So until that teacher forced me, I didn't write, and then I started writing. I like right and wrong answer things—like spelling and math.

By the way, the word "misspell" is easy to misspell, isn't it? I'm good at seeing other people's mistakes, but not my own. I can't write a second draft. It's not productive. I won't change anything because I'll like it all.

I asked Michael if he ever learned to plan his answer before writing an essay.

Michael: Planning won't work for me. I'm very linear—more than most. Just to get going is a problem. The issue of remembering the topic is another problem for me. For example, in a literature exam I knew that I was behind and when I was writing I tried to make a straight outline and tried to figure out how much time to spend on each part. But when I wrote the beginning, I'd remember other topics and deviate from the list I made. It just didn't work.

By the end of the undergraduate years Michael had developed facility with writing in terms of self-expression, mechanics, and language use. Organization of thought took time to develop, but Michael's willingness to rework his written assignments using feedback from his teachers was another positive aspect of his learning style. While some college students bridle at teachers' comments, and are not motivated to redo work, this wasn't true of Michael.

Prof. R of the honors college: In time, his work improved considerably: it became more focused, more consistently pertinent to the works and ideas central to the course, more developed. He was dogged in his willingness to rewrite. And that doggedness paid off so that he began to get better than C grades from time to time, not least because his participation in class discussion improved in quantity and quality, moving from sometimes pained questions about what was just said, to targeted reactions to the remarks of other students, or to my exposition of the texts before us.

While he says that he struggles with editing his own work Michael volunteered to be the editor of a School of Education publication and became a competent editor and a better writer himself. He was assigned an empty storeroom as an "office," where he proudly posted "office hours" on the door, and was given a mailbox along with other faculty and staff. He loved this recognition!

> *Dean of the School of Education*: Michael volunteered for the very demanding job of editing the School of Education's newsletter published twice a year. He organized his time most effectively so that he was in the "office" several hours a week to communicate with faculty and staff about the content of the publication. He was effective in motivating faculty to write columns and submit these in keeping with the deadlines. Overall, Michael proved to be a very effective manager and editor.

Part of the job of editing this newsletter was interviewing new faculty and soliciting articles. Michael sent out a barrage of e-mails to the faculty requesting articles, and posted deadlines for submission of their work. This officious style on the part of an undergraduate "turned off" some faculty, and in accord with typical behavior, deadlines for submission of articles were often ignored. Michael had difficulty understanding how faculty, whom he held in high regard, were derelict in turning in their work on time.

Michael edited a column I submitted to the newsletter and he and I debated the organization of what I had written. I had to justify why I developed the piece as I did. Initially, Michael's questions seem to challenge, but subsequently, I've discovered that Michael's endless questions are really an important means for him to learn how others do things. Unfortunately, some have perceived the questioning as being confrontational, because Michael doesn't make his underlying purpose for asking so many questions clear. He can also appear too persistent in his questioning style, which can make others defensive.

Michael wrote a column for the newsletter as he finished his stint as editor and was preparing to graduate and begin a teaching career:

> *From the Editor's Desk*
>
> The time as editor was definitely a learning experience for me. The process that I described two years ago of making the newsletter whole is definitely true. Trying to make the connections between articles to portray an image of the school as a whole was far more difficult than anticipated, but I hope I provided the best portrait possible.
>
> My experience with faculty and friends has been life altering to say the least. First, thank you to all that have managed to put up with me through my troubles with the newsletter, studies, family, and life as a whole. I hope as my adolescence closed, I was not too bizarre to anyone. I've grown up now, whatever that means. There are more people to help grow up, so I'm ready to

journey out into the world of education. I will miss you all, but hope to see you soon.

To demonstrate how Michael's writing ability developed, the following is an excerpt from the paper he submitted for the education autobiography assignment described previously. This section is about how his college years impacted on his thoughts about teaching. Michael came to the realization that mathematics was too separate from other disciplines and later in the paper presented a recommendation for more inter-disciplinary studies allied with mathematics. Michael seeks connections on many levels:

> My collegiate studies are further pressing my vision of teaching. While I was always good at mathematics, it was not until recent months that I became avidly engaged with the ideas of mathematical physics, mathematical psychology, and other mathematical sciences. I feel mathematics is a tool or methodology, but not an isolated subject. My experiences throughout school and discontent with separating the disciplines in high school along with the applied orientation of the college math and computer department contribute to this evolving vision.
>
> It is my view that people in literature and the humanities feel mathematics is sacrosanct and not for them to use or even question. This is illustrated in such sayings as "Ouch, math" or "Ouch, calculus." People say, "If you know it, that's great, but not me." Until these statements become the exception rather than the norm in collegiate institutions and larger society, the twenty-first century will not be all it can be, as the borders between disciplines will restrict the expansion of knowledge and therefore of society.

The true meaning of a question

Michael has often said that he just doesn't "get" it, when discussing many things and this often applies to his restricted and literal comprehension of language. As children mature they learn that language has both nuance and subtlety and words often have both literal and connotative meaning. This was not true for Michael who used language bluntly or sometimes just didn't understand what others meant. Often Michael struggled to understand the focus or actual intent of questions posed to him. This was especially true in oral conversation that required "give and take" between listener and speaker. On written exams and college papers, he worked hard to develop appropriate answers with the correct focus. While Michael had abundant information to convey (and perhaps too much information, resulting from his focus on detail), he had trouble focusing on the thesis of his answer, difficulty organizing the information, and knowing when to omit irrelevant or tangential detail.

I asked Michael to talk about his academic experience and focus on his comment that some things that seemed obvious to other students were not clear to him.

> *Michael*: Sometimes I just miss simple things. I tend to look at things holistically and it's hard because it's the way I think. There are things I get and things I just can't get. I want precision. I don't want to leave things unresolved. I can't tolerate ambiguity. Sometimes I miss a small part of something in math and I can't go on until that part is answered.
>
> I would say I am holistic in the sense that when I begin and while I work on something, I tend not to work in a structured, logical order. Often I do not use an outline for writing for instance. Sometimes a minor detail at the end seems more important for me to tend to first than a major issue at the beginning. In the end, I need every detail to be explored and understood, but to get to that end I do not go in any particular order. Just as things pop out at me, I would say I develop them.

Professors with "holier than thou" attitudes and feeling rejected by some

An informal poll of Michael's professors revealed their genuine affection for him. When I asked many faculty about their experiences with Michael, they most often responded that he was one of their all-time favorite students. Most teachers were delighted to have such an inspired and motivated student in their classes, and saw that he was without guile in his questions and concerns. He was viewed as a very intelligent student, who was so sincerely motivated to learn. Obviously, almost all of the math and computer science faculty had special delight in Michael's mathematical brilliance and his love for the subject. However, there were some few faculty with whom Michael couldn't connect easily. Michael knows that one faculty member lost patience with his endless questions and they had a more brittle relationship than he had with other teachers. Michael eventually realized that this faculty member didn't want to be interrupted, because it interfered with his style of teaching. Michael quickly learned not to "stand out" in this professor's class, or be subject to critical attention.

Michael also complained about another faculty member, who he felt didn't treat the class fairly. He identified several problems with this teacher: she gave unexpected tests, changed course assignments mid semester, test contents didn't represent subjects covered in class, and she argued with students about the accuracy of her lecture material. In the large class this young professor taught there were many difficulties with classroom conduct. The professor had difficulty winning the students' respect and unfortunately took retaliatory measures against them. This atmosphere upset Michael tremendously and he complained directly to her several times that he wasn't learning what he wanted to learn, and that the professor wasn't teaching what she should be covering. This did not engender any sympathy from this faculty member. In fact, she didn't distinguish Michael's genuine concern about learning from the negative feedback, complaints and questions she was getting from other students. Michael's perceptions of this faculty member were "on target" and she resigned her position shortly thereafter citing her own dissatisfaction and the complaints of many students.

Extra-curricular activities

Michael desired connections with other students and learned, as many freshmen do, that getting involved in extra-curricular activities that occurred outside the classroom would be a way to accomplish this. He joined one club that organized events revolving around Michael's religion. Even after graduation, Michael returned to the campus to participate in events sponsored by the club. While Michael has never identified himself as a religious person, throughout his childhood he participated in events sponsored by his local temple and was an excellent religious school student. The cultural connection of religious events seemed to be a good bridge to others in college.

Michael was also a frequent contributor to the college newspaper and this came about in a curious way. When the advisor to the campus paper, who was also a professor of journalism, sent out a campus-wide e-mail soliciting an aide for her 16-year-old, severely autistic son, this resonated with Michael and he contacted her. Michael told her that because he was too busy he didn't want the job as an aide, but he wanted her to know about his story, hoping that it would be encouraging. Thus began their special friendship.

> *Prof. F*: I found [his e-mail message] warm, heartfelt and generous. So much for the theory that autistics do not have sympathetic feelings. I think that in that e-mail he mentioned that he might contact me in my role as advisor to the newspaper, since he wanted to work on his writing. I encouraged him to do that and actually, we wound up having some sessions in my office that summer.

Michael found his own unique niche when he contributed to the campus paper.

> *Prof. F:* That began Michael's "career" in writing. He was a hard worker, not the best writer in the world, a fact he will probably tell you himself. But he cared about the words, about *each* word. He liked to write what I'd call "number stories," why the academic calendar was not convenient or fair, and why it should be changed is the one I recall now. He seemed to have a fascination with those kinds of stories not a lot of people do. But they were very useful stories for the paper and I understood very well his fascination with them. It often works when people use their autistic tendencies to create. I think that Michael did that in writing for the paper.

When his classmate, Rosemarie, began a club for students interested in teaching careers, Michael eagerly joined and became a very active member. However, during an emotional crisis that occurred mid junior year, he found himself ostracized by some club members and he became very disillusioned. Rosemarie comments on why Michael dropped out of the club and the difficulty he had with other club members.

> *Rosemarie:* He left the club for a combination of reasons. His points and ideas weren't being brought across clearly to the other students. He didn't feel that the club was as organized or structured as he wanted it to be. He had lots of ideas, but others didn't give him a chance and listen to him and work through the ideas. He always wanted to know exactly how we would do things. He was so structured and everything had to be very focused.
>
> He put lots of time in one activity, working on a website, and others didn't check it and he became upset. When he stopped involvement in the club during junior year, he wrote a letter to the club and one member read it. He had wonderful ideas for the club, but implementation was difficult and he had a hard time motivating people to follow his ideas. We were doing more social activities with children in the schools and he felt that lots of events weren't academic enough and we weren't devoting time to secondary students.

Michael provided a list of problems related to this extra-curricular involvement that reinforces the social awkwardness that he felt: feeling on the outside, often having a minority opinion about many things, and causing disruptions in meetings.

A more successful extra-curricular experience for Michael was becoming a paid tutor in the math and computer science department. It was evident that his teaching skills showed a talent. I asked Michael what made him a good tutor.

> *Michael*: For lack of a better word, I obsess on each step of a problem in mathematics. This ensures that students spend ample time and understand each and every step. Lastly, because I think holistically, I frame a student's difficulty in the overall context of what they are learning (i.e., a particular unit or course). This often allows them to realize their difficulty is in one small area of a large topic. And, for many students I explain something this way: "Although your solutions are often wrong, it is because you are making the same mistake(s) in different areas and not because of overall difficulty with mathematics. So while you may think you made 26 mistakes, you really made only 3 different mistakes, but you made them several times."

Students requested Michael as a tutor because of his remarkable math skills, but also because he was very patient with them. How interesting that what Michael knew intuitively in mathematical reasoning, he could convey to others even though verbal fluency is not one of his strengths.

When reflecting on his college experience, it's clear that Michael did not truly feel comfortable with many kinds of social interaction. However, when I asked him to list fond or special memories about college, he did provide the following positive thoughts: joining clubs, becoming co-secretary of the honors council, knowing more people I passed on campus, and taking over the education newsletter. Poignantly, Michael responded to the question about how his college experiences differed from what he thinks is the typical student's experiences with this list: many adolescent and high school experiences I had in college, but not in high school, my immaturity, and being socially confused with peers especially when people thought I disrespected them without my knowing.

There are multiple indicators of Michael's success at college: overall grade point average of A-, completion of the honors college program, acceptance into a competitive graduate school (where he recently completed a master's degree in secondary math education with an A- grade point average), and honors received for both academic performance and service given by the math and education departments. In addition to the academic accomplishments, there were many extra-curricular activities that Michael participated in and thoroughly enjoyed. College was a time of academic learning and social growth!

Getting along with college peers

Michael, what do you think the other college students thought about you?

Michael: I think that everyone thinks I'm different, but at the same time intellectually I know that some people see no difference. I just assume that I'm different from everybody else and that's how I've always thought since I was very young. I'm not unique, but I'm different. Everyone is in one group and I'm in another.

Issues with socialization are at the very heart of the autism disorder. Autistic individuals struggle to connect appropriately and meaningfully with others and often appear isolated and totally self-absorbed. When he was a student in the special education high school, Michael found a group of peers who accepted him. These high school students needed special education for their academic needs, but allied behavioral disorders typically accompanied whatever learning disability they had. In that group of special education students, all of whom seemed different, Michael was not very different at all. Getting along with college peers was a challenge for Michael and no one could anticipate what would be the social outcome of the college experience. All wondered how he would adjust to the college environment, and also wondered how he would be treated by regular students. I inquired about how Michael was generally treated by other children.

Michael: I was always with kids in special education and I was never that different from them. Probably, other individuals, people who I didn't like anyway, used my being in special ed to foster their judgments about me. But this was not a major issue in general. Those who thought positively about me, still thought positively. Those who didn't, didn't; and those who didn't care, still didn't care.

When Michael began college, he clearly looked different from most other college students. He was stocky, awkward, a sloppy dresser, and clearly had no interest in wearing stylish clothes or following trends. He walked with a heavy-footed gait and often kept his head down. When I first met him, Michael paced in circles and seemed like a very troubled young man. During freshman year, he walked around campus alone listening to a Walkman radio and seemed to be in his own world. Michael was not often aware of how other students viewed him and treated him. The friendships that eventually developed were with particularly sensitive people. But there were also times when others shunned him, and it had to be hurtful.

Through the years in college, both Michael's demeanor and his ability to relate to other students changed dramatically. According to his uncle, with whom he has a close relationship, college was definitely a turning point in Michael's life. There were more lessons that Michael learned at college than those related to academics.

> *Uncle Joe*: I'm very proud of the many outstanding things that happened when Michael was at college, but at the same time, I could have cried when he told me some of the stuff that went on in college. In general kids can be cruel and he told me that there were some who called him "Forrest" for Forrest Gump. And you knew that stuff was going on without him talking about it, and he shrugged a lot of it off.

During the college years, Michael gradually formed friendships and by the time he was a junior he no longer walked across campus isolated from others. He was recognized by many who greeted him with friendly remarks. Michael joined extra-curricular clubs and took leadership roles in student activities. In his junior year, Michael began living on campus and shared a dorm room with a student who knew nothing about his disability. Living away from his family was a formidable challenge. At college, Michael did find a "home" for himself in the math and education departments and formed friendships with other serious students and had very personal and deep relationships with some faculty. College was a remarkable time of growth and change—a laboratory for learning "normal" behavior.

I asked Michael about how he got along with other students and what particular problems he had.

> *Michael*: I guess I had a hard time with some. My voice—it bothers people. Routine things get in the way. I've always had trouble with time. I was late and disruptive in terms of arrivals. It's a klutziness situation; and literally I often couldn't find a place in the classroom to squeeze into. Sometimes I don't know when to talk and either I interrupt other people or I think I'm talking and I'm actually not. Life with other students—it was part of being an outsider. I probably didn't always know that they were giving me a hard time.
>
> Here's something that I'll never forget—the first semester in my first calculus class. I had a big paper cup of soda—46 oz—that I carried into class. I often carried food and drink with me, sometimes because I didn't have time to eat before class and I was late, but sometimes just in case I got

thirsty. I took one sip from the cup and plop, it dropped. Everyone sat in the class with their feet up the rest of the day. It was flowing. I made a river out of the business school building. Many still talk about that cup of soda.

The spilled soda story became a family "legend"; Uncle Joe comments about Michael and the event:

Michael can be a charming guy, but people must understand that every day is different for him; and for his two-liter bottle of soda!

I asked Michael why he wore a Walkman so often during the first year at college.

Michael: I listened to music and wanted everything to be quiet. No one would be talking to me and no one knew me. I felt more normal, when I was listening to something.

Listening to a Walkman was a habit. I always did this on the bus—school bus, or city bus. When I went to high school, I didn't like the bus driver and it was such a long ride so I just put on the Walkman and started doing schoolwork. I just don't like total quiet. I usually only listen to mellow music on the radio, but sometimes I'll listen to the kind of music others listen to. I wouldn't wear a Walkman in class.

I asked Michael if he was often lonely.

Michael: I guess.

Others view Michael at college

I wanted to learn others' perspectives about how Michael fared socially in college. Michael's friend, Rosemarie, spent a great deal of time with Michael in a variety of in-class and out of class settings.

Rosemarie: I know for a fact that some students did make lots of fun of him, and some were very cruel behind his back. I'm not sure if they were aware of his diagnosis. I know instances with other students in the same major who tended to use him. Michael's really a brilliant young man and the other students asked for help with the homework. He would work through it with them and behind his back they would make fun of him—the way he walks, talks, and projects himself. I got into verbal confrontations with these people. I feel that everyone has some disability, to some extent. I think he was aware of this, because after an education club activity he asked me, "Do people notice that I'm different? Do people like me?" I was just taken aback—to just self-reflect like that; it's painful and I think to some extent he realized that others think he's different and he cared about this.

In the education club, I think at times he could handle it, but at other times people couldn't handle his presence. They didn't understand him—why he would walk fast, disappear and then come back. People thought it was odd behavior. Others couldn't embrace his quirks.

As with all autistic individuals forming appropriate peer relations was always a problem for Michael.

Michael's maternal grandmother. When Michael was a college senior and just after his birthday in April, he told me that he wanted a party. At that time, he was living with his grandfather and me on weekends, because he wasn't getting along with his mother and his parents were having their own problems.

It would be a combination graduation and birthday party we decided. He took charge of everything: invitations, menu, etc. We were all very concerned and weren't sure if anyone would turn up for this party he wanted to have. You see Michael never really had friends. He didn't have neighborhood friends, because he went to the special schools. And of course, most other children didn't want to be Michael's friend, when he was young.

So the invitations were sent out, the food was purchased, and we kept our fingers crossed. And they did come, and they seemed like regular college students, and we were so delighted for him. It was a regular party.

Prof. S of the math dept (who has an autistic son): A couple of students refer to him as the ultimate nerd. He was always friendly and helpful. In a social setting, he was very wary before going in and interacting. He doesn't do it easily. One of the things you learn when you are young when you have social-dysfunctional issues, especially if your behavior is good, is that older people are a lot more tolerant of you than your peers; dealing with peers is always an issue.

Prof. Q of the School of Education: Michael was adept in the realm of abstract ideas and intellectual queries. I think he was far less skilled in personal domains. I found his participation in class welcome—his questions and insights were provocative and wonderful for class discussions. However, I believe that his peers may have found him argumentative in this way, and perhaps overly critical and overly interruptive of class activities.

Prof. S of the School of Education: In class, Michael was inquisitive, thoughtful, and had an insatiable appetite for knowledge. He also had little if any sense of inappropriateness and often said things that other students found silly, offensive, or childish. When they laughed, sometimes at him, he did not seem to be offended, or perhaps he did not notice. Since the students were a cohort that had been together since freshman year, they appeared to have formed a bond with Michael, and treated him as a mascot, but in a kind, not a cruel way.

Prof. R of the School of Education: At times it was less easy for other students to tolerate Michael. This was especially true during stressful periods in the course. Regarding his need to have questions answered and often asking for clarification, they would say, "Stop that—we don't have time." Students always want to end class early so they tend not to disrupt the instructor to ask questions that would keep the class going over time. But at other times, they were by and large patient and understanding and occasionally there was a little bit of teasing. They were good natured towards him, but might say: "Did you come up with that answer yet, Michael?" because they expected him to always get the right answer and do it quickly.

Living independently on campus

Until he entered the very last semester of college, Michael did not drive a car. He either got rides to and from school from his parents, or used public transportation, which was both inconvenient and time consuming. Michael took academics very seriously and devoted lots of time to studying, which he preferred doing at the college. Consequently Michael spent very long hours at school and some students even called him a "resident commuter."

Jake, Michael's father: Sometime I'd go at 2:00 a.m. and pick him up at the library. He was always a student and that was him. Intellectually, I've never known anyone who was a better student.

When he reached the third year of college, Michael's mother suggested that he live in the college dorm. Michael's conduct towards his mother and aggressive behavior at home continued during the college years, and his mother thought that perhaps it was the right time for Michael to try independent living. She and the family also needed a break from the turmoil that Michael could create at home. On a practical level, she also thought it would be more convenient for Michael to live at school. Michael had many concerns about living away from home, especially because he was accustomed to being catered to by the family.

Uncle Joe: I was a huge advocate for getting him into the dorms to learn how to take care of himself. Also, there was no change in his behavior towards his mother at home, and she needed relief. He did say a few "fine" words to me, when I pushed the issue of his living at school, and he said, "I'm not ready and just butt out."

Michael's college is located only about fifteen miles from his home and because of a shortage of dorm rooms and the proximity of his home to campus, he was ineligible for living in the college dorms. The dean of students was told about Michael's inability to drive a car as well as his diagnosis. After meeting with Michael and his mother the dean and director of residential life decided that they would try to accommodate Michael's application for dorm space.

Michael had always lived at home, but did spend time with his grandparents at their home and also had one difficult month at a residential camp for handicapped children. Michael's family had grown accustomed to meeting all of his needs and life at home was structured to avoid his tantrums. Michael was a difficult person to live with: he was hypersensitive to sounds (especially his mother's voice on the telephone), he had special dietary needs, he would often sleep a tremendous number of hours, and he could not share space or attention with his brother. Michael was both demanding and intolerant of those he lived with. In summary, the prognosis for Michael's adjustment to living on campus did not appear to be good.

When Michael was informed that there was a dorm room available, he was randomly assigned a college room-mate named Ted. Ted was a biology major, chemistry minor and came from a state out west. He was also two years younger than Michael. I asked Ted why he chose to go to a school in New York and asked him about himself.

> *Ted*: I wanted to see what life was like on the east coast and see what New York City was all about. I have been described as an old-fashioned guy, because I am respectful toward all of my peers and my colleagues. I also believe that everyone should be held to their actions and they should be aware of this fact. I was able to obtain a scholarship for swimming and academics so I packed my bags and came to this college. After I receive my biology degree I plan to go into veterinary medicine.

Michael has told me that he and Ted got along well as room-mates, but that they didn't spend much time together. Ted's involvement in competitive swimming and pre-medical studies were all consuming. I was skeptical about how well these two very different people related to each other, especially considering their very different cultural, regional, and life experiences. Michael was difficult for anyone to live with and I asked Ted about his first impressions of Michael.

> *Ted*: When I first saw Michael I did not know what to expect, because the people out here [in the east] were already a lot different from what I was used to. The reason for this is because everyone out here runs at such a fast pace and it's very stressful. I didn't have any expectations.

I asked Ted to describe Michael as a room-mate.

> *Ted*: All I wanted from a room-mate was for him to be clean and not a smoker. When Michael walked in, my first impression was a positive one. He was very intelligent and his family seemed to be pleasant. He was very respectful toward me and was always concerned to make sure that whatever he was doing did not bother me. Michael was extremely organized, however he was rarely on time and we always had a good laugh about that.

Michael was committed to making this living arrangement work, and apparently the two didn't have problems getting along. Ted told me that because of his demanding schedule and swim practice, he often wouldn't return to the dorm until nine or ten in the evening and Michael was busy doing school work at that time. He and Michael consequently didn't spend much time together in their dorm room, nor did they eat together. Ted was unaware of Michael's diagnosis and his history of attending special schools. Luckily for Michael, he was assigned a room-mate whose expectations were quite minimal and easily met.

> *Ted*: Living with Michael was a good experience. He was very respectful and was always willing to talk to me. He always had many things going on in his life and was always ready to talk about it.
>
> He was very different from other kids that I have roomed with. This is because he was very reserved. I never felt that I could really joke with him like just giving him a hard time. I just did not feel that he was the type of kid that you could give a hard time without hurting his feelings.

Expecting that Michael might have exhibited some unusual behavior in the dorm I asked Ted if there were any outstanding incidents:

> *Ted*: One night the phone rang at like four in the morning. I hopped out of bed to answer it and when I was walking over to get the phone, Michael woke up and freaked out. He gave out a shriek and pushed himself against the wall on his bed. I nearly had a heart attack and told him that I was just getting the phone. I never really asked him what made him do that, because

I figured that he just woke up and saw a figure in the dark, but now I've learned that he had a rough childhood so maybe it was due to something else.

Michael had difficulty relating to people on an emotional level and I wondered how he truly got along with Ted. Evidently their relationship was more positive than anyone could have predicted, given Michael's disorder and his lack of experience living with someone outside his family.

> *Ted*: I never saw Michael in a bad mood or being sad. I'm sure that he had his moments, but we always were on a good note with each other. I will never forget Michael and his positive outlook on things.

Because Ted lived far from college, he was invited to holiday meals with Michael's family. Ted became aware that Michael's parents were having difficulty and, while Michael was willing to talk with him about other topics, he refused to discuss his parents. Although Michael's parents were barely speaking with each other during the Thanksgiving holiday, the family put up a "good front" and Ted related that visiting with Michael's family was a very positive experience. He also said that because the whole family were such good cooks, he "stuffed himself" at the holiday meal. I asked Ted if he had anything else to say about Michael and he offered this advice to Michael.

> *Ted*: One thing that I think that Michael should do is stand up for himself more. I always tell him that since he respects others, they, in turn, should respect him.

Ted is now very curious about Michael and his history. While he sensed that Michael was "different" from others and wondered why he was this way, he never got very personal with him. The chance pairing of these two very different fellows worked out better than anyone would have predicted. Each was respectful of the other and was reserved.

> *Ted*: I just thought that Michael was distant from me and maybe that was why I never felt comfortable about joking with him a lot. Now I'd like to know more about his childhood to help me understand him better. I wonder if his childhood was bad, or what happened.

Living on campus posed other challenges for Michael, who says that he was shy and didn't know the appropriate etiquette about group living. Even something as simple as using a microwave oven in the common room, or operating a washing machine, were experiences Michael had never had. There was also a "tug of war" between Michael and his mother about laundry, which reflected the difficulty Michael had becoming independent and his resentment of his mother when she didn't comply with all of his requests. Initially, Michael's mother supplied him with clean laundry each week, but for a variety of reasons she asked him to take more responsibility for learning to do his own laundry at the college. This became a tremendous battle between them. Michael was accustomed to pampering by his mother, and he was totally unwilling to do laundry, and became very angry. Michael even offered to pay his mother for doing his laundry and was furious with her when she declined.

Michael was never good at keeping track of his money. Frugal by nature and having little interest in clothes or entertainment, he never spent much money when he lived at home. At college, budget became a problem. Michael literally kept losing money, which was a familiar pattern for him. When he did have money, Michael splurged on buying food both from the cafeteria and nearby fast-food places. Due to his frequency in the cafeteria and his pleasant demeanor, Michael made friends with the food staff, who quickly became familiar with his dietary quirks and desires. Michael's funds quickly depleted.

Getting to class on time continued to vex Michael. Ironically, even though he was living at the college, he was still frequently late to classes. When he lived at home, Michael made deliberate efforts to leave on time to catch the right bus to campus, or his family arranged to drop him off in plenty of time. Living at school, Michael became less disciplined about getting up and out with sufficient time to make class and he often rushed to classes late and poorly groomed. Michael's room-mate discussed the problem about Michael's chronic lateness and said that Michael would always stop and talk to someone instead of saying he had to go to class. This behavior might be attributed to Michael's intense desire to get to know others, or simply that he did not know how to tell someone gracefully that he didn't have the time to talk.

Michael's grooming and appearance also deteriorated at school. Without oversight by his mother and family, his typical attire became rumpled sweat pants, a baggy tee shirt, and flip-flop sandals. His hair was rarely combed. Both because of Michael's hypersensitivity to touch and because he's admittedly lazy, this wardrobe was soft, unrestricting, and easy to put on quickly when he was late for class. Michael preferred to wear flip-flop rubber sandals instead of taking trouble to put on socks and tie sneakers, and went outside with bare feet in open sandals well into the cold, winter months. He didn't seem to mind when others commented on his unusual dress code. The combination of hypersensitivity to touch and rough textures along with insensitivity to some stimuli, such as cold weather, is common with autistic individuals.

Friendships and relationships

I asked Michael to describe college life and tell me about his friends. I wondered if there were any girlfriends.

> *Michael:* Friendships are hard. People think that I'm either smothering them or ignoring them. I haven't had a girlfriend since high school and she went to my school and she had lots of her own problems.
>
> This is just another whole set of rules I don't know about. Just like I don't know what it's like to have a billion dollars. I never pursue girls. I would only consider it, if they ask me. I don't pursue that kind of thing because I don't get it. I have girls who are friends, but they aren't girlfriends.

> *Michael's friend, Rosemarie:* He had a structured organization chart, a table, about friends. He e-mailed it to me. There were friends with different values: friends, friendly acquaintances, acquaintances, and people you'd see everyday. He's very into structure.

Michael did form a couple of friendships at college that continued even after graduation. While he was insecure about knowing how to approach new people, Michael's desire to have friends and his involvement in campus life did result in his meeting and knowing many new people. These friends did not initially know about Michael's diagnosis and many never suspected that his background and experiences were so different from their own. When I asked Michael to tell me who were the people with whom he was especially close, the group of friends was composed of very caring and decent people. One young lady was well known on campus, and had a severe physical disability. She and Michael became close friends and her warmth, independence, spirit and outgoing manner endeared her to all who knew her. Another young woman was quiet and introspective, but was a student of remarkable academic ability who loved to write poetry and was especially soft-spoken and reserved.

Michael joined the Hillel club (an organization for Jewish students) and met Craig, who was a communications major and two years younger than Michael. I asked Craig about his impressions of Michael.

Craig: Michael was quiet, shy, and friendly. Out of all the people in the organization, he stood out. The other people were very social and outgoing. But he didn't say much, and didn't draw much attention to himself. A lot of time he'd sit alone at the Friday night dinners that the club would have, or at meetings, but he seemed content and comfortable. Later, when he made more friends in the club, he did become more outgoing and sociable. But when I first met him, he was very quiet. When I did talk to him he'd be as friendly and talkative as anyone. After being school friends we became good friends and have been ever since.

I wondered if Michael told Craig anything about his background.

Craig: I didn't know about his autistic background until May the following year. He didn't mention it, or talk about his past. He did say that he went to special schools growing up, but never said why. I found out about him when I read the article in the local newspaper at graduation. It said that Michael didn't talk until about age seven. I was shocked! After that article came out he became more open about his autism.

I inquired about what Craig thought of Michael.

Craig: He's altruistic and always willing to help someone or do a big favor. Sometimes I think he puts other people's needs before his own. He never gets worked up, or very stressed. I've been in tense moments with him, but he always remains calm. He can take the bad for what it is, and move on. Or in a bad situation he tries to be funny.

What about Michael as a student?

Craig: He works harder than almost anyone I've seen. He always talks about the time he was writing a paper the night of game 5 of the 2000 Yankee vs. Mets World Series, when everyone else was watching the game. He prides himself on being a good student, but he doesn't brag though, ever.

I always saw him help his peers (other math students). Whether he was tutoring them or not, he'd always offer to help them, too.

He's very organized. I know he's handed in papers late, but yet he's always on top of his work. In his dorm he used to have schedules of when things were due and what order he should do his assignments.

Did Craig note any weaknesses or differences in Michael?

Craig: Hmmm, not sure if it's a weaknesses or whether it's due to his autism. At times he looks at things too narrowly and logically. For example, I once asked him advice on how I should pursue a girl I liked. I told him there's no way she and I could have lunch alone at school, because our schedules just didn't match. But instead of thinking of another way for me to pursue her, he tried for the next 30 minutes to figure out a way for our schedules to match. Michael will take the time to help a friend and to try and understand a situation and give the best answer or advice he can give.

A crisis in his junior year

During Michael's junior (third) year at college, his friend, Rosemarie, came to talk with me. She was very troubled and didn't know how to begin the conversation. I was a coordinator and advisor for the program Rosemarie was in and we knew each other. She also knew that I was close with Michael and finally she told me that she needed some help. Rosemarie had known Michael since they were both freshmen and by the third year they had a very close relationship. However, Rosemarie was now uncomfortable with Michael, because of a significant change in his behavior and she thought he was "stalking" her. She told me that she could no longer handle the intensity of their friendship and she was receiving endless phone calls and e-mails from him and couldn't get him to stop. When she discussed this with him, he became angry.

I spoke to Michael and he was very distressed. He said to me, "Okay, I'll never talk to her again," and denied that he was stalking her. He attributed his almost constant appearance at her classrooms to the coincidence of having classes in the same buildings. It was clear to me that this relationship was fraught with problems and that Michael had gone overboard in being "too present" in Rosemarie's life. He would not admit to being obsessive with Rosemarie, which is what she thought was happening.

More recently, I said to Michael, "You've been friends with Rosemarie for a long time and I know that there was a serious problem in this relationship during the third year of school. What happened?"

> *Michael*: She was the one who noticed the issue. It's hard for me to say what she noticed. Sort of like a time warp. What's an hour for someone else is like days to me. If I don't see someone in two days, it's like two months—I don't have that time grasp. I don't think I called her or e-mailed her or saw her too often.

According to Rosemarie this is what happened:

> *Rosemarie*: Michael was going through a lot with his parents and we spent time in the dorm talking about five hours at a time. He would misunderstand a comment of mine. Then he would write or e-mail me. I felt that I provoked negative feelings in him and it became very difficult. I had

thought of him as a very close friend and at some point I think he felt that I was trying to hurt him and turn against him. There were so many confrontations.

He would call me nonstop and many, many e-mails—pages and pages of e-mails—and he didn't understand why I wasn't reading it all. He was very argumentative and a burden. He knew my schedule better than I did and I would see him passing outside my classes. He was so focused. There would be some miniscule thing and he would blow it up. We needed time apart.

I subsequently asked Rosemarie what happened to mend their friendship.

Rosemarie: After I talked to you he stopped all contact with me, but about a month later we started to talk again. It was a mutual thing. I was going out to eat with friends and I invited him. I went to study abroad the next semester and everything was fine when I got back.

Some months later, I learned that there was a general pattern of deterioration at that time in the middle of Michael's junior year. Several factors seem to have contributed to what would be a "breakdown" during the January intersession. This was the first year that Michael was living away from home. At that same time he became aware that his parents were experiencing a significant recurrence of marital problems. Michael had also decided to stop taking medication to see what he would be like without it. (During the college years, Michael's psychiatrist prescribed Prozac to help stabilize moods and to avoid cyclical depression.) As a result Michael went into a severe depression once classes were over for the mid-year break. This continued for several months until the resumption of medication alleviated the anxiety, depression, and compulsions Michael was experiencing. By spring Michael's typical behavior resumed. The obsessive behavior with Rosemarie was part of a larger problem that got out of hand. Even though Michael had difficulty with his mood that semester, he was able to focus on academic work and did well.

In a conversation with Michael he admitted that it was a mistake to stop taking his medication that semester. He said that he learned an important lesson and would never make that mistake again. I suspect that because Michael wasn't living at home, his mother could not monitor him closely. She didn't see his deterioration until it reached the crisis level, when he was home for intersession.

Even without the crisis that occurred when Michael stopped taking his medication, having friendships and relating socially has been an ongoing challenge. I discussed the problem Michael has always had with friendships with his Uncle Joe, who provided some interesting observations.

> *Uncle Joe*: Friends in Michael's world are so different. His brother knows how to work a crowd and is a master at it. With Michael it's so different. I've included him when I have my adult friends around and he's really good company. He'll ask people questions about what they do and really tries to find out about them. But he's more uncomfortable doing this when he's with people he doesn't know. He definitely likes to hang out with the adults. Guys his age are in a different place and that's not a comfortable zone for him. My favorite expression is that he knows to expect less and be disappointed less, especially about friends.

Uncle Joe has been very helpful to Michael throughout his life in many different ways. Uncle Joe is a bachelor, who Michael jokes was actually married for about 30 seconds. Uncle Joe relates that Michael often discusses sensitive topics about relationships with him that he would not raise with his mother or father, either because it would be very awkward, or because he thinks that they wouldn't provide the right advice. Uncle Joe enjoyed including Michael in his adult, social world to help Michael develop social skills in what he calls a "toolbox" of experiences. One evening Michael had dinner along with his uncle and several friends, one of whom is a school psychologist. The guests were not aware of Michael's disability and were dismayed at his strange dinner manners. Michael was accustomed to indulging his food cravings and chocolate chip cookies were a frequent accompaniment to the main course in any meal.

Uncle Joe takes note of Michael's keen intellectual awareness coupled with an inability to know what's appropriate.

> *Uncle Joe*: Michael is incredibly self-aware—who he is, what his condition is, his place in the world. He asks many questions so he can try to understand other people. It's amazing that he's so self-aware in certain areas and so oblivious in other areas. Someone seeing him for the first time during a meal didn't know how to react to him—always needing his chocolate chip cookies and his other obsessions. He told them about himself and then they understood. But he doesn't get the social manners.
>
> There's a five to six year lag with him as he continues to experience things—things that kids usually experience as teenagers. Social issues have been and will continue to be a prolonged event for him and a problem for him. I don't know where his relationships will go. We all have this stereotype of what people need or do in order to be happy. We can be sad for

Michael, but his expectations are different. He truly sees things differently. Michael's also at the point where he's thinking about relationships with girls and trying to discover how to look for female relationships.

Michael's uncle is a keen observer of his nephew's development and makes an important point when he acknowledges that what Michael knows about social behavior is intellectually acquired and not intuitive. It's clear that Michael has wanted to expand his life to include relationships, but struggles with knowing how to do so. The college years were the time when this desire was most acute and where new behavior was acquired.

> *Uncle Joe:* Michael has the ability to intellectually understand his emotions and social skills or lack of them. This is a constant conflict with him. When you point things out to him in certain arenas, he'll listen and say, "okay" and then he'll change something about himself. But the timing and how to present this to him are the key in getting him to change.

Being part of the family in which Michael was raised, Uncle Joe comments that Michael has been exposed to a family that by and large has been solution oriented and tackles problems directly.

> *Uncle Joe:* The "juice" he got from everybody in the family was to learn how to figure things out and I'm constantly amazed about his desire to do just that—even with social relationships.

Uncle Joe feels that the likelihood of continued, social growth is most favorable, especially considering the changes that occurred in Michael during his college experience.

College graduation

What had started as a glorious day ended badly. It was the perfect weather for the large outdoor May graduation—bright blue sky, sunny, cool, and clear. I saw Michael at the education graduation ceremony at mid-day and took pictures of him along with other students. He was beaming after receiving awards in both education and mathematics. Later that day, when I stopped by his home to give him a graduation gift, I could see that he was very troubled. He didn't make eye contact, seemed sullen, and wouldn't talk. I later learned what happened.

According to Michael's mother and grandmother, Michael had a tantrum when the family wanted to leave the college campus after graduation. This is a hectic time for both students and their families. After the graduation ceremony there's always a great rush to get into cars and proceed in the slow and long procession towards the campus exits. It can be a poignant time for students—saying good-byes to friends and faculty—but most relish moving on to parties and family celebrations. Initially, Michael refused to get into his family's car. He yelled and made quite a scene, but after coaxing, he got into the car and the family left the campus. Michael's violent temper did not subside and when the car stopped for a red light a short distance from campus, he abruptly got out of the car. Michael walked back to the college. This was both frightening and upsetting for the family, who, although experienced with handling Michael's tantrums, wanted to celebrate the day in fine fashion and good humor.

> *Michael*: My family wanted to leave very quickly after graduation and I wanted to stay a few minutes. I don't like endings. They rushed me. I got really angry and I didn't talk to my mother for weeks. They rushed me. They didn't respect me.

A year after this event, I again questioned Michael about what happened on that day and wondered if there was more insight on his part with time having past. Michael still insisted that he was in the right and that the family was wrong in having rushed him. Stubbornness and inflexibility are very much a part of Michael's personality. He felt that graduation was "his day" and therefore anything and everything he wanted should have been fulfilled. He did not care that his family was eager to avoid the congestion leaving campus and also concerned about getting to the restaurant where they had reservations. Michael and I talked about transitions always being hard for him. I asked him to think about whether the reason for the outburst might have been a reaction to the physical departure from college that day, knowing that this wonderful time in his life was now over. He responded that he still believed that his family didn't honor him by rushing him off campus. We joked that perhaps he was correct and the family was wrong, or that the family was correct and he was wrong. After extended silence, Michael commented that they were both right and wrong. Michael still wouldn't acknowledge the discomfort and embarrassment his very inappropriate behavior had caused everyone that day.

The four years at college proved to be a deeply rewarding experience for Michael and during that time he matured tremendously in terms of his social adjustment and ability to fend for himself. In spite of Michael's tremendous growth at college there are specific issues related to social adjustment that he continues to deal with. Michael is insecure about how to talk with others, he has difficulty with friendships, and even touching or being touched by others, and maintaining direct eye contact are problems that persist. While living away from home is a rich experience for all college students, it was truly a remarkable achievement for Michael.

Author's reflection

Intellectually Michael has always known that a diagnosis of autism makes him different from others, and he has always felt like an outsider. After attending special schools all his life, Michael told few people at his college that he is autistic, hoping that college would be an opportunity to be like everyone else. As a college freshman Michael was accustomed to feeling separated from others, but similar to many students, Michael changed dramatically during the college years.

Acknowledging a separate school history

Michael attended special schools from preschool through high school. In those years including an autistic child in general education was unheard of. The special schools provided tangible benefits, including intense language development in early childhood, small classes and individual attention, teachers sensitized and trained to deal with unique students, a curriculum geared to individual students' learning capacities with realistic expectations, and an accepting peer group where everyone was different. Yet Michael's description of "gaps" in his education demonstrates that attending special schools can have drawbacks: not having typical school experiences, not being exposed to a full standard curriculum, not getting academic enrichment and, most importantly, little or no experience with non-handicapped peers.

Michael continued to attend special education schools before college, because of the severity of his problems during childhood, his success in these programs, and his family's fear about his adjustment in a regular school setting. Much of the literature on inclusion has focused on the gains students derive from the social and emotional benefits of being with non-handicapped peers. Michael, however, stresses the academic deficits of the modified curriculum in a special education setting that he feels left him not fully prepared for college.

The outcome if Michael had been included and if he had attended a "regular" secondary school is speculative. While such an education might have provided Michael with a superior academic background, there is still concern about his ability to adjust to the stressful world of a large high school. Michael's experience suggests that the decision of whether or not to include a special child in a general education setting should include consideration of a child's academic potential, post-high school expectations, typical behavior, and the quality of available support services. With hindsight and with the positive experiences of many special needs children now enrolled in inclusion programs, it is likely that students similar to Michael do profit in many ways from typical school experience. Although inclusion could have resulted in social adjustment problems, one college professor who knows Michael well commented that he "is an inspiration and a 'poster boy' for the use of mainstreaming and inclusion, where appropriate." But for Michael, inclusion did not occur until college.

In college, Michael first confronted his special education history when a professor asked her students to write their education autobiographies. The assignment forced Michael to think about what he had been trying to camouflage, and the professor was not prepared for the emotional "meltdown" that resulted from this routine assignment. Michael cried when he met with his professor privately and related his school history to her. He suffered from doing the assignment and this episode reminds us of the stigma students may feel whenever they are singled out, labeled, and treated differently.

Interactions with faculty and behavior in the classroom

Before college Michael had always attended special schools with small classes taught by faculty who were trained and sensitive to the unique learning needs and behavior of their students. The choice of this small liberal arts college was very appropriate, because the college prides itself on the faculty's "open door" policy for students, smaller classes than many other universities, and a "student-friendly" atmosphere. While Michael was not part of this college's program for learning disabled students, many of the faculty had experience relating to students with special needs and may have been more attuned to Michael's differences because of this. Several commented that they noticed Michael's odd behavior and mannerisms and this suggested to them that he might have been in the special program. Sometimes, Michael tested his professors' patience by coming late to class, asking too many questions, obsessing on details, and challenging others. Michael did benefit from being in the honors college, because it signaled his high academic ability. A poll of many of his professors reveals that most found Michael quirky but delightful, because of his love of learning. Michael formed close relationships with many faculty, who valued him both as a person and as a student.

Michael wanted to be treated the same way as other students, but did not always "blend" into the background. By his own admission, Michael often does not "get it," and he had difficulty acting like other students in class. For example, most faculty expect that students make eye contact with them, indicating that the student is paying attention and giving the teacher non-verbal feedback about whether the student understands what is being taught. Michael has difficulty making eye contact, because he says that it disturbs his concentration. This might have resulted in some faculty assuming that Michael was daydreaming, disrespectful, or bored. Several faculty have mentioned Michael's perpetually smiling face and recognize that most college students don't always appear to be so happy. Unfortunately, the smiling often masked the sadness that Michael felt.

Michael's extraordinary desire to achieve helped him to overcome many barriers. For example, during his freshman year the associate dean of the honors college expressed doubts that Michael would be able to complete the demanding program, and he suggested that Michael withdraw. This confirmed Michael's worse fears and self-doubts, but also fueled his tremendous motivation to succeed and caused him to work even harder.

The college experience also showed Michael that he has the capacity to learn appropriate social behavior in class. He recognized that his college peers did not accept the behavior that had previously worked well for Michael in his special schools. For example, because autistic individuals need clarity, structure, and rules, Michael pursued precision with incessant questioning. Initially, he did not recognize that asking complex questions, especially at the end of class, is "bad form" and can annoy both teachers and students. Michael developed some insight regarding social aspects of classroom dynamics, because he eventually learned to modify his behavior to some extent. This change in behavior required concentration and deliberate effort not to fall back on old behavior patterns in each new classroom situation.

College programs that provide support services for students with special needs can be helpful in assisting students like Michael with strategies for interacting by giving constructive feedback about behavior, as well as providing guidance and support. Michael wanted to be a "regular" college student and did not want special services. He learned appropriate behavior by trial and error.

Learning attributes

Michael's superior intelligence and ability to use it distinguishes him from many other autistic individuals. It has been estimated that only a portion of the autistic population has a "normal" IQ and Michael's superior intellectual ability clearly places him in a very small group. He excelled academically in college, a source of tremendous pleasure and recognition for him and a fundamental part of his sense of self. His choice of the math major, with a minor in computer science, naturally fitted his need for precision. The rigorous curriculum in the honors college also provided an enriched learning opportunity, so that by graduation Michael was well educated in the liberal arts. Michael's additional minor in secondary education was a logical outcome of his comfort with schools and a practical answer to his goal of becoming financially independent after college. In summary, Michael made good academic choices throughout his college career.

Some aspects of being autistic enabled Michael to be an excellent student. Michael is very intense and can focus on learning with more sincerity and effort than many other students. He doesn't fatigue easily and pursued academic assignments with tremendous commitment. As one faculty member described it, Michael could sit in front of a computer screen and work out problems long after others would have quit. Michael also expected to be an independent learner. If he didn't know something, Michael pursued his own investigation until he was satisfied that he understood. Michael is tenacious and strong-minded. While at times and in some situations Michael's conduct could be seen as obsessive, at other times and in other situations his conduct was considered persistent and focused.

Michael claims that he is a holistic learner, who needs everything to fit into a big picture. A jigsaw puzzle is easier to assemble when you know what the completed picture looks like, and similarly Michael seeks a "map" of how various aspects of knowledge fit together. At the same time, Michael's need for precision, his focus on detail, and intolerance for ambiguity also caused "roadblocks" to learning. Michael can get "hung up" on one piece of a puzzle. More than missing the forest for the trees, Michael can dwell too long on each branch, twig, or leaf. A math professor related that during one class Michael fixated on solving a problem regarding a topic that mathematicians know is considered unanswerable. Other students accepted this, but Michael didn't. He obsessed on the topic and wasn't able to move on and profit from the remainder of the class.

Michael also has tremendous problems with time management. He can get lost in a task and ignore other priorities, or simply withdraw and let time pass without notice. Michael addressed this problem with a self-devised system of creating and displaying a large chart that divided each day into half-hour time slots. He improved managing his time during test sessions, and refused to self-identify his disability to qualify for untimed exams, or use a word processor, or other technological aids.

Michael also had a compulsive need to know his schedule well in advance so that he could organize his time. This worked well for him when he did his honors thesis during the summer. Unfortunately, this need caused great anxiety when the information wasn't available at the time he wanted it. Michael also had difficulty with unstructured free time, and could not just "hang out" and relax the way his peers did. He managed this by keeping himself busy with extremely full academic and extra-curricular schedules.

Michael has never learned to take notes in class. He says that everything seems to be equally important and it's impossible to decide what to record in a notebook. Instead, Michael chose to only listen. Fortunately, he was able to retain lecture content with precision, because of his extremely good auditory memory. A college level learning skills course, such as those provided for incoming freshmen and learning disabled students, might have helped develop the study skills Michael could have used in college. Such a course was not part of the honors college curriculum, because it was assumed unnecessary for these successful students.

There is growing awareness that more students with autism spectrum disorders are entering college with the resulting need that college programs provide non-traditional support services to help them succeed. In addition to the academic support that colleges provide whenever students have difficulty, some schools now provide guidance on social situations and managing the college experience. For Michael, identifying himself as a "special needs" student was out of the question; he wanted to be like everyone else.

Extra-curricular activities
Michael was determined to form relationships with other students and joined clubs that complemented his cultural and academic interests. He brought the

same single-mindedness to these activities that he did to his academic studies. Michael did not shy away from attempting to connect with his college peers, and while he has leadership qualities, he was not always successful, because he lacked flexibility and spontaneity.

According to one of Michael's math professors, Michael does *not* stand out as markedly different in the world of mathematicians and computer scientists, where his personality traits and idiosyncratic behavior are fairly common. Another professor commented about the high potential for Michael to fit into an academic community where his unusual behavior is less likely to be a problem:

> Although he wants to be a secondary mathematics teacher, and I think he will be an outstanding one, eventually he wants to become a mathematics professor. He will be a natural. With his brilliance, lack of social skills and idiosyncratic quirkiness, he will fit right in as a member of academe.

Michael voluntarily served as editor for a newsletter distributed to students, faculty and alumni. His need for approval and desire to be helpful were manifest in his willingness to take on the demanding job. He performed well, considering his inexperience, disability, and full academic schedule, but he encountered some difficulties negotiating the interpersonal aspects of working with faculty members and others who contributed articles. The recognition Michael received from editing the newsletter satisfied his desire for approval.

Friendships and socialization

The college years are a time to test out social acceptance. Most college students arrive with a social sense gained from prior interactions, which allows them to continue to develop their social skills. Michael entered college with a desire for friendship, but without the skills and experiences that would have helped him know how to do this. For example, Michael cannot deviate from telling the truth. The art of using "white lies" in socially appropriate situations, to avoid unnecessarily hurtful comments, requires subtlety and insight that Michael lacks.

Michael never had nondisabled friends before college and he tried to regulate the world of friendships by creating a chart to help him organize the dynamics of different kinds of relationships. His "friendship rules" were poor substitutes for what other college age students know intuitively, or have learned from past experience. This is an area of struggle for Michael that has gotten far better, but still requires time and conscious attention. When Michael does connect with others, it is the result of deliberate action, rehearsal, and much thinking. This "create a rule and practice approach" is a good example of how Michael tries to manage the effects of his disability.

College was also a time of emotional and physical separation from Michael's family. While Michael relates that he felt like an outsider at college, he did make friends, who were remarkable for their decency and sensitivity. Michael did not surround himself with a large peer group, but found companionship with a few special friends, who think of him as an outstanding person. It is interesting to consider whether Michael had a special affinity for befriending students who were especially caring, or whether he developed these friendships because it takes a certain kind of person to overlook Michael's deficiencies and see his many admirable characteristics.

Dating and girlfriends were not part of Michael's college experience. He has difficulty understanding the "rules" of girlfriend–boyfriend relationships and Michael's discomfort with being physically close to others or being touched is a barrier to a romantic relationship. Nevertheless, Michael's ability to form male–female relationships definitely improved while he was in college, and today he is very motivated to find a meaningful relationship with a young woman. Biographies written by other high-functioning autistic individuals reveal that some have found meaningful life partners, while others say that this is an area in which they are not successful. Michael has changed tremendously, because of his desire to become a fully socialized person, but this is an area that is still evolving.

Today there is far greater awareness and increased knowledge of the social needs of autistic children, and many school programs include training in this regard. Michael did not have the benefit of being exposed to and learning the "scripts" of social interaction through a formal process, but his college experience became a "classroom" for social learning from which he benefited.

Recognizing emotional needs

The college experience can be an emotional time with both positive and negative experiences. While most other college students are keenly aware of their emotional sides, Michael, like other autistic individuals, intellectualizes his feelings, but does not, or cannot, acknowledge the importance of emotions in his life. For example, Michael denies feeling nervous or worried when he started college, which are typical emotions of almost all freshmen.

Michael has difficulty relating spontaneously to others and this can make him appear stilted and guarded. A classic aspect of Michael's autism is his inability to "read" people's faces and this creates more problems in responding to others. To test this out Michael was shown two similar, full-face pictures of the same young child, each expressing a very different emotion. When asked to differentiate between the pictures, and after studying them carefully, Michael said that a part of a hand was shown in the corner of one picture and not the other. He totally ignored the very different facial cues to the emotional reactions of the child. The exercise was also an opportunity to discuss appropriate social behavior, such as saying, "That's such a cute baby!" Autistic individuals need to be taught and reminded to look at faces and think about the feelings of others.

Psychotherapy and counseling are traditionally recommended to help with emotional adjustment. "Talk therapy" was tried when Michael was a college junior, but he had little confidence in the process and was unable to be as self-reflective then as he is today. Choosing the right therapy modality and supportive interventions for an autistic person is very important. Autistic individuals are less likely to profit from therapy based on the ability to be insightful about behavior, because they lack emotional intuition. Instead, therapy that focuses on learning problem-solving approaches and getting objective feedback about behavior is likely to be helpful.

Independent living

College is a time for all students to learn how to manage more independently, whether they live at the college or commute from home. Michael had the benefit of both experiences, because he commuted from home for the first two years and then lived in the dorm. College life, especially living on campus, required Michael to exercise basic independent living skills: remembering to eat, having clean clothes, managing pocket money, not losing things, etc. Michael was poorly prepared for this independence, because previously his family catered to all of his desires, needs and habits.

Michael learned to be independent of his family in some ways, such as commuting and studying, but he refused to take responsibility for some daily living skills such as learning to do laundry. It's interesting that unlike many of their peers, Michael and his room-mate kept their dorm room unusually neat, which demonstrates that Michael can be appropriate in daily living skills when he is motivated to do so. Michael expected that his mother would provide the same level of attention and care that he had been accustomed to, and was very angry when this didn't happen. Michael's journey to independent living engendered familial conflict as his family sought to promote his growth by providing support in a different way. Michael interpreted this as less care. This weaning process must be especially difficult for any disabled child, who is likely to have depended on others in so many ways throughout their childhood and adolescence. Ironically, this conflict may not be so different from the experience of many adolescents who demand to be treated as an adult in some respects, but still remain dependent on their families in other ways.

Michael had poor insight about the changing dynamics occurring within his family, especially between his father and mother, and viewed his family members' concerns as time taken away from him. This was especially true of Michael's difficult relationship with his mother. While Michael was successful at learning the "script" for social behavior with the students and faculty at college, he still had difficulty being calm at home. Although Michael disputes this, his family reports that during the college years he still exhibited aggressive behavior at home, especially towards his mother. This is in stark contrast to the well-mannered, calm person Michael was at college.

Advances in understanding autism

Michael entered college a "pioneer," as prior to that time very few autistic individuals were academically successful enough to go to college. Due to the significant increase in the number of individuals diagnosed with autism and greater awareness of the spectrum of disability within autism, it's likely that Michael's path to college will be followed by many others.

Until the 1990s mainstreaming handicapped children, especially those diagnosed with autism, was the exception rather than the rule and past generations of special education students often did not have choices in education placements. A special education diagnosis could easily result in a bleak prognosis. The inclusion of children with a wide range of disabilities into general education is now a reality for many. Although his special schooling did not adequately prepare Michael for social interactions at college, he did profit from his pre-college education, which provided many good learning opportunities, while attending to his behavioral needs.

Like others, Michael also benefited from new generations of medication prescribed to help reduce symptoms of his disability. During college Michael greatly profited from medication that decreased anxiety and depression. Michael stopped taking his medication during his third year of college, a fairly common occurrence with people with emotional problems, who are not realistic about the importance of medication in their lives. The message for others like Michael is to work closely with the appropriate physician to monitor their well-being and medication needs.

The college years: A lab for learning

There is objective evidence that Michael profited and learned both from the academic and social aspects of college life. Michael thinks that when he started college, he was developmentally at least four years behind other college students in social skills. When Michael graduated, he said that he wished he could start college over again, at a time in his life when he would be better prepared to experience it both socially and academically.

Michael believes that his college experience was very different from the experiences of most other college students. Although he surely was different, it is not self-evident that Michael's experience was completely unique. Many college freshmen are not mature, may feel like outsiders, and need a period of adjustment to settle into college. They do develop and mature over the course of the college years. Michael benefited from the enriched academic program in the honors college, fully participated in various dimensions of college life, and gained significant acceptance and recognition in many ways. Part of Michael's feeling of being so different from others is likely to be a result of his inability to understand how others feel. It may be that Michael was more like everyone else than he imagined and that in real and important ways, he succeeded in his desire to be a "regular" college student in a regular school.

Chapter 3

From Birth through the Early Childhood Years to Diagnosis

He was a very smiley baby—a very fun baby. You could make him laugh, and giggle, but soon Shari, his mother, noticed that something wasn't quite right.

Uncle Joe

The couple meet and marry

Shari met her husband, Jake, when she was 14 and he was 18, while she worked at a bungalow colony, where city families went for a summer in the mountains. She thought he was the biggest "nerd" in the crowd, with black plastic glasses and polyester pants, but he was certainly interested in her. After that summer they continued the friendship talking all night on the phone. Jake was going to a city college and Shari was still in high school. She had great ambition and planned to become a nurse, because she thought that if she became a doctor it would be too time consuming to maintain a quality family life. Jake planned to be a math teacher. When Shari was only 17, Jake gave her an engagement ring, and although they didn't plan to marry soon, they were considered a couple by everyone. Two years later they broke up, but Jake's persistent calls and letters renewed the relationship.

Shari was always an excellent student and proudly remembers getting the math medal in junior high school and graduating number 5 out of a class of 1100 from high school. Jake's plans to be a math teacher didn't materialize and after college he took a job with a drug store chain. Shari was concerned about Jake's future and encouraged him to go back to school to prepare for a professional career. In frustration Jake told her that he could sell vacuum cleaners or even be a garbage man, but Shari kept insisting that he return to school. Eventually the couple decided to marry and in April 1976 the ceremony took place. As newlyweds, Shari worked as a hospital nurse and Jake worked and studied accounting at night.

Michael is born: April 21, 1980

When Jake graduated from the accounting program, he began work as a junior accountant at a large medical center. Four years later, Shari delayed her plans to return to school for a bachelor's degree, because she wanted to have a baby. Shari became pregnant. The couple lived in a large, one-bedroom apartment and looked forward to the birth of their first child. Thinking back, Shari admits that they could have waited longer, but they did not know how difficult their life was to be:

> *Shari*: You don't know what life is going to bring you. You think you have plans, and then things change forever.

During the pregnancy Shari continued to work until her eighth month. She felt good and the pregnancy had gone well. During her eighth month, she stopped working, because her "belly was big," the demands of hospital nursing became taxing, and she had concerns about exposure to illnesses. Shari and Jake purchased a crib and awaited the birth of their first child.

Shari's due date came and passed, while she continued to get bigger and bigger. Her contractions started on a Saturday night, but she didn't enter the hospital until Sunday. Awaiting the first grandchild on both sides of the family, the extended family gathered in the hospital waiting room and the lengthy labor caused them great concern. The contractions continued with little progress and after 14 hours in the labor room, the doctor decided to perform a Caesarian section. Michael was born on Monday night at 10:20 p.m. He was 7 lb 11 oz and 20 inches long. Great joy and expectations surrounded the birth.

> *Shari*: With a beautiful face and a pointy cone head and there he was.

Shari ran a fever and stayed in the hospital five days, but eventually the new family went home to their apartment. She decided to nurse Michael, but due to the fever she had to stop nursing. To help with the baby, Shari's mother, Helen, stayed with them for the first week. Shari remembers Michael being such a good baby.

> *Shari*: He'd sleep; he'd eat. After two weeks he was sleeping from 7 p.m. until 5 a.m. and was easy to take care of.

Shari thought she wouldn't return to work as quickly as she had anticipated, because she wanted time to enjoy being a mother. Michael was doing well and he was a gorgeous baby.

> *Shari*: His head got beautiful. Blond hair and blue eyes and fair skin, and he filled out nicely.

Not long after, Shari began to experience bouts of post partum depression. She also noticed that Michael didn't suck well and she switched bottle nipples many times until he seemed more comfortable. She says that she didn't like the way he would drink and later this observation became the first thing that Shari noticed that caused her concern about the beautiful baby. At six weeks, Michael was started on food and things seemed to get easier. At four months, he had two teeth. He was a "smiley baby" and the family remarked that he looked just like the adorable baby on the label of the Gerber baby food jar. Michael made good eye contact, gurgled, seemed happy, and responded well to people.

Concerns

When Michael was four months old, Shari returned to her nursing position and the baby was cared for by his great-grandmother, who found him to be a good baby, who was very active. Shari remembers that Michael sat up at five and half months and by eight months he actually walked across the living room. He smiled and responded to people, babbled a bit and even made sounds similar to "ma-ma." He was the delight of the whole family.

Perhaps because she is a nurse, Shari was even more vigilant about Michael's development and she became concerned that the baby made no sounds that resembled language. Jake didn't think there was anything to be worried about and he was a real "hands-on" daddy, while Shari worked late hours. Shari's mother remembered that her other daughter was also a late talker and reassured her daughter that Michael was a healthy boy. But Shari's concerns about Michael continued.

> *Shari*: When he was past a year, I was watching for language. I watched his play and I watched him retreat. He'd bang on the pots and pans. He went to the cabinet where I kept the [plastic containers], which made my mother-in-law think he was brilliant. He'd take the top off the round bowl and stand it on

its side and spin it. And then the flapping started. This was during the second year.

Shari became aware that Michael loved to watch television, but he didn't care for the usual children's programs. Game shows were his favorite. He was most interested in staring at the credits as they rolled down the screen at the end of a show and he would sit in front of the television totally absorbed, flapping his arms with his mouth wide open.

Shari was seeing a pediatrician who had been her own childhood doctor and therefore she felt especially close to him. When Shari saw the doctor for one of Michael's regular check-ups, she described her concerns in detail, including the fact that at about 18 months of age Michael's eye contact was decreasing, and there was still no language, or sounds that resembled language. The doctor did not comment. When Michael reached age two, Shari was convinced that something was wrong because at times Michael seemed lost in his own world and wasn't developing age-appropriate language. Because little Michael was able to make his needs known, the family dismissed Shari's concerns.

Shari: Mother's intuition. I knew something was wrong.

Shari continued to share her concerns about Michael with the pediatrician who suggested that she observe him carefully and keep detailed records. Shari noted that at two years and nine months Michael didn't respond to loud sounds. He didn't play the way that other children his age did and he couldn't be left alone at all. At the next doctor's appointment, the physician spent a full half hour observing Michael. He finally agreed that it would be helpful to get other doctors' opinions and thus the round of appointments with specialists began. The family became aware that the baby did have problems.

Uncle Joe: Eventually, Michael became a stereotype with hand flapping, little or no eye contact. Little things would bother him and Shari jumped on all of that and really started a lifetime commitment to finding out what needed to be done.

The perfect baby is autistic

When Michael was two years and nine months old, the first specialist was consulted. He was a pediatric neurologist located at a prestigious New York City hospital. The doctor concluded that Michael was neurologically intact and while there was nothing remarkable in the physical exam, his diagnosis was infantile autism. The dreaded words appeared in writing for the first time: *infantile autism*. The doctor's report included the following information:

> On examination Michael was an alert, bright eyed child who readily played with blocks, toys and other objects. He did make a variety of sounds including fragments of words but only rarely a complete word such as "car"…"mommy." He paid little or no attention to specific requests made by his mother or by the examiner. He was able to place different shaped blocks into appropriate spaces. He also filled in missing letters in a word. He tended to talk in a sing-song voice. He was able to arrange puzzles at age level. At times, he walked off by himself waving his arms and jumping tiptoe. When he was refused a toy, he screamed loudly in frustration. There was little eye contact.

> Impression: The history and findings are indicative of infantile autism. The pace of his early development and the acquisition of skills, if not language, suggest that he has normal intelligence. The neurological status is normal.

Many, many doctors

The circuit of doctors' appointments continued for approximately six months, with each specialist confirming the diagnosis of autism. The news was stunning. Although medically trained in nursing, autism was a disorder that Shari and the family knew little about. Shari and her mother sought opinions from other experts with the faint hope of discounting the first diagnosis, but also to learn more about Michael and autism. They proceeded to make the rounds of many specialists at hospitals that Shari knew were prestigious.

Two weeks after seeing the first specialist, and at his recommendation, Shari and her mother took Michael to a psychiatrist at a large medical school. In a two-page report this doctor confirmed many of the initial findings with the following concluding paragraph:

> Michael made no eye contact with me. He made fleeting eye contact with his mother and grandmother. He babbled a lot and said several words; he occasionally echoed. He did not seem to understand anything I said to him. He related poorly and seemed to involve himself with his mother or grandmother only when he wanted something done, like to open the door.

> Diagnostic impression: Pervasive Developmental Disorder–Infantile Autism.

This specialist referred Shari to a therapeutic nursery program at an adjacent hospital to consider a residential placement for Michael in their hospital-based program. The visit to that program had a profoundly negative impact on both Shari and her mother. They felt that the hospital environment was forbidding and they were especially upset to learn that many of the children were given strong psychotropic medications. Shari's mother even recalls witnessing a nurse smack a child. This was no place for their child and the two women fled the hospital.

> *Helen, Shari's mother:* Up to 18 months Michael didn't seem that different. But when he was about two years old we made the rounds of doctors. It was a grim prognosis. When one doctor told us that Michael was autistic, we went next door to his hospital to see a program for special children. They wanted to put him into the hospital. I'll never forget what we saw. Their cribs were like cages and it was primitive. That unit was frightening. One of us grabbed the stroller and the other grabbed Michael and we literally ran out of that building. It was freezing cold and we were crying. We were sick at what we saw. We ran out of there so quickly.

> *Jake, Michael's father:* When he was so young, the doctors at one hospital wanted Michael on a locked ward. Shari wouldn't put up with that. But from that time on we knew Michael would always be different.

Unwilling to admit Michael to this residential program, Shari and her mother took Michael to another specialist in a pediatrics department at a different medical center two weeks later. Shari was not going to be satisfied with any doctor or program that didn't offer help and information. Again, the diagnosis was confirmed.

> *From the report:* My examination revealed a well-developed, well-nourished, handsome young man with a screeching, shrieking cry. He never made eye contact and never related to the examiner in the sense of an interpersonal relationship.
>
> His general behavior and lack of relatedness strongly suggests the presence of Autism. If this is the case, he appears to be rather high functioning, and it is somewhat encouraging to note that he has developed some language at this time. I have referred him to [this hospital's] Child Development and Learning Center for extensive psychological and psychiatric workup. The objective is to evaluate his current status and recommend the most optimal setting for him to be placed in, to enhance his future progress.

Shari: From January to June we spent the six months seeing specialists. He was almost three years old when we began the round of doctors. Every kind of specialist examined him and he was even admitted to a hospital for a day. He was tested for fragile X and other chromosome disorders. He had a CAT scan of his head and we met with a geneticist who wanted to map his genes.

I walked around with a pad of paper to write down every word I heard Michael say. He had about 30 single words, but we didn't hear him use the words every day.

I didn't know anyone else who was going through what we were going through at the time. I was searching. I did whatever they asked me, whatever they told me, as long as it felt right. I did see a lot of people over the years where I walked right out on them, if it didn't seem right to me.

So after all that testing, it was autism.

Uncle Joe: My sister didn't know that what she was doing was right, but it turns out that everything she did was right. She sought the best advice and became a Sherlock Holmes. Her background was outstanding and it's almost like she was prepared to take on this role.

Michael presented a repertoire of behaviors that are both typical and unusual for autistic toddlers, including what one specialist labeled "precocious linguistic ability." Michael's behavior was very inconsistent. At times he would get excited to see family members, but then would quickly lose interest and play alone. He exhibited toe-walking and would often twirl and pirouette. He was a very poor eater, refusing all meat and vegetables and since his first birthday his primary food was plain bread.

Jake: I have a younger brother who is 10 years younger than me and I remember him growing up. I remember my brother's first words, but not with Michael. His eating habits were terrible and he couldn't stand the texture of food. He couldn't drink from a straw until he was about 10 or 11.

At age two and a half, Michael climbed out of his crib and later slept on a mattress on the floor. The whole apartment had to be child-proofed, because he didn't learn to follow rules and was "into" whatever interested him. By age two years and ten months, Michael had a vocabulary of almost 30 words, but used them in an echolalic manner and did not use language to communicate with people or to express his needs. Michael had a fascination with the alphabet, which he could recite accurately in rote fashion and he could even spell the words "mommy," "daddy," and "nanny" on his magnetic board with dimensional letters. He was able to count from 1 to 20 and used numbers to count objects showing that he understood numeration. Michael was able to assemble 12-piece puzzles and was fascinated and skillful with shape-sorting toys. Other behavior was especially problematic, including incessant ripping of paper, spinning objects, flapping his hands in the air, and often just appearing lost in his own world.

> *Shari:* I want to say that at home he was a good baby, but he screamed and cried and banged his head. And he had tantrums. But I want to say that he was really a good baby. He was quiet a lot of the time except when he'd stand in front of the TV and he'd flap and make noises.
>
> I also remember that he liked magazines, but what he did with them was shred them. I'd come home from work on a Saturday and his Dad had him all day and I had to wade through the shredded papers in the living room. I had heard about another child who would take boxes of food out of the cabinets and break them. That child would also open the refrigerator and pour everything out of the containers. Or he would smash eggs. But Michael didn't do food, he did paper—newspapers, magazines, decks of cards, which he shredded. For a long time, he just wanted to shred paper.
>
> He liked spinning things, figuring things out, putting things together. He loved puzzles and playing with the telephone. His favorite thing was playing with magnetic letters. He could spell before he could talk. There were letters all over my refrigerator. He would just sit and spell and he'd be tuned out from us. Sometimes he'd sit by the refrigerator and play with letters and sometimes he'd be sitting and spelling and flapping and making grimacing faces. We'd call to him and got no response. He was so tuned out wherever he was. He didn't like crowds and he didn't like company in the house. It wasn't easy.
>
> *Jake:* He was a problem. He used to spin things a lot. He walked very early, but he really ran, not walked. But it wasn't like a kid chasing something, because he'd run around in circles. We lived in an apartment with a kitchen with two entrances and you could walk around through them. He'd just run around and around until he'd run smack into the walls. And he'd do it just every day.

Accepting the diagnosis was very difficult. While Shari and her mother began to use the term "autistic," both Michael's father and grandfather were in denial about the diagnosis for about six months longer.

> *Jake:* Shari took him around from place to place. She was very good with him and spent an inordinate amount of time with him trying to get him to

make eye contact. Michael's condition had a tremendous impact on the whole family. It was upsetting thinking that it's possible he wouldn't have a so-called normal life, but I thought that doctors aren't always right. Are they?

Michael's great-grandmother, who had cared for him until he was about three years old, never truly believed that anything was wrong with this beautiful child she adored. Her daughter, Michael's grandmother, says this about her mother and her relationship with Michael:

> *Grandmother Helen*: My mother, his great-grandmother, took care of him for the first three years of his life and she never believed that there was anything wrong with him. She was very intelligent, but practiced denial. She treated him like you do with all kids and you couldn't talk to her about Michael's autism. She'd say, "I know it, but I can't believe it," and she gave him that extra measure of love.

When Shari tried to explain Michael's unusual behavior to others, she told them that he had a language delay. Shari thought that people recognized that Michael was a bright child, especially when they saw him focusing on puzzles. People outside the immediate family had never witnessed his self-stimulating behavior. They didn't question Shari or the family further about the language delay. Shari did not use the term "autistic" with non-family members and she tried to focus on the positives, including Michael's fascination with letters and numbers and his use of a magnetic board on which he learned to spell simple words.

> *Jake*: When I came home from work and he was very young, he wasn't saying anything. But then he'd start spelling with magnetic letters. I always thought that the intelligence was there, but nothing about him was the normal way of doing things.
>
> I remember his third birthday party. We made him a party and had other children in the house. He locked himself in his room, because he couldn't stand the noise and he didn't want any part of it. That's not what you would call normal.

Getting help

Everyone realized that special services were needed for Michael to progress and the search for appropriate programs began. The first intervention program was started when Michael was a little over three years of age. He was brought to a developmental center associated with a hospital where Shari had seen a respected specialist. During the summer months, Shari brought Michael to the hospital's speech and hearing center twice a week. By the end of the summer, Michael's language was actually starting to develop. Shari recalls the first time that Michael used two connected words. He said "Bye-bye car," and that occurred during the winter just before he was four.

Shari expected that Michael would be enrolled in the school located in the same hospital as the speech center, but she was told that it wasn't the right environment for him. One of the staff provided Shari with the names of several programs including a special learning center.

> *Shari:* The first appointment for a program interview was at the special learning center and he was accepted that same day. I instantly bonded with the social worker when we did the intake and she remained a dear person in our lives for many, many years. It is a place for emotionally disturbed and learning disabled children. An autism diagnosis wasn't enough for admission, but with Michael's behavior and tantrums, he was accepted. In those days we needed to be certified by the Family Court to be eligible for funding. We applied and he was funded.

> *Grandmother Helen:* Someone up there was looking over and my daughter found that center, but it wasn't easy. And doors were closed to Michael in so many schools. The center was literally Shari's lifeline.

> *Uncle Joe:* I remember the earliest time when Michael was in school at the center. The social worker was a savior for them. Michael looked like such an unhappy child, but I don't know if he was really unhappy, but he was locked in his own world. His mother is the reason that he's out of that world and not institutionalized. She worked with him constantly and never gave up.

The Center for Child Development: Preschool program (ages 3–5)

Michael attended the Center from preschool throughout his childhood years, until he entered another school for high school. The Center is a nonprofit, non-public school funded by the State Education Department and the Office of Mental Health. It is both a day treatment center and a special school and has served seriously emotionally disturbed children and their families since 1959. The early intervention program currently addresses children from birth through age three, the preschool program enrolls children from ages three to five, and the upper school population is for ages five to sixteen. When Michael attended the preschool program, there were approximately 24 children enrolled, but today there are 66 children registered. The Center is devoted to treating children whose primary diagnosis is emotionally based, and the children typically have other characteristics including: attention deficit/hyperactivity disorders, oppositional/defiant disorders, Asperger's disorder, post-traumatic stress disorder, and pervasive developmental delays along with other disorders.

When Michael began at the Center, the school accepted children who were autistic if they also had significant emotional problems. Today, with many other programs designed specifically for autistic children, this is no longer typical. The Center's resources now include specialists from many disciplines to provide specialized services for a wide range of disabilities. When Michael attended the school approximately 20 years ago, he was enrolled in a very small, preschool class along with other very disabled children. He also received services from a speech and language teacher. At the Center Michael was enrolled in Mrs. L's preschool class for two years. She is now the principal of the school and remembers Michael very well.

> *Mrs. L:* At that time [Michael began with us] the Center didn't do extensive screening of the children who applied, and it may have just been a telephone call that got him admitted to the school. Today, of course, there's a full evaluation. In those days, I didn't know the children until they actually came into school and started.
>
> We didn't start a whole class of six children all at the same time. I do remember that Michael started in September and I have a strong memory of two things especially: his mother and his behavior.

Many of the children who attended the Center came from poverty families, were in foster care, or had families with significant mental health and social problems. Michael and his family were different, because they were educated, middle-class people with a very disabled child.

> *Mrs. L:* His mother was not typical of the type of parent we were used to dealing with. It's very scary when you meet someone who is just like you. It was one of my first experiences with someone with a disabled child who was like me. I remember that she brought Michael to school and she stayed to see how things were going. Most parents would just want to leave the child and escape. Shari did what you or I would have done.

The Center and its staff had a tremendous impact on Michael and his family, because of the wonderful support and services they received.

Shari: At age three and a half Michael entered preschool and both my husband and I received the beginning of the emotional support and professional guidance that continued throughout those many years.

We were isolated by our ignorance about Michael's problem and lost in the pain of our fear for his future. A social worker, Mrs. R, entered our lives and gave us hope. She counseled us and encouraged us to attend her parent support groups. She has made herself available to every member of my family including my mother, father, sister, and brother and helped them to understand the disorder so as to be a supportive factor in Michael's education. She remains a meaningful guide and a valued friend.

I asked Mrs. L, Michael's preschool teacher, to describe Michael when he entered the program.

Mrs. L: He was like an animal, but not in a bad way. He was unsocialized, like a little puppy, and he was a biter and a pincher.

On the first day he attended school, we had a fire drill early in the morning. I had to get this child out of the building and I just couldn't do it. He was having tantrums and he wouldn't walk and I couldn't carry him, because he was biting and pinching. I remember walking outside the building and holding him at arm's length. I was thinking that I'm walking in front of the whole school and I didn't want everybody thinking that this was a terrible child. It was his first day of school and he was having a really hard time. Eventually, another woman came over and helped me and together we got him out of the building.

It was just so physically hard to hold him and deal with him. Can you picture sharp, little teeth and fingers just grabbing at you? I remember trying to hold him in a nurturing way, which was impossible, and feeling really bad for him that this was his introduction to school.

There were two possible class placements for children of Michael's age. For the first year, he was placed in a class of very low-functioning children.

Mrs. L: He belonged in that class at that time. He wasn't too aware of the other children. He was a real behavior child at the beginning and I don't think he had much language at that time.

His program was very individualized and language-based. But first I had to get him to stop biting and pinching me. Eventually, he did stop. Some children you could feel guilty about, because you didn't want them in your class. You couldn't deal with the child and the parent was a nightmare. But that wasn't Michael. Eventually, everything you tried to get Michael to do, you could get him to do. He achieved so much that first year and he really started to pick up.

The program was very structured and language-based and extremely consistent. But you had to be careful with Michael. He would learn everything by rote, and therefore you had to change your materials. He developed very good concrete knowledge, but it was a challenge to get him into more abstract concepts. But he did.

Of course, there was no ABA at that time. [Applied Behavioral Analysis is a stimulus-response program widely used with autistic children today.] I did a lot of "look and say" and as an old time teacher I now realize that what I did was the foundation of today's programs for autistic children. There was lots of reinforcement and repetition.

Today it is recognized that the family of autistic children play a central part in their child's program. At the time that Michael attended the Center, there was no formal parent education component, but Shari wanted to learn and do all she could to help her child.

Mrs. L: A lot of what Michael achieved was because of Shari. This was a mother who was grateful for everything you did. In those days, being a mother of an autistic child was a pretty thankless job and some people were still blaming mothers for the child's disability. Shari was so intelligent and we bonded on many levels. Michael was a difficult child, but he had a mother who was wonderful to work with and she would follow through on things we had done in school. It made a difference—a big difference. These are the kind of children who do better and in those days a parent who came in and said, "What can I do?" was a pleasure!

It's difficult to visualize Michael as a preschooler, so I asked Mrs. L to describe Michael during that first year.

Mrs. L: What sticks in my mind is that he had the TV Guide memorized and that's how he knew the events in his life. When such and such was on, that's when Daddy would come home, and if Daddy was late—tantrums!! He also liked coupons. From talking with him today I realize that he was the kind of child who structured his environment so he could function. He worked like a computer.

Mrs. L provided more detail about the difference between Michael's preschool program and the program today.

Mrs. L: We know so much more now and have so many more resources for teaching and have many specialists from different areas as well. For example, if Michael were to come in today, then he'd be put into a class with a modification-teach model where each child has a strip with his or her daily plan on it. The cues would help the child structure the day. It would cut out some of the problems he always had with transitions.

Today, we also teach children social stories. There's a program where the child is exposed to different kinds of situations and the child is taught how to respond. If a person says this, then you say that. For Michael, we never knew what he was thinking. It was a world all about him.

At the end of his first year, I saw a child with a lot of potential and he really responded very well and we worked well together. I have to admit that I loved him. He was very adorable once he stopped biting—a wonderful kid with a wonderful mother. I saw him succeeding. I tell my teachers, you're the child's first teacher and you have the blank slate and you're setting that child up for life.

I asked Shari about Michael's adjustment to preschool.

Shari: His transition was very difficult and his separation from me was very difficult. He was not toilet trained and he was three and a half and we were nowhere near getting him trained. When I took him the first week, mommies were allowed on the school bus. We went on the school bus together for the first few days and I stayed with him in the classroom, and then I stayed in the hall. He spent time in the classroom screaming for me while I sat in the hall. They had a one-way mirror and it was hard for me to watch him scream.

The second week of school he was put on the bus without me which was torture. For the first few days I followed the bus in my car to see if he was okay. It took a month or two of screaming to get him on the bus. I couldn't get his hat and coat on. He knew he was supposed to go to school, but he wouldn't let me dress him. I could barely pick him up and he did every kind of body contortion to stop me. I remember handing him kicking and screaming to the bus matron. Then I'd go upstairs to our apartment and call my mother and cry. I called my husband and just cried. He always had trouble separating. If I'd go to the bathroom, he'd bang on the door.

I asked Shari how she and her husband managed this difficult child. One significant change was Shari's work schedule and the subsequent decision to stop working.

Shari: My job in the hospital was falling apart. I couldn't handle it any more. Michael was put on the bus and traveled to school for an hour each way. He was at school from about eight to two. I wanted to resign from the hospital. They didn't want me to leave so they asked me to work out a schedule around Michael's school. I said I could work when my husband was home at night. So I worked four nights a week and every Saturday and every other Sunday.

I did that for a while, but by the time I got to the hospital it was just too much. Several times my supervisor had to take me off the unit, because I was crying. I worked in the ICU [Intensive Care Unit] and I just couldn't do it. It just got to be too hard. I went to talk with the hospital psychiatrist who told me to take a six-month leave. I was burned out. When six months were up, I took another six months and I didn't go back to working for some time.

I wondered if the family saw changes in Michael during that preschool year.

Shari: Michael started blossoming. The language started to come. By four he could put two words together and there was no medication needed. He was trained by the time he was four and the school helped me with this.

But there were still tantrums in school. He would throw things, turn over chairs and turn over the desks. He went through biting and he bit kids in school. He also bit us. It wasn't always in anger and I almost think it was his way of making contact.

The family services provided by the Center offered much assistance.

Shari: From the very beginning it was apparent that Michael was to benefit from this very special school and its entire staff—therapists, teachers, doctors, and social workers. He also benefited from the training that his father and I received that prepared us to continue the education at home. They had a mother's group, a father's group, and a couple's group. We went to every support group that the school offered. I was a fixture in the school.

We were determined that Michael would have the command of language. We spoke to him every waking moment, gave him opportunity for socialization away from school, and provided continuous stimuli to prevent him from retreating into his own little world.

The second year of preschool

At the conclusion of the first year of preschool, there was discussion about Michael's placement for the next year. Because of the progress Mrs. L had seen during the first year, she decided to "move him up" to a different kind of class the next year.

Mrs. L: I moved him to my other class with higher-functioning children for the next year. They were as dissimilar from Michael as you could imagine, with very dysfunctional families, but they were higher functioning than the previous class in terms of cognition. They were more social than his first year's class as well. I thought we'd see if he would rise to the occasion with this new group.

In the first class he never connected to the other children. He never knew their names and each child in that class really did their own thing and was pretty unrelated to each other. He was different from them, because he functioned on a robotic level.

In Michael's second year, he was in a class that I loved so much, because these kids were great. But they had suffered so; it was heartbreaking to hear their backgrounds. After being a teacher for so many years, this was the one group that I still think about and remember.

In the new class he was very much the odd man out. These children were very social and connected to each other. The children would talk to him and they could get him to get somewhat involved in the group activities. He was so young and it was so early and he hadn't really developed into a person and we were pushing him to be social. He wasn't really part of this group, but he was there and he had his own set of social rules and we tried to fit him in and he tried to make sense of what was going on.

I've read books written by autistic people and it's clear that their anger and frustration come from their very different view of things around them. From their point of view, they are entitled to be angry. The other children were different from Michael in many ways. If they didn't fit a particular need for him, he acted out. His negative or isolated behavior was because he didn't think that the others were doing what he thought they should be doing.

When I asked Michael about his preschool memories he said that he doesn't recall a great deal, but a couple of incidents do stand out. One memory was the physical sense of walking down a long corridor in the school carrying a box of cereal. He brought that "important" box with him from home and held it on the school bus and carried it into his classroom. Another memory is especially interesting, because it exemplifies how Michael interpreted events around him.

This was an incident regarding Theresa, who was a child in Michael's second class. While this is "Theresa's story," Michael thought that the incident was really about him. Michael relates that one day he bit Theresa's ear and after that she never returned to school. Even now Michael believes that his behavior caused Theresa's departure from the school, which isn't correct.

Mrs. L: There is one day I'll never forget during Michael's second year in school. Frankly, I don't remember Michael even being part of the events that occurred. It was the day of Theresa's birthday and we always had parties for the children and made it a big deal. Another child, who was a real heartbreaker because of his family's poverty and many problems, even brought Theresa a home-made present that he wrapped by himself and I thought how sweet it was. It was her fifth birthday and he gave her the present.

There were many terrible things going on in Theresa's family and on her fifth birthday she was removed from her home. This was one of the few times that social services came here and actually took a child. It was an awful coincidence that this happened on her birthday. We never saw her again and it just breaks your heart. This child and the other children had no closure and I often wonder what happened to Theresa.

Mrs. L had the opportunity to discuss this sad day with Michael, when he visited the preschool 20 years later. He told her that he thought his behavior caused the child to leave, and Mrs. L corrected his interpretation of Theresa's departure from the school.

Mrs. L: It's 18 to 20 years later and Michael still thinks it's all about him. He thought she left because he bit her. I don't remember that happening, but he was certainly a biter during the first year of school. The events of the day really had nothing to do with him, but I remember the impact of that day on all of us.

At the end of preschool a decision had to be made regarding Michael's next school placement. While he was still an isolated and difficult child, the school staff realized that he had high potential and acknowledged the significant amount of progress he had made.

Mrs. L: I remember it was time for him to move on and I was just projecting my own feelings. He had done so well and I was so proud of him. I was hoping that he wouldn't have to stay in our center's upper school and that he could move out into the regular world of school. Others didn't agree. He was promoted into our upper school and honestly, he was well placed there.

I was caught up in my own defense of him because I saw his potential and was so proud of him. I was hoping he could go somewhere else, but he did stay in our upper school until his high school placement. This is unusual because children come and go from the school at different times, because they need different kinds of environments. Because we have group meetings, I was aware that Michael had lots of issues and behavior problems all throughout the elementary school years.

I wondered if Mrs. L was aware of problems that persisted with Michael's behavior at home. While he did well in the structured setting of the Center, Michael remained aggressive and angry at home.

> *Mrs. L:* It was typical that kids would fall apart when they got home. School is a very structured setting and they hold it together here. When they get home it's fatigue, or they don't have to behave at home, and they often know that they can get away with things at home that we don't allow in school.
>
> Sometimes, we forget that these children have such a full day and it's hard for them when they get home from school. There's also that emotionality between a mother and child. I can send a child home if he or she is out of control on a given day. A teacher's day has boundaries, but at home it's different for the child and the family.

Now there is consensus about the importance of early intervention for children with disabilities. When Michael was a toddler, there were few programs designed for autistic children, and finding an appropriate one was difficult. Michael's preschool experience did make a significant difference for both him and his family. I asked Mrs. L to comment about this time in Michael's life.

> *Mrs. L:* When the parent comes here this is the time that they are raw. Shari came here and said, "Help my child." She was desperate. We do a lot of parent support. It's the first time that the child is "in the system" and their needs are so different. Michael's preschool years were tough ones, but he did well.

At a recent visit to the Center Mrs. L showed me pictures of Michael's preschool classes. Michael was a very cute, well-built child. In the photos Michael didn't look straight forward or at the other children, and appeared sad. Was he ever happy, I wondered, and I asked Mrs. L.

> *Mrs. L:* For Michael, happiness appeared to be nebulous; and now, of course, he's not the child I knew then.

Author's reflection: The journey from diagnosis to intervention

A child with a major disability such as autism creates enormous issues and stress for the entire family. Families are central to the well-being and progress of all children and even more so for the autistic child. They are the child's first care-givers and can be the child's lifelong advocates. They also provide the child with knowledge about the culture and values of society.

Michael's family went through definite stages in the path from his diagnosis to treatment, which may be informative for others who learn that their child is disabled.

Anticipation and delight

Awaiting the birth of their first child and especially the first grandchild in the family filled Michael's parents and relatives with anticipation and delight. After four years of marriage Michael's parents were ready to become parents. Great joy surrounded the pregnancy and the entire family looked forward to the baby's birth. Shari's medical training kept her well informed about the stages in her pregnancy and there was every reason to believe that there would be a healthy baby.

When the labor went on for too long and Michael was delivered by Caesarian section there was concern. Michael was a sweet infant. Shari called him the "Gerber baby," because he closely resembled the beautiful child on the label of the Gerber baby food jars. New babies are such fun and Michael's birth was symbolic of the family's optimism about the future.

Concern, anxiety, and mother's instincts

All new mothers, especially first-time mothers, have concerns about their infants. There are many questions: Are they sleeping enough? Are they eating correctly? Are they gaining enough weight? Most mothers recall particular anxieties about their child. Some children are fussy eaters; some children don't sleep enough; and some children run high fevers or have chronic illness. Each child is unique and may not achieve the typical milestones at the same time in the same way. It's natural for parents to be concerned about a young child.

Shari was vigilant about Michael and his early problems sucking from a bottle caused her anxiety. As he approached age one, he seemed to be doing well except for unusual feeding habits. He was physically active and walked early. Michael was adored by the entire family, who celebrated each accomplishment.

Between 12 and 18 months, Shari noticed aspects of Michael's behavior that caused her concern. When other children started to babble and make language sounds, Michael didn't. Sometimes he was overly sensitive to sounds, but sometimes Michael wasn't responsive at all. When Michael began to flap his arms in front of the television and "tuned out" his environment, Shari knew that this was significant and needed to be investigated.

Talking about these concerns with both the family and Michael's pediatrician did not help Shari. Initially, they were all dismissive of her concerns and everyone tried to be reassuring. They told her what she already knew: many children don't talk early, especially boys, and all children develop differently. Shari says that her "mother's instincts" guided her to be even more vigilant about Michael, and she continued to question aspects of Michael's development. While others in the family denied that there was anything to be concerned about, Shari persisted in her search for answers to her questions and concerns about Michael. This is a common pattern in the families of autistic children. Often one parent is very concerned about the child, while others in the family deny or don't recognize that there's a problem.

Confusion, fear, and confirmation

Parents of many autistic children recount the frustration they felt when they suspected that their children were significantly different, while others discounted the concerns. The parental confusion and frustration then often turns to despair, when the fears are confirmed that their children are different. The diagnosis of autism is profound and the reality of the diagnosis causes tremendous heartache.

Michael was born in 1980 and less was known about autism then as compared to today. In one respect, Shari was fortunate in her quest for information, because she had a sophisticated knowledge of the medical world. She also lived in a metropolitan area with access to well-regarded hospitals and doctors. Shari, like others, suffered from the fear and sadness over the new term, "autism," that would be permanently attached to her beautiful child. Identifying specialists and the many appointments with different doctors to provide and then confirm a diagnosis, is a common pattern in the lives of these children and their families. While the family doctor or pediatrician may have concerns about a child's development, the formal diagnosis is usually provided by a specialist.

Seeing specialists can cause both confusion and anxiety for the family. Sometimes, various specialists have differing opinions about a child. Simply understanding medical terminology can be overwhelming to a family that is already under emotional stress. The manner in which a specialist relates to a family can also vary widely with different consequences. Families can wonder whom to trust and whose advice is most important. The formal evaluation of a child with autism creates a new world with the introduction of unfamiliar terminology, multiple and sometimes conflicting recommendations, and too little or too much information. How best to negotiate this path to formal diagnosis is a tremendous challenge.

When several specialists confirmed the autism diagnosis for Michael, there was tremendous despair. The birth of a child is the cause for celebration, but when the child is disabled joy turns to sadness. The manner in which each family member comes to terms with the diagnosis may vary tremendously. In Michael's family some were in denial, some could not use the word "autism," but all were sad and fearful. As Michael's father related, it is so difficult to accept that your child may never have a normal life.

Acceptance, determination, and assistance

In Michael's family, there is a strong bond between Shari and her mother. Their instincts set the direction for Michael's future. Shari and her mother are people who face problems head-on, but the support system of the whole family provided tremendous help. Once the two women accepted that Michael was autistic, they were determined to find the best help. When one specialist wanted Michael placed in a residential program, Shari and her mother were horrified by what they saw and rejected the recommendation. The women continued to look for individuals who could provide the help and insights that they needed to aid their beloved child.

At that time resources for the treatment of autism were limited and locating appropriate programs was difficult. Information about autism today is far easier to access and there are many organizations and support groups devoted to assisting families. Due to the marked increase in numbers of children diagnosed with autism spectrum disorders, there are now many specialized programs. Because the quality and approach of programs can vary tremendously, parents still describe their frustration locating appropriate services and programs with which they are comfortable.

Deciding on the best help for Michael was primarily determined by his mother's instincts. It was apparent to Shari that speech and language therapy was a priority for the child and therefore this was the first interventional service that was utilized. Michael's subsequent placement at the Center, which appears to have been a combination of luck and circumstance, was of tremendous benefit to all. Even though the state of knowledge about the treatment of autism was different in those years, it is evident that due to the good will and professionalism of the staff at the Center, Michael progressed and his family had a support structure to help them.

Twenty years ago autism was a disorder that some had read about, but few knew first hand. The number of cases of diagnosed autism has increased enormously in recent years, whether because of better identification, more children fit into the broader category of having an autism spectrum disorder, or because there are truly more cases. One expert has called the high increase in autism a public health crisis. Providing information and resources can do a great deal to assist families in the process from diagnosis to intervention. It is so important that those who work with these children and their families truly understand the poignancy, frustration, confusion, and sadness that families experience.

Chapter 4

The Most Difficult Years of Childhood

He once had a tantrum in the classroom that was so bad that they cleared the room. He destroyed it. Michael remembers when he went berserk. He had a tantrum wherever we were. His father and I picked him up and carried him out of every place we were—every shopping mall, every restaurant. We never knew what triggered him. When he got a little older he would hold himself together until he got home, then he would be hell on earth in the house, but he stopped acting out in the street when he was maybe eight or nine. He only did it in the house or in school. It was safe in those places.

Shari

Michael's years from kindergarten through his graduation from the Center in ninth grade contained many dramatic events including the birth of a sibling, academic progress, deteriorating behavior, a Bar Mitzvah, and most importantly, a two-month hospitalization at age nine. The hospitalization was so critical in Michael's perception of his development that he describes his childhood as having two parts: time before the hospital and time after. Michael's behavior was so problematic during his childhood years that it disrupted every phase of his life, but the childhood educational experiences also laid the groundwork for the very productive secondary school years that would follow.

Before the hospital: Scot enters the family

When Michael was six, his parents had another son, Scot, and Michael's world was forever changed. Michael's mother had deep concerns about having a second child:

Shari: Everybody told me to have another baby. I said I didn't want to have another child. I didn't think I could give Michael what he needed if there was a baby, and I was afraid it [the autism] would happen again. We did the chromosome tests, and there was nothing they could see. Everybody said it would be good for Michael to have a brother or a sister—to see that there are other people and other things going on in the family. But Michael's world was all Michael. It didn't work. Michael's whole world is still Michael.

Shari tried to prepare Michael for the arrival of the baby.

Shari: When I was pregnant he was six and he didn't understand there was going to be a baby. I tried to explain it to him. It took him a while to understand. When Scot was born, I asked special permission for Michael to see me in the hospital, because he was worried that something was wrong with me. They gave us special permission. They took him to the nursery to see the baby. The nurses fussed over Michael, but he was worried that something was wrong with me.

Shari recalls Michael's initial reaction to Scot.

Shari: At first, when I came home, he was okay with the baby. I was in the hospital for only two days and then we all stayed at my mother's house for a week. Michael had a lot of people around him, and he seemed okay. We took Scot to Michael's school to show everyone Michael's brother. The baby slept in our bedroom, but Michael wanted to know when the baby was going to sleep in his room. I waited about a month and I put him in Michael's room. At first, Michael was doing okay.

The baby was born in April and initially Michael seemed to adjust to the change in his family. That summer Michael attended a regular day camp and the camp personnel were not told about Michael's special needs and his diagnosis. They were told that Michael was a sensitive and immature child who was very shy. All things considered, the summer went fairly well. Shari remembers Michael's camp experience:

Shari: He had an okay summer and he was very quiet. At camp he went off by himself, but he didn't tantrum. The counselors liked him and he was really a very good little boy. But he didn't want to play sports; he wanted to dig holes. There was another little boy there that liked to dig holes also, and while the others were playing sports, the two of them dug a hole to China.

In the fall, it became clear to everyone that Michael began to regress. His behavior deteriorated and even his language skills took a step backward.

Michael's behavior was characterized by temper tantrums and violent outbursts that occurred both in and out of school. While Michael initially appeared to have positive feelings for his baby brother, concerns soon developed about how Michael would treat his brother, because of his own very difficult behavior which included hitting and biting.

> *Shari:* When Scot was six months old, Michael said he loved him. He held him and gave him the bottle. By the time Scot was two, we were in trouble. While I didn't think he would intentionally hurt the baby, I never left Michael alone with him. He tried to love him, but he was mad at me for bringing this baby home and eventually it came out just how mad he was at me.

> *Jake, Michael's father:* Back when he was a child, Michael said he wanted a brother or sister. He only wanted the baby to be in his bedroom and wanted to feed him. We had fears that there would be danger, because of Michael's tantrums and hitting. As he got older Scot became a fighter and didn't want to put up with Michael. Scot would hit Michael over the head with a baseball bat if he got angry. When they were older and if they were alone together, Scot would actually take care of Michael.

Michael freely admits that Scot's birth had a strong and negative impact on him. As an adult Michael reflects on his brother's birth and the resulting change in his own behavior.

> *Michael:* At that time, Scot ruined my life. I lost my parents when Scot was born, because they were with him. I had no understanding of dual attention and if he was there, it was all about him. It was a change from how things had been before. I resented all the attention he was getting and that was actually the true reason that I behaved the way I did. I felt that my mother's concern wasn't me; it was my brother. My mother's concern in life was to make sure he was okay, not me. I always demanded a lot and she always did it, because there was nothing competing. I had no qualms about reacting physically instead of reacting verbally.

The complex and troubled relationship between Michael and Scot is discussed in Chapter 10.

Before the hospital: School and more doctors

Michael did well academically in the primary grades. He developed verbal ability and speech therapy was no longer needed.

Shari: He was the shining star of the school. He responded to whatever they were working on with him. Everything they did with him, he learned. He was always so good at math, but his IQ was low because he tested so poorly. The scores were so low, maybe 40 or 50, but they knew he was bright. He loved school.

The area of greatest concern was Michael's behavior, especially at home. When Michael was approximately six and a half, a pediatric neurologist was consulted, because of his inconsistent behavior, poor impulse control, and aggression at home and at school. For the first time medication was prescribed to reduce the violent behavior.

From the neurologist's report: Michael has made great strides in language development and is particularly good at mathematics. Last year he began having temper tantrums and even striking out when upset. He became irrational under stress. His school indicates that he is distractible, has difficulty staying on task, yet has difficulty changing tasks and also has problems with eye/hand coordination.

However, Michael made an overall favorable impression on this neurologist.

From the report: Michael presented as a pleasant, cooperative, fidgety boy who was easily distracted. He insisted that my scale was wrong because it was three pounds different from another scale. His observations were interesting as were his comments. For example, he asked me if I was running behind in my schedule. He talked well and had a good fund of knowledge. He could read a second and third grade paragraph quickly but did not pay attention well enough to answer the questions.

This specialist's overall diagnostic impression of Michael was "pervasive developmental disorder with poor impulse control." Medication was prescribed to address the behavioral issues and there was a referral to a psychologist who specialized in behavior modification. Months later, when Michael was eight years old, the family consulted Dr. B, a psychiatrist, because of continuing deterioration in Michael's behavior both at home and at school. Dr. B is a very caring and dedicated professional and has remained Michael's psychiatrist through adulthood and knows him intimately. In his first diagnostic report, Dr. B indicated that Michael appeared to be significantly depressed and reported that the child made statements indicating that he wished to die. But again, Michael made an overall favorable impression:

From Dr. B's report: Michael appears to be a very friendly (overly friendly?) almost eight-year-old boy. He appears to be bright and was surprisingly articulate, expressing himself very clearly. Given the past history of the pervasive development disorder, I was quite surprised at how well he related to me. Most striking was his marked high level of activity. He has extreme difficulty sitting still even for a short period of time. He is extremely fidgety and constantly walking around the room needing to touch everything he sees.

Michael acknowledged frequently feeling unhappy and even depressed. He has had thoughts of wanting to die, although [he] denies ever actually thinking of killing himself. He feels very badly about the fact that he is always getting into trouble. In fact, one of his three wishes was that he was "a different person and didn't have to go to a million doctors." He readily acknowledges that he has difficulty controlling his anger and wants to get some type of help. He asks intelligent questions [about] how medication works to help control anger.

What was especially striking about this evaluation was Dr. B's reaction to a figure drawing Michael did at this consultation:

Dr. B: Until I saw the figure drawings there was really nothing to indicate the severity of Michael's difficulty. However, his drawings were quite bizarre. For example, when asked to draw a person he drew the face, a long neck, and then proceeded to draw two circles which he told me were the belly button and the penis. He "forgot" to draw the frame of the body and would have left the umbilicus and penis isolated from the head and neck if it weren't for my reminder. When he did complete the drawing, he drew no arms but large hands with enormous fingers. Given the fact that he is an intelligent youngster this is a strikingly bizarre drawing.

Dr. B's overall clinical impression, while noting the early childhood history and Michael's current level of functioning, was that Michael had an "atypical-pervasive developmental disorder." It was clear to both Dr. B and Michael's parents that in his early years Michael made dramatic improvement in many areas, but this stopped when his brother was born and there was severe regression. The new course of treatment prescribed by Dr. B was different medication, individual cognitive-behavior therapy, and parent counseling.

Michael had always been a very interesting child, who seemed to be both similar and different from many other autistic children. Early on he displayed some of the "classic" traits of autism such as language delay, hand flapping, showing obsessive behavior, and being totally self-absorbed. He also had special talents described in some autistic children including superb geographic memory and incredible mathematical talent. His father recalls one example of this:

> *Jake:* He seemed to have a photographic memory. One time when he was very young, we had to go to an office for handicapped children in order to keep him qualified for special education. We were discussing it, but we weren't sure how to find the office. Michael told us how to get there, because he saw it when his bus passed it on his way to school. He gave us specific directions for the route we needed to take.

Michael's Uncle Joe remembers another trait:

> *Uncle Joe:* He was an incredible kid. When he was young you could tell him someone's date of birth, and he'd tell you how many days old they were. He also could figure out which day of the week the birth date fell on.

School took on tremendous importance in Michael's life and in the life of the family. School structured Michael's day and gave Shari needed respite from his outbursts and demands and also provided time for Shari to devote to her younger child. The personnel at the school also provided enormous support for the family and gave them advice about strategies to handle such a difficult child. Even though Michael had behavior problems at school, he truly enjoyed attending.

> *Jake:* Once Shari got him to go, he wouldn't miss a day of school. Once he literally cut off part of his finger, but he wouldn't miss school. He was attending a Sunday program to develop the social aspects of handicapped children. He was walking along the wall with his finger touching the wall and a door closed on it and the finger was cut off. We took him from the place and rushed him in an ambulance to the hospital where they sewed the finger back on. The next day he wanted to go to school and he did return in a couple of days and he wrote with his other hand. Michael's life was all about school.

Before the hospital: Grades 1–3

Michael doesn't have a great deal of detailed memory about his school experience prior to the hospitalization when he was nine. He does recall having had the same teacher for first and second grade. I asked him about his school experience in the primary grades:

> *Michael:* I don't remember much, but sometimes we watched *Sesame Street*. I know that we copied the morning message first thing each day to practice

penmanship. I didn't talk to other kids much, but I shared chips with another boy and I never saw those kids outside of school.

I didn't like having a new teacher in third grade and I think she was strict. I would yell, flap, hit, or bite, or run out of the room. I know I had to be carried out of the classroom to the time out room. In that room I would kick the door and when I was older I scratched on the wall.

There are several themes that emerge from interviews with Michael's childhood teachers and the school psychologist. They remembered incredible problems with Michael's outbursts, aggression, and unpredictable behavior in the primary grades, but all remarked about his intelligence, academic ability, and often charming personality. I asked Michael if he remembers what caused his outbursts.

> *Michael*: Anything would set me off: my books out of order, if the school bus was out of order in the line, if I wasn't ready to leave the classroom. There was physical aggression. Being the age that I am now and being analytic, I can't say that my behavior at eight was part of a deep thought process. I was unhappy and I would do what would make me not unhappy. I didn't get my way all of the time and I felt that it was worse than during previous years.
>
> I think that medication worked for me from about age seven to eight. But later the effects wore off and they couldn't increase the dosage. I know that in the spring before the hospital I tried lots of medicines. Even then they wanted me to be in the hospital, but the hospital unit was too full.

Michael's teachers have keen memories of Michael throughout his many years at the Center and especially his extreme behavior problems prior to the hospitalization.

> *Ms. B, who is a crisis teacher*: When you mention Michael's name, my whole face just brightens up because Michael always had a smile on his face even when he was angry. He was one of a kind. Even when he did something that he knew was wrong, he would always turn it around. One time he swung at a teacher and tried to hit her, and then he said, "Do you think it's going to rain today?" And I said, "You did something wrong." He said, "Let's forget about that," and then continued to talk about the weather.

I asked Ms. B what provoked the outbursts.

> *Ms. B*: Anything. If the weather was bad and we had to change from going outside to inside, he couldn't accept it. He would try to control himself, but he would start shaking and grit his teeth and try to restrain himself so no one else would have to. At dismissal we had 14 buses and his bus usually

came first, but if his bus wasn't first, that would set him off. He'd say that he had to be home by 3:00 to watch a TV program, and he'd go off. He was the type of child that even if he got upset or excited you could switch it around and he would try to listen to you. You could work with him, but he couldn't accept changes.

I asked about his overall ability.

Ms B: You always saw his intelligence. He wasn't only book smart. He was a manipulator and he could talk his way into everything and you could really have a conversation with him.

Ms. L, who worked as a teacher's assistant in kindergarten and in the primary grades: We used to physically have to pull him into and out of the classroom because of his tantrums. After he had an outburst he'd say, "It's over, just forget about it. Don't bring it up. I'm sorry."

One thing I must say is that he was the most beautiful child. In preschool he really had a lot of autistic traits, and I would see him with his mother and just want to say hello, because he was a gorgeous baby. When he was older, he got so upset that he would cry a little, smile a little and this would go back and forth. But his face would be like sunshine. He really had a sense of humor and could come up with things and you'd wonder where did he get that from.

Twenty years from now, if you ask if I remember him, I'd say, "You can't forget him." He was the most quick-witted child and what made him stand out among the other children was that he was extremely bright.

Dr. J is presently the chief psychologist at the Center and saw Michael for therapy for many years. He remembers Michael well. I asked him about his initial impressions of Michael.

Dr. J: It seems as if I've had a whole lifetime of knowing Michael. I tested him when he was four years old and I saw him for individual therapy from ages 11 to 15. He's brilliant with math and his math skills were unbelievable even at age four. In his early childhood he had many autistic features: violent tantrums, speech delay, very oppositional, outbursts, and echolalia. He made tremendous progress here and he responded very well, but he needed the right situation to bring out his best elements.

Before the hospital: Behavior at home

At home, dreadful behavior problems between Michael and his brother and tantrums persisted. As Scot got older, he invaded Michael's space and the boys competed for their mother's attention. When this happened, Michael reacted violently.

> *Shari*: He was terrible to Scot even when he was only three years old. The baby would go over to his brother and say "Hi" and Michael would take the door and slam it in his face. And he really hit him. In the beginning it was "My baby, my baby." That lasted until Scot started to become a person and then it all changed. As soon as Scot walked and talked, it changed.

While Michael counted on his mother's undivided attention during his early childhood years, with the birth of his brother he was no longer the total focus of her life. While all siblings compete for parental attention, Michael's anger at his mother turned into increasingly violent behavior. When Michael's aggression was exhibited at school, there was a team of people who was frequently enlisted to handle him, but this wasn't true at home where his behavior become especially frightening.

> *Shari*: I was his security and his whipping post. I was the one to come to, when he was sick or in trouble and I took care of everything, but I was also to blame for everything.
>
> And he hit me, and he was getting bigger. And he hurt me. And I learned to get him on his stomach with his hands behind his back and physically sit on him until I could talk to him and calm him down. He hit Scot and he hurt him and I would have to restrain him. His tantrums were unbelievable sometimes.
>
> When Michael was nine, it was a terrible year, a horrible year. Sometimes I'd get a sheet around him to restrain him, so that he wouldn't hurt us. I knew I had to stop him before he hurt himself or hurt us or broke things. Every doorjamb in my house was cracked from slamming doors.

> *Uncle Joe*: His violence was tough and I remember getting calls and I'd go over and just sit on him. There were many family interventions on many levels. We were all running over to the house and I even stayed at any hour. But for us it was normal. We're all family and that's what you do for your family.

> *Jake*: When he was with his mother he expected her to do everything for him and she always did. And if she couldn't do something, he just couldn't handle it. His temper was mostly directed at Shari, and occasionally toward Scot. He was physical and verbal and then I had to step in and I'd get the worst of it. The only time he was physical with me was when I was trying to protect Shari and when he was older he just picked me up and threw me into the wall.

In the spring, just as Michael was turning nine, his parents sought assistance from the specialists they were seeing, because they no longer knew how to handle his behavior and were concerned that Michael would hurt his brother. They were also fearful of hurting Michael, because physical restraint was needed to contain his outbursts and they were afraid that in their frustration they might abuse him. Michael was especially physical with his mother who bore bruises from his aggressive behavior. Dr. B, Michael's psychiatrist, commented on Michael's status at that age and for the first time raised the issue of hospitalization, as well as the possibility of a residential placement for Michael.

> *From Dr. B's report:* Overall I do not feel that medications have been particularly helpful. Clearly he has done better while on medication, but I question whether the benefits outweigh the risks. At this time I am recommending an inpatient hospitalization to see how he responds to structure and discipline. I would hope that we could observe him medication free during the hospital stay. It may also be possible during the inpatient program to do more intensive work with the parents. During the hospital stay consideration may need to be given to the possibility of residential treatment in the future.

Dr. B recommended Michael's admission into a children's psychiatric hospital, but there was no space available. Michael had a different idea. He thought it would be good for him to go to a residential summer camp.

> *Shari:* He got it into his head that he wanted to go to sleep-away camp that summer. He came up with this idea by himself, but probably heard about it from my friends' kids. We found a special camp, but it was very expensive. It was a therapeutic camp for children in special education and one month cost what a whole summer would cost at a regular camp. We tried to figure out how to pay for it and it became a family project. We paid for part, my parents paid for part and even my sister's first husband put in money. Everyone was sending Michael to camp. Four weeks away for Michael and for four weeks Scot was going to be an only child, which would be a treat for him.
>
> The camp was very far upstate, but Michael was "psyched" to go. We bought the trunk and got everything together. The day to leave arrived and Michael marched off onto his bus with a backpack. My mother, Jake, and I were crying hysterically, and Jake was worse than me. We didn't let Michael see us cry, but there was no separation problem for him. Then we cried all the way home.
>
> Because of the camp policy we couldn't call him. The camp called us, when Michael finally realized what he had done—the reality of going away.

And he had a tough time with it. He sent postcards that said, "Take me home." I called the camp and they said he was fine, and doing okay.

On visiting day we told Michael that he could stay for the rest of the summer, if he wanted to. He was torn. It was a fantasy camp and they had everything including psychologists and psychiatrists. There was swimming, which he loved, and a lake, and arts and crafts. It was everything you could imagine. The social worker took a liking to Michael and he was good while he was there. But he doesn't take change well, and he decided he wanted to come home after the month and finish the summer at the Center.

From the day he returned he was totally off.

Before the hospital: The crisis

Michael recalls leaving camp after one month, but thinks that he was sent home for poor behavior, because he bit a counselor. Michael returned to his regular school program at the Center for the month of August, but exhibited the worst behavior they had ever seen from him and he tried to harm himself.

> *Shari*: Every day I got a phone call that Michael was in trouble. He could not get himself together and he was getting into arguments and fights. He was angry and very difficult. And then the call came that he was threatening to kill himself.

> *Jake*: He always threatened that he would kill himself, but I think he did it only with his mother to upset her.

Michael has very detailed memory of the suicide attempt.

> *Michael*: I tried throwing myself out a window on the second floor at school. First, I remember getting put into the quiet room and then they wanted me to sit in the administrator's office. After time in the quiet room, I often went to that office and did some work under her desk. But that day I had enough and I wanted to do something different, and the window was there. The window seemed bigger than it does now, and there was no air conditioner in it. I was thinking—get it over with. I had enough of everything. I climbed on the radiator by the window and I leaned out and said I was going to jump. Someone from the other side of the room came and pulled me back in and calmed me down.

I asked Michael if he truly intended to kill himself and what prompted this. He replied that he remembers thinking that his life was getting worse and worse, because he wasn't getting his way about anything. He also said that he decided that he might as well kill himself and get it over with. The

psychologist who was seeing Michael for behavioral therapy, Dr. G, has a slightly different account of the same day:

> *From Dr. G's report:* On August 1 Michael had two episodes of suicide attempts at school witnessed by teachers and other persons in the school office. The school director knows Michael well and indicated that he has never seen Michael behave in such a manner. Previously, Michael has complained that he is unhappy and has made suicidal statements since a young age (four years old), but has never taken action. He attempted to throw himself out a window and fall over a railing on a high staircase. Adults had to pull him away from both places.

Obviously, this dramatic event required immediate attention. Dr. G was consulted and saw Michael.

> *From Dr. G's report:* Michael was interviewed by himself. He expressed that he wanted to be dead because he was not happy and he believed others wanted him dead including his parents and people at school. He was confusing anger with wishes that he would be dead and exaggerating punishments directed toward him. He could find no advantages to living except to take a trip to Disneyland. Michael had plans for further suicide attempts. It seemed that he would be at risk for self harm in an impulsive fashion if he was confronted with a stressful event. Michael also expressed homicidal interests directed toward his brother who he perceived as constantly bothering him.

Hospitalization was clearly required, but unfortunately again there was no space available in the hospital that was most desirable. An emergency plan of how Michael's parents should deal with him was put into place to maintain Michael at home until admission into the hospital. In the report written by Dr. G just prior to Michael's hospitalization, there is mention of a new issue, Michael's report of hearing voices:

> *From Dr. G's report:* Michael acknowledged and described auditory hallucinations. He stated that he had been hearing some voices. They may have been command hallucinations. However, he showed no other evidence of delusion or thought control problems as his discussion and responses were appropriate and goal directed. Michael was oriented and clearly alert and appropriate.

Michael remembers the voices:

> *Michael:* I had six people in my head—always six. It's a good number. They didn't have names. I gave them numbers: 1, 2, 3, 4, 5, 6. When I got upset I'd

talk to them and they'd tell me what to do. I had an evil one who would like to beat my mom; and another one who would say, "You shouldn't do that." And another voice: "Oh, it's your dad's fault." And another voice: "You're just upset today, calm down." They'd all tell me different things and they all had a different character. I don't remember too much now, but a number of years ago I could have told you about each one. These were just voices.

While "voices" are not typically thought of as one manifestation of the autism syndrome, there is speculation that other high-functioning autistic individuals have also experienced this phenomenon, or it may be associated with a separate disorder entirely. Michael's hearing voices will be more fully explored in Chapter 10 with insights about Michael and autism from multiple perspectives.

Hospitalization

Shari clearly recalls the crisis that the suicide attempt created and the need to have Michael admitted to the hospital. Again, she was determined to find the right place for her son and consulted the very experienced psychiatric social worker from the Center with whom she had formed a close relationship. Although she had just retired from her social work position at the Center, Mrs. R was most helpful and accompanied Shari to see a children's psychiatric facility with which she was familiar.

> *Shari*: Mrs. R was an amazing woman and went with me to look at the hospital. He wasn't admitted right away. We had to wait for a bed and we kept Michael at home. He couldn't go back to school, because it was too much of a risk.

The decision to admit Michael to a psychiatric hospital was painful for the family, but all agreed that it was necessary. Michael was nine years and four months old. Shari recalls the admission process:

> *Shari*: Michael held himself together and he knew he was going in. Jake and I took him in with all his stuff to admit him. We went through the process and we sat in a room full of specialists and Michael revealed that he heard voices, and he went on and on. And the voices didn't stop in his head, so that's why he did bad things. Jake and I sat there looking at each other like we didn't know this child that we were bringing to the hospital. And he acted things out, and I didn't know all this stuff was coming out of him and we didn't even know where it was coming from.

But even in the most dire situations, there was some levity when the family recalled the hospital admission:

> *Jake*: I remember the day we took him to the hospital and you know that you have to go through all these things before you're admitted and talk to all these different people. All these people spoke to us and Michael. They showed us around the hospital. Michael asked them if they had a swimming pool there. It was like he thought he was going on vacation.

> *Shari*: We took him on a tour with the nurses, and he walked around with a notebook like he was in school, and he was asking questions: "Is there a swimming pool, and what do I get to do?" He was really calm, and took a liking to one of the nurses who was very sweet.

Michael has precise memory of the day of the hospitalization.

> *Michael*: I think I was told about it. My parents drove me to the hospital and I thought it was like going to summer camp. And I didn't get it. And when I got there I asked where the swimming pool was. They left me. The first night I tried to get used to it and the next day I did something—physical aggression—and I got four hours locked in my room and then again the next day. And also I was a head banger. At the hospital if I got out of control, they would wrap me in sheets really tight so I couldn't move.

I asked Michael about his hospital experience and what his day was like.

> *Michael*: It was organized like a school day. Classes were in the morning and in the afternoon we would have groups, meetings, visiting hour and p.m. snack. Bedtime was at 9:00. There were two people in a room like a dorm room, but there was a large opening in the door so that they could give you food without letting you out if you had to stay in the room. My mom would come, because I couldn't shower myself in those days. I couldn't figure out what to do in a different shower and I didn't want to put all the effort together needed to shower myself. If I was punished, she couldn't come.

Shari remembers how she felt leaving Michael at the hospital.

> *Shari*: When we left, he kissed us goodbye. He was fine. It was like camp and this was only two weeks after we brought him home from camp. We left him and went home.
>
> Visiting was twice a day. In the afternoon it was for an hour and at night for an hour. And the rules were that if the kids acted out, they would be punished. There were very strong punishments, and they lost visitation. Michael did lose it often.

Michael spent approximately ten weeks in the hospital. During that time he was taken off all medication and put on a strict behavior modification plan with significant "time out" consequences for aggressive behavior. I asked him about his progress in the hospital. It was his opinion that his stay was longer than most of the other children, who seemed to come and go while he was still there.

> *Michael:* I stayed there for over two months, which I think is considered a long stay. There's no set length, but you need sufficient improvement to leave. I would always have a setback or something. I got used to that structure.
>
> I started to get lonely and miss home and different people got out of the hospital. So I wanted to figure out a way to get home and I asked myself "What do I have to do? How do I have to behave?" That's when the behavior system started to work. I had to behave in a certain way to get out. They used the behavior mod system and then I could do it at home. All my meds were stopped and then they started new meds.
>
> I missed my mom's supervision: taking care of my showering, my clothes and all that stuff.

I wondered if Michael missed his family.

> *Michael:* I don't think so. I was more wrapped up in what they did for me; what their actions were and not my feelings.

I asked if he was lonely.

> *Michael:* Sometimes. The first week was very bad, when I got four to eight hours time out for physical aggression. At home I would only get 20 minutes for the same behavior.

Michael and I discussed whether he was aware that he used tantrums to manipulate his family so that they would comply with his every wish. He said that he realized this was true and that he couldn't do this with the people in the hospital. I also wondered if he had been aware that his tantrums and aggressive behavior made him different from most children.

> *Michael:* Yeah, but I thought it was just normal that they [his family] did whatever I wanted.

I wondered if Michael felt anger towards his family for having him hospitalized and asked how he reacted to them, when they visited.

Michael: I was angry then. And I was angry for many years, but not now. [In the hospital] we got along fine. We played games and it was like my normal times. But if I misbehaved they wouldn't let me see my family. My misbehaving was usually physical—hitting and then they wouldn't let me see my family.

As an adult Michael reflects on the hospitalization as one of the two worst points in his life. The other very negative time occurred during the depression he experienced in the middle of his junior year in college. Michael feels that the hospitalization had critical consequences for him and changed the direction of his behavior and ultimately his life. I asked what the hospital stay meant to him.

Michael: I guess I realized that actions have consequences; other people would realize this younger. I think the hospital woke me up to the severity of punishment for particular actions. Maybe in the hospital I just became used to functioning in society as it is, as compared to my own little world at home and at school. Maybe I just found out about expectations in the hospital stay.

It was the first time that my behavior had consequences. Until then I always thought I was normal. I didn't know about autism. [Being in the hospital] turned my world upside down, because I realized that I wasn't normal.

I discussed the hospital stay with Shari.

Shari: He was punished a lot. He acted out a lot. When we would come, we could sit in the day room with him. If he was punished, I was devastated to not see him and to know that he was punished.

He lost weight because he really didn't like the food. They tried to accommodate him to a point, but they also tried to get him to learn and to eat other foods. But he was stuck. For example, he would always eat only waffles. Thinking of eating an orange would make him gag. When I'd come, I'd bring him a container of chocolate milk and a bagel. I guess I always just gave into him and did whatever he wanted.

He was in the hospital for ten weeks. They used to wrap him in wet sheets when he was completely berserk. There was a lot of crying. All of us cried.

By the time we finished with him in the hospital they said, "This is autism."

Author's reflection

Michael's childhood years were highlighted by pivotal events. While both the family and the professionals that worked with Michael expected that the progress they saw in his early childhood would continue, this did not happen in all respects. Michael's language and learning skills continued to improve, but managing the increasing frequency of violent and unpredictable behavior became the dominant theme for much of Michael's childhood. The birth of Michael's brother and the impact another child had on the family dynamics coincided with Michael's accelerating aggression and attempts at self-injury. Michael attributes this deterioration to his anger towards his brother and his inability to share parental attention.

Sibling rivalry

Children who are first born have the undivided attention of their parents. When a sibling arrives, there is a natural progression from being the family's only focus to sharing the "limelight." Michael was six years old when his brother was born, but because of his autism, he was not an independent and well-adjusted child. Most children eventually accommodate to the arrival of a brother or sister and their initial negative behavior diminishes. The birth of a brother seems to have had a devastating effect on Michael that continued throughout Michael's life up until adulthood. It would be highly speculative to attribute Michael's behavioral deterioration at that time solely to the birth of his brother. It may have been that the nature of Michael's autistic symptoms changed as he was growing older, but Michael blames the arrival of another child for the problems he experienced. The ability of Michael's parents, especially his mother, to provide undivided attention to Michael was markedly reduced when care had to be given to the sibling. The relationship between Michael and his brother, Scot, has been problematic from Scot's infancy up until adulthood. Michael, like other autistic children, was unable to share his mother, because he was accustomed to and required complete parental attention.

As children grow older they benefit from their relationship with siblings in many ways. The quality of sibling relationships does change throughout an individual's life, and these relationships are likely to continue past the relationship with parents. Therefore brothers and sisters can provide comfort and support throughout one's life. For autistic children sibling relations are full of problems. A disabled brother or sister can be a huge embarrassment to the nondisabled sibling and certainly having a child with special needs substantially changes the quality of family life. Scot comments about his embarrassment over his older brother's appearance and behavior and relates that even inviting friends to his house was a tremendous problem because of his concern that Michael might act out. As nondisabled siblings mature, they are often given more responsibility for taking care of the disabled child, which can ultimately result in their providing total care and decision making if they become guardians after the parents are deceased.

Interaction with his brother was difficult for Michael, who had trouble getting along with any child even for a short time. This problem was exaggerated at home, where Scot's presence was continual and interrupted a world that had previously been only about Michael. Likewise, the baby brother had no ability to understand Michael's hostile behavior towards him, and Scot soon developed aggressive behavior towards his brother as well. The stress within the family had to be enormous, given competing concerns: protecting and nurturing the younger child while still devoting enormous time and attention to the older, difficult sibling. Parents are especially anxious to see if the later-born child develops normally or evidences the problems of the older child. It is also not unusual for the younger child, who may be developing normally, to imitate the autistic behaviors of the older child, causing concern and frustration for the family.

It is apparent today that even if Michael was not autistic, he and his brother are very different people with different personalities, views about life, and goals. Today the brothers no longer live in the same household, due to the parents' divorce. There appears to be more tolerance for each other, and time apart from each other has eliminated the daily battles that occurred in childhood. As many of Michael's autistic traits have reduced and as Scot has gotten older there is an intellectual understanding of each other, but sibling rivalry and competition for attention are still issues between them.

Behavioral issues

Autistic children are known to have very difficult behavior. They can be rigid, non-communicative, defiant, aloof, aggressive, and just difficult to manage. Michael had been a demanding preschooler who frequently had tantrums and was both a biter and pincher, but his early behavior was not especially frightening for the family. This pattern markedly changed after Scot's birth, when

Michael's tantrums often resulted in physically aggressive behavior, most often directed at his mother. These outbursts became more uncontrollable, and were dangerous. While Michael was initially able to control much of his aggression in the primary school grades, this also changed and he became very, very difficult to manage both at school and at home. The school setting provided multiple personnel to deal with this disruptive child, but at home fewer resources were available, even though the extended family was frequently enlisted to help out.

The path to understanding and managing Michael's behavior led to consultations with many experts who recommended various treatment modalities including therapy and medication. When Michael's outwardly aggressive behavior turned into self-destructive tendencies, another avenue of help was needed and Michael went into a hospital setting.

Michael's disruptive behavior at home and in school was a pattern that existed throughout his childhood. It continued at home during adolescence and even into young adulthood years. As a result of hospitalization and the implementation of the strict behavior modification plan, Michael realized that there were consequences for his behavior, which did change his conduct at school. Few people outside the family would have thought that the mild-mannered adolescent who diligently attended school and did so well academically could still be frightening at home when a "meltdown" occurred. Michael's self-regulation has changed remarkably through the years, which may be attributed to medication, maturity, and better insight on his part.

Experts and specialists

Another theme that emerges from Michael's childhood is the family's unrelenting search for assistance from experts and specialists. When problems were noted early on, Shari and her mother avidly sought help and turned to the medical community. The family continued to seek the advice of medical and psychological experts to assist them in the management of their difficult child. Locating and relating to a variety of specialists can be a hurdle, but assisted by Shari's determination and medical background, this family was able to locate and choose between multiple resources in a large metropolitan area. Shari was viewed by the school personnel as sympathetic and caring and she developed a close relationship with them. This provided an excellent support structure with a network for advice, help, and referrals.

The multiple consultations and appointments with Michael's treating doctors and psychologists were both wearing and expensive. Another concern for the family was weighing the differing perspectives of experts who recommended various approaches and offered different advice. It is impossible for the family to predict the success of these different recommendations and it takes astute judgment and knowledge to decide on which advice to follow.

Michael's hospitalization was both a climax to a cycle of deterioration and a source of new information and approaches. It was emotionally devastating to turn this child over to the care of others, but all in the family recognized that something new and drastic was definitely needed. The hospitalization had a profound and long-lasting effect on Michael, who still talks about it with sadness. From the time of his hospitalization Michael no longer thought of himself as "normal."

Chapter 5

Childhood after the Hospital

I lived with a notebook for two years. He had to earn points for everything. I had a board up in the kitchen. Everything was behavior mod.

Shari

The behavior modification plan that was established for Michael in the hospital was closely followed both at home and at school, and there was progress.

Shari: Finally, we brought him home and he went back to school and for two years we lived on the behavior mod system and there were points for everything. He came home with no medication. They tried different things. We went through all the meds and we were trying every drug until we settled in the routine. Some of them were awful and one gave him tics. He had to touch his finger, and touch his nose, and then he had to go through a whole sequence in a certain order. I thought I'd lose my mind watching him.

He went through different stages. For example, he became obsessed with different things at different times and he just couldn't tolerate some things. For several weeks it was if the fringe on the rug wasn't straight, or during another period it was if the sliding doors weren't closed enough, or then it was if the cheese on the pizza was crooked, he couldn't take it.

Michael: I wasn't always bothered by many different things at the same time, but rather I remember that I had very narrow obsessions.

I asked Shari how things progressed.

Shari: When he came home things were pretty good and he went back to his school and continued to see Dr. B [the psychiatrist] and Dr. G [the psychologist]. And we did what we had to do. He was functioning. The house was calmer and for a while he stopped hitting me.

At one point, I had both of my children going to that hospital for therapy. I think I spent more time in that hospital than anyone else between upstairs for one and downstairs for the other. But it was a good place.

Scot was in therapy when he was five, because he was acting out. I was told he was so angry at what his brother had done to him, and to me, and to all of us, and that any sibling with a brother like Michael needed therapy. And he had poor impulse control too and later was diagnosed with ADHD [attention deficit hyperactive disorder]. I always thought that Scot would have a bigger heart for people with disabilities. But sometimes there's so much anger in him about his brother. And I spoiled him then and some say I still spoil him to make up for what he was living with. And I was so burned out from dealing with Michael.

I asked if Michael's "voices" continued after the hospital.

Shari: He'd still talk about voices even when he was in college, but it got better. Sometimes he said he heard them more than other times. We'd say, "Are you just thinking?" He'd say, "It's a voice; it's not thinking."

Meeting Michael today you would have no sense of the very troubled, aggressive, and violent child that he had been.

Shari: Even Dr. B [the psychiatrist], when he sees Michael today and knows how well he's done, wonders about him and his original diagnosis. I think he's a mixed bag of problems. But without any question, Michael was autistic and today they would probably say he is somewhere on the PDD [pervasive developmental disorder] spectrum.

Back to school

After more than two months in the hospital Michael relished getting back to school. He recalls his first day back:

Michael: I came home on Columbus Day and it was also a religious holiday. I loved going back to school, especially my first day back. I felt that I was supposed to be there. It was October and school started without me and it was kind of like going back to school after you've been sick. I felt it was where I was supposed to go. I really liked school—different subjects, working towards a goal, finishing a math problem, reading or anything else.

It's where I did some things right.

Michael stayed with one teacher, Mrs. G, for most of grades four, five, and six. According to Michael in each grade there was a mixed group of children with an age range of approximately two to three years. Some children remained in the class from year to year, but others changed classes or transferred to other schools. Michael's classes generally had six to eight children, who were frequently divided into ability groups for various subjects so that the class work was at the appropriate level. Michael recalls a great deal of individual work with two to three adults (a special education teacher and aides) usually present.

> *Mrs. G*: Michael came from the hospital with a behavior mod plan. I felt that if he could comply with the plan in the hospital, he could do it in school. For example, if he cursed he got 20 minutes in the quiet room. For hitting, it meant four hours. His mom and grandmother were really helpful, because they would pick him up if he had to be sent home.

Michael recalls the behavior modification plan at school.

> *Michael*: Positive behaviors earned points and negative behaviors lost points. For example a brief yell deducted two points and a push or slap were ten points. There was a list with the exact number of points for different behaviors. Points earned could be spent on rewards and there was also a list of specific rewards and the point amounts I needed for each. If I spent all my points one day on rewards, and earned no points the next day and also lost points for negative behavior, my point total would go below zero and I would have to earn my way back to zero. At some points, probably half the time or more, my point totals were in the negatives.

I asked how Michael's behavior after the hospital compared to his behavior before.

> *Mrs. G*: In the previous grades he was wild: hitting, kicking, acting out. One teacher made a mistake of turning her back while she was sitting on his legs trying to take his shoes off during one of his outbursts. He reached around and grabbed her throat. Truthfully, I was almost afraid to get him. You could see him getting angry and all of a sudden something would fly at your head. One time he threw something at me and I made him spend four hours in the time out room and we never had a problem after that.

I asked if Michael's behavior changed that year.

> *Mrs. G*: We had the plan on the wall and he knew that I would follow it. After a while, he wouldn't even argue with us about the plan and the time out. We'd say "Come on, let's walk out," and he would just walk out with me or the person who accompanied him. He knew that we weren't going to tolerate his behavior. I remember one time when he was going through a

cursing episode, he just went to the door and he said he was going to the time out room on his own. His extreme anger problems really got better after he came out of the hospital.

I asked if there were any outstanding events during the time she taught Michael and Mrs. G had strong memories of a class trip to Washington, D.C., and problems with Michael.

> *Mrs. G:* There was a benefactor who planned an entire trip to Washington, D.C., including staying in a motel and he was also our guide. I had three boys with me, but the aide had Michael in the next room. All the boys wanted to stay with me except Michael who wanted to be alone. The other boys had a great time, but for Michael it was really difficult.
>
> Part of the trip was a visit to Capitol Building. Michael asked the guide where we were going next and he wouldn't tell him, because he wanted it to be a surprise. The guide didn't understand that Michael couldn't deal with change. Michael had a temper tantrum on the lawn and we even followed the behavior mod plan there. We made him return to the hotel room and while the other kids went swimming, he sat in his room for several hours.

> *Mrs. B, the class aide:* I think that Michael wanted to do the trip to Washington as if he was going himself and he wanted to be in charge and get his own way. In his mind he knew what he wanted to do, and if we weren't following his schedule, it would set him off. At one point he just sat himself down in the middle of everything and he would not move. He was like lead and he just sat there and crossed his legs. As he got bigger and older, the funnier this behavior looked to everyone else. When I told him that he looked funny just sitting, he said, "Maybe, I'll stand up and pout instead." He certainly had a way with words.

Michael also recalls the trip to Washington, D.C., with a distinct memory of pulling flowers out of the ground and throwing them at the Capitol Building, because he was so enraged. He also remembers the "time out" at the hotel. Michael seems emotionally detached from the memory of the out of control person he had been when he was younger. I asked him what he remembers about that "other" Michael.

> *Michael:* I don't think back at these things. I'm so factual. I've been told about this, and I have a factual memory, but it's not a real memory. I remember requesting to sleep in the other room [at the motel], because closeness with other people was disturbing to me. I didn't want to sleep near other people. You know I never had friends over to my house when I was young.

I also remember the way that I looked. I had very smooth skin and red hair when I was younger. My mother made sure that everything looked right—haircut and all that.

Mrs. B, who had been the "crisis teacher" and aide when Michael was in the elementary grades, recalled another incident when Michael couldn't control his anger.

> *Mrs. B*: We had a field trip to the Hall of Science [a local museum]. The trip was organized by having the children go from one section to another with a museum guide. Michael wanted to go some place different from the other children and he was told that he couldn't. That was it! He wanted to follow his own plan and go at his own pace and he couldn't do it, and he refused to follow the group. I was with him and he told me "You're an adult, and you should tell these people that they can't tell you what to do." I told him that we both had to follow the group. He didn't understand that and he became so angry. He got so upset that he snatched at me and pulled my skirt off. [She laughed loudly when she says the following.] But luckily I had a long slip on that day.
>
> Because of his behavior, he and I had to leave the trip and return to the school. When he would "rev" up like that, it was very hard to get him to calm down. He had to run through the whole course of his routine, and if he said he would be angry or cry for the next half hour, that's exactly what he'd do to the minute.

I inquired about Michael's academic skills in the upper elementary grades, wondering at what point his extraordinary ability became evident.

> *Mrs. G*: He was bright and he always did his work. But he didn't like to hear any noise when he worked and this caused a problem with others in the room. He was always very strong in math and in computation, but we had to help him with other things. Logical reasoning wasn't there. Even his English skills were poor. He could retell a story, but couldn't go further than that.
>
> I really don't think that he learned much academically during those years with me. The standards and expectations for these children were so different then. We didn't have sufficient materials and often we reused old workbooks and erased some of the answers in them. Today things are much more academic.
>
> Michael always wanted to do his work. Even with his behavior problem he could learn, but you needed to get his attention. School work seemed to calm him and he enjoyed doing very tedious work. There was so much

rigidity. If I gave him a list of words and one was out of order, it was a catastrophe.

At the beginning of sixth grade Michael's class was changed and he was moved to another teacher, but his behavior deteriorated and he returned to Mrs. G's classroom where he stayed throughout sixth grade. Mrs. G feels that the new teacher wasn't firm enough and didn't adhere closely enough to the behavior mod plan, but Michael attributes his behavior problems to another cause. He remembers that there were two boys who goaded him in the new class, and he couldn't handle their taunts. He was relieved to go back to Mrs. G and the children he knew well in her class.

I asked Michael about the change in his behavior during the time after the hospital.

> *Michael*: There were fewer behavior problems, because I wasn't the same person after the hospital. It was the fear of going back there and I didn't want to take that step back. I realized that I wasn't normal and I wanted to be normal.
>
> Schoolwork always calmed me down. I liked writing my spelling words ten times each. It was something that was tangible. I didn't like writing sentences, because it took more time for thinking and I didn't produce as much concrete work. But I could write a whole page of words in a short time. Tangible results have always been important to me and writing sentences didn't look like I did so much work.

I asked Mrs. G and Mrs. B to tell me about Michael, as a person, during those years.

> *Mrs. G*: There was a part of him that was so sweet. He was very comical and he made me laugh so much that I would cry. I remember his saying that he wanted me to date his uncle, and he and I would really laugh about that. I also have a memory of Michael standing on the radiator and screaming. There were definitely two different sides to Michael. He had a strange diet and would only eat bagels and cream cheese. Really, that's all he would eat.

> *Mrs. B*: If you stood firm, he respected you, but if something set him off, then he'd be in a rage. He could pull himself out of it, but only if he wanted to. For example, if he was in a rage, I would ask him a riddle. He would stop his tantrum, answer the riddle, and then go back into his rage.

I asked how Michael got along with the other students.

Mrs. G: He really didn't relate to the others. He might sit and do work with his neighbor, if I told him to. Michael was brighter than the other children, but he was more violent and didn't spend time with his classmates.

Towards the end of his college years, Michael and I visited this school so that he could introduce me to his former teachers. When we walked through the building, he was very focused on the physical changes in the facility and he especially wanted to show me the time out room where he had spent so many hours. He noticed that it had been repainted and that you could no longer see the scratches in the wall that he remembered making.

Mrs. G: When he came to visit after many years this May, it was very weird to me until we were alone in my classroom and it was the old Michael—joking and talking. In the hallway with the others around, he seemed to be uncomfortable or embarrassed.

He was a great student to have.

I asked Michael about his recollection of the academic part of the upper elementary school years. It wasn't at all surprising that he focused on talking about math.

Michael: In first grade I used the fifth grade math book and I used that same math book for many years. I must have learned something, because when I entered high school I did go into regular high school math classes, but for other subjects I was placed in ninth grade classes when I really should have been in tenth grade.

Maybe I just knew all the math stuff and other things. In the elementary grades, I don't remember the teachers teaching. I do remember sitting in my seat and the teacher would go over something simple such as how you spell a particular word. But I don't remember ever sitting through a math class or a history class, where I was taught something new. We did a lot of workbook stuff, but there wasn't traditional teaching such as when the teacher stands in front of the group or class. I'm having trouble trying to remember what we actually did all of those days.

I asked about reading and writing.

Michael: I was good at pronouncing words and remembering details, but poor at inferential thinking and that was true even when I got to high school. In seventh grade I was forced to write sentences and even a paragraph. But I really didn't write or understand writing. When I was in the high school, the teacher was surprised that I said that I never really wrote before that year.

Since Michael's time in elementary school significant changes in special education programs have resulted in a more rigorous curriculum with academic goals and expectations that are far more advanced than the program that existed for Michael in the elementary and junior high school grades.

Michael had a close relationship with the physical education teacher, Mr. H, and was insistent that I meet and interview him.

> *Mr. H*: We both love sports and we became very close because of it. When he was young, he was really hard to manage, but this changed when he got older. Every week he would take the newspaper and would give me his predictions for every game in every sport. Each Friday he would have his predictions planned out for the weekend games that were scheduled. We called it "predictions," and he would predict the scores for the weekend games. It was all about numbers. On Mondays we'd compare notes to see how each of our predictions turned out, and he had it ready for me. He did this for every game, every weekend.

I asked how Michael did with the physical education program, because he was an awkward, uncoordinated child. I also wondered about his relationships with other students.

> *Mr. H*: [In those years] there was no gym and we'd be in the cafeteria or we would go outside all the time. It didn't matter to Michael how cold it was outside. It could be 15 degrees and the first thing he did was take his jacket off and be in his shirtsleeves. He was so comfortable outside.
>
> Because of him we started teams and intramural kickball was the first one. He wasn't athletic, but he was the manager and scorekeeper. He was brilliant in keeping the stats. The team would travel to other special schools that were close by, and he would come to all the games and keep the scores. It was a behavioral plan too, because if someone didn't behave in school, I wouldn't let them travel with us. I felt that sportsmanship was important and Michael was great. I could see that he was really progressing. When he was young, there were lots of problems with anger, but as he got to be a teenager he was progressing.

Therapy

Support services are an essential component of a special education school setting and Michael was involved in therapy at school. The chief psychologist at Michael's school, Dr. J, first met Michael when he evaluated him at age four. He knew Michael through the childhood years, but was especially involved with him from ages 11 to 15, when he saw him for individual therapy. I asked Dr. J about his impressions of Michael:

> *Dr. J:* Michael has done really, really well. He's so bright and brilliant with math. He was unbelievable with math even when he was four and I first met him. I loved working with him. In the end, there was such a good result.

I was also curious if Dr. J had been involved with Michael's family during those years.

> *Dr. J:* In our school the social worker does the family contact. This is done so that the child can trust that the therapy is separate and private from the family. This is their space. With Michael's family, it was unusual that the social worker stayed with them from early childhood until she retired from the school, when he was much older. She wanted to provide consistency and do all that she could do for this family. She wanted to give them every service. It was evident that Michael's family, especially his mother, reached out to us and was responded to by all of our staff.

I asked Dr. J about the strategies he used with Michael to address the tantrums and violence.

> *Dr. J:* It's an important question, how to help the child reduce outbursts over certain issues. I devised a plan and I called it the OBA—Outburst Average technique. We called this his batting average with outbursts and he was very excited about it. It was a hook to his fascination with numbers and baseball. He loved it and he was very honest about it. What he would do was to keep track and record the number of his outbursts. I remember him saying, "I had half an outburst," which was funny and interesting. Michael always needed to be precise and literal. It seemed to work along with the other strategies that were used.

Dr. J also commented that the hospitalization was important to stabilize Michael so that he could return to school. The behavior modification plan used in the hospital was very strict, and the school personnel used it as well, but less strictly. Some even questioned whether it was "fair" to expect this child to comply with all the rules and regulations of the plan, and there was some debate about it.

While Michael's behavior at school seemed to improve, Dr. J was aware that there was still a significant problem with his outbursts at home, and special sensitivity to the sound of his mother's voice. Just hearing his mother speak on the phone could cause Michael to go "beserk." Dr. J also discussed the topic of Michael's "voices" and I wondered if this was noted in his experience with other autistic children.

> *Dr. J*: Michael never told me about his voices, but it is reported with other autistic individuals—sometimes, but it's not common. A low percentage do this. Of course with the high-functioning individuals, they can articulate about this. Many others are trapped in their inner world and can be haunted by voices without anyone knowing about it. Michael's so bright, but others may not realize this is occurring.

I asked Dr. J to speculate about the reasons for Michael's dramatic improvement and his very positive outcome.

> *Dr. J*: He made tremendous progress at this school and he responded very well. When he left, I felt that there was a really good chance of his succeeding and was cautiously optimistic about his future. I had concerns about people bothering him and how he would handle it. His situation needed the right elements for success.
>
> There are typically a combination of factors if things work out well: medication, family support, behavior modification (which is crucial for a child with autistic features), therapy, and circumstances (for example a change in his classroom when there were concerns about bullying or being tormented by others). This school was the link for him and his family in so many ways.

I asked Dr. J to comment on Michael's rich fantasy life during his childhood years, and the pretend play that featured a tree.

> *Dr. J*: Michael was always a loner, and during recreation time I became aware that he had a fantasy about a tree in the yard. Each day he would get onto the tree and pretend that it was the school bus and he was the bus driver.

Others at school were well aware of Michael's tree ritual and had mentioned it to me, so I asked Michael to tell me about it. He did so with precision and delight.

> *Michael*: Outside the school there was a tree that almost looked like a school bus. There were even bumps in the tree that could be like the radio. There was a pole on the tree that looked like the thing you use to open the door on a bus. Somehow this tree had all the physical characteristics of a school bus—just like the one I was taking to school. In later years pieces would fall off and it wasn't the same. [On our visit to the school Michael pointed out where the tree had been located. It was apparently removed for new construction.]

I would sit on this tree and flap for the entire lunch hour. And it was just the most fun thing to be alone and sit on this tree and steer. And there was a piece of wood that was almost round and I would use it to steer. In those days the school buses were old and they would squeak when you'd stop, and I'd make the squeaking sound too.

I suggested to Michael that many young boys are fascinated by trucks and buses and asked what was the special attraction for him. I also speculated that the motion of the wheels on a bus would have been especially appealing to an autistic child.

Michael: I was just interested in the school bus route. I'd imagine myself just going through the streets and picking the kids up—they'd be early, they'd be late and I would wait for them. It wasn't about trucks and things that moved. It was about the process of picking up the kids and the schedule. That's what it was for me.

I asked Michael how long this ritual continued and what other students thought of it.

Michael: I did this for most of my time at the school—from age seven until the end, when I was about 12. Sometimes the other kids would come over and ask "Did you get there yet? Where are you going? Where are you up to?"

Dr. J provided an overall reflection about Michael during these years.

Dr. J: I was delighted to work with him because of his upbeat personality. He always had a smile, and even in an outburst, once you'd stabilized him, he would smile. Everyone realized that the tantrums weren't his fault and everyone liked him. A truly remarkable individual!

It is especially interesting to learn about a child's perception of therapy and I asked Michael about his relationship with Dr. J and what the therapy might have meant to him.

Michael: Dr. J was more the supervisor, because there were other psychologists, but he had a few special cases and I was one of the special cases. Usually, I had him once a week and we'd play baseball outside, or if we weren't outside, then it was playing a board game. It was a lot of play therapy and some talking about issues.

I do remember that in fifth grade I learned to tie my shoes, when I was with him. We had a puzzle of a shoe with laces.

We joked at this point that Michael is still not adept at tying his shoe laces and resents the extra work this takes. He laughed about his wanting to wear sneakers with Velcro closings, although his mother didn't think it was fashionable. When he moved away from his mother's home, he went back to wearing Velcro shoes.

I asked Michael if he thought play therapy sessions were beneficial, but he didn't answer the question directly.

> *Michael*: We'd have about a half hour and sometimes we'd play a board game and it would take about three weeks to finish—and he [Dr. J] would save it during the week. When I got upset at losing, we'd talk about that. It was usually individual therapy at this school, but they had group therapy when I was in high school.

Again I asked if he thought that the therapy approaches helped.

> *Michael*: I guess [it helped]. They'd see you individually and it would help them assess what to do in the classroom.

Junior high school grades and graduation

At the end of Michael's eighth grade year, his family bought a house and moved to a suburban community. The Committee on Special Education in the new community had to review Michael's school placement, and based on Michael's success at this school, they decided that he continue there through the ninth grade.

> *Michael*: At the end of eighth grade I was academically ready to leave the Center and a lot of kids who were academically below me did leave the school at that point. The school at the Center goes up to age 16, but they really didn't have ninth grade materials. Ninth grade was a boring year, because I was in the same class with the same teacher. She gave me lots of stuff to do, but academically it was a lost year and I should have moved on.

Graduation is always a time of reflection and for Michael and his family graduation from the Center was a most significant event. Michael began his school years at this same facility as a most troubled and disabled autistic child. By the time he completed ninth grade, many of the most difficult behavioral problems were significantly reduced. Michael made progress in school and was experiencing success academically as well as in his emotional adjustment. Violence in the household, especially directed towards his brother and mother, unfortunately still continued. I asked Michael about this and wondered why he was able to control his anger at school, but not at home.

> *Michael*: It took about three to four years for my outbursts to wean off at school, but it took basically until I moved out from home for this to stop with my family. Aggression at home was mostly about my mother, but a little bit about my brother—about how tied at the hip he and Mom are. I called them Siamese twins.

Michael disputes the level of violence in the home that all of his family report but acknowledges his ongoing anger towards his mother.

> *Michael*: The only time I was aggressive was when someone would do something that I wanted stopped. And Mom would do things that I wanted stopped. My dad would do whatever I wanted and he wasn't around as much as my mother.

The family took pride in Michael's graduation from ninth grade.

> *Mrs. L, Michael's preschool teacher*: When he graduated, we were all there. It was a very proud day and we all cried—all of us. His graduation was really a very special day. He was loved! It wasn't just the teachers that were proud. The whole family was there and the school was so proud of him. He was part of who we were and part of me and part of me as a teacher. He was a hard kid and because he did well, I did well too. I've taught for a number of years and with some they come in and it's another child and a new year. But I can remember thinking so many years before that this child has potential. I've taught a lot of special children and I can't say that about a lot of children. I felt really good that he had done so well and I was proud to look at the whole picture.

> *Michael's grandmother*: School is and always has been his "everything"! Michael was their star and he might have been their most difficult situation. And teachers got abused by him. But their techniques and their affection for him and their devotion were incredible! The school environment is everything for Michael.

I asked Shari, Michael's mother, to reflect on Michael's progress at the Center. I asked her what she felt had made the tremendous difference in her son that was evident by the time of his graduation.

> *Shari*: It was absolutely the program and the people. Without them, I don't know what would have happened. It was also the family commitment. I think we were lucky. It's his intelligence. A lot of time his intelligence is

going to win out over his problem. I can't say what broke his wall down totally. I don't know why us and why we were lucky.

There were certain things we always worked on. The social worker could get you all the information you needed. And the teachers and the administrators—they all cared and they all helped. He loved that school.

Michael remembers this school graduation.

Michael: I actually had a state test that morning that went right up to graduation. They gave me all the awards and I was obviously very recognized: physical education, French (which I took for seven years and today I can say "good-bye" and count some numbers), and even home economics. All the kids get awards, but I got eight awards. Especially math was my subject. About 20 kids graduated that day.

My parents thought I was the star at graduation and that's how people made me feel. It was important for me and I think that I was there the longest out of all the people graduating. People who were graduating with me—I called them the new students—they were there three years and I thought they were new! Only the building was there longer than me—just two years more! At that time I was their longest-lasting student. Graduation was very important to my family and they felt honored.

I asked Michael to reflect on the likely causes for the positive change in his behavior during those years.

Michael: The main thing was the hospital and the behavior mod plan–also keeping it up and fine tuning it at school and by Mrs. G. Those three years after the hospital were important. The last time I really acted up outside my home was the middle of seventh grade, after I left Mrs. G. I bit the teaching assistant. She annoyed me. She wouldn't give me credit [on a spelling test] for spelling a word that I thought was right. So I bit her arm.

I would always get harder words [than the other students]. She gave me a 95 on that test, not the 100 I thought I deserved. She argued that my "a" and "o" were sloppy and wouldn't give me the five points. So I grabbed her arm and bit it. I remember doing it. I'm the kind of person that when I get upset I like to grab.

I'm much more under control now, but that was me then.

Author's reflection

Academics

Michael's attendance at the Center provided many positive features, but Michael feels that the academic aspects of his education were not as rigorous as they should have been. This may be attributed to the enormous difficulty the teachers had managing Michael's behavior. It can also be a result of the limited expectations that educators had at that time for very disabled children. Resources, including textbooks, supplies, and other teaching materials, were limited at Michael's school as they were at most institutions that educated special education students. In retrospect, Michael's teachers freely admit that the curriculum for special education students, academic expectations, and availability of resources have changed dramatically in more recent times. Adherence to the legal protections and compliance with the provisions of the Individuals with Disabilities Education Act go far to ensure that a special child's education will receive appropriate institutional resources and full attention.

Behavior

It is well recognized that children with autism display behavior patterns that not only interfere with learning, but create tremendous management problems at home and at school. Michael's extremely aggressive behavior at school negatively impacted on his success during the childhood years. While most of his teachers in the elementary grades fully suspected that Michael was very intelligent and had high academic ability, his behavior prevented him from fulfilling this potential. Anger, tantrums, and violence persisted through most of the upper elementary grades and therefore managing Michael's behavior became the primary focus both at home and at school. It should also be emphasized that Michael's teachers had tremendous fondness for him. They said that when inappropriate behavior did not interfere, Michael could be engaging, funny, and clever. In many ways these positive personal attributes may have given these professionals even more incentive to tolerate and work with such a disruptive child. It reminds us of the old nursery rhyme that when the child was good, [he] was very, very good, but when [he] was bad, [he] was horrid.

Michael's serious attempts at self-destruction appeared when he was nine years old. Stronger measures to address his behavior were needed. In Michael's history there are many trends that echo the experience of other autistic individuals including depression and inability to manage himself. Michael's comments about his suicidal attempts indicated his tremendous despair and frustration with life. Today psychologists and psychiatrists who work with autistic children are much more attuned to addressing the "co-morbidity" issues (existence of other conditions) that accompany autism. They recognize that anxiety and depression are very prevalent in this population. With the widespread use and acceptance of drugs that are well suited for treatment of mood disorders, tremendous progress has been made. Medications that were prescribed for Michael through most of his childhood sought to ameliorate anger, reduce his obsessive-compulsive disorder and focus attention, but did not treat depression.

Hospitalization and behavior modification

It is an extreme intervention to have a child hospitalized, but this was necessary for Michael, because at nine years of age his violent behavior and suicide attempts required that something more was needed. Michael's family was most fortunate to have a network of trusted professionals that helped them locate a hospital not far from their home that specialized in treating psychiatric disorders for children and adolescents. The treatment administered to Michael was "state of the art" for that time and was primarily based on behavior modification, group therapy, and wrapping him in sheets when he was most out of control. The behavior modification plan begun at the hospital and continued in school and at home replaced the many medications that had previously been ineffective and caused many unpleasant side effects.

The concept of "generalization," getting the child to transfer behaviors learned in one setting to another setting, is regarded today as necessary to the success of the autistic child. Following the behavior modification plan at home as well as in school increased the likelihood that Michael would move forward. Michael and his family lived a life dominated by points and rewards for many, many years and it took great commitment for the family to follow the plan. Because of Michael's need for precision and his skills in math, the point system of the plan was especially well suited for him and provided a means by which he could clearly see specific consequences of his behavior.

The hospitalization had a dramatic and profound effect on Michael's view of himself. No longer could he pretend that he was similar to other children and, even within the population of hospitalized children, he had more difficulty than most. Being in the hospital taught Michael that his behavior had significant consequences and this set a new direction for his life.

Chapter 6

Becoming a "Man" at Age 13

All along he went to Hebrew school, which was amazing, but he liked it. He took to reading Hebrew very well, and with his obsessions and compulsions, when the teacher said you read ten minutes of Hebrew every day, Michael read ten minutes every day. And we all know that no other kids listen to their Hebrew teachers so well. Michael reads Hebrew incredibly well.

Shari

For every Jewish child raised in a home with traditional religious values, turning 13 is especially important. During childhood, Jewish children are not expected to be able to fully observe the commandments of their religion, although it's expected that they will learn about what the commandments mean and conduct themselves in a moral fashion. When a child becomes 13, the obligation changes, because this is considered the age at which a child can participate as an "adult." After age 13 the child is expected to devote him or herself to becoming a Jewish "adult." This is especially true for the male child, who traditionally was the significant person in terms of a public, religious role. While no family actually believes that a young teenager can truly understand or assume the responsibilities of adult life, nevertheless becoming 13 involves an important rite of passage.

The thirteenth birthday is marked by a religious ceremony, called the Bar Mitzvah [or Bat Mitzvah for a female]. Becoming a Bar Mitzvah means being a son [or daughter] of the commandment. The religious ceremony is the first time at which the child can be called to read from the Torah (the Old Testament Bible and a primary source of religious beliefs), lead part of the prayer service including chanting a portion of the Haftorah (Jewish scripture containing the writings of the Prophets), and be fully counted as an adult member of the Jewish community. During the service, the child usually speaks about the meaning of that week's Torah or Haftorah portion, acknowledges the family and significant others who helped prepare him or her for the event, talks about dedicating his or her life to moral causes, and announces to the congregation "Today I am a Man [or Woman]."

Jewish families and their children look at the Bar Mitzvah as an important event in a child's life and one that requires not only extensive preparation, but public acknowledgement. For the child, there is often anxiety, given the responsibilities of reading and chanting in Hebrew as well as being the center of attention of both the immediate and extended family, invited guests, and the whole congregation. The event also symbolizes that a child is now inducted into the world of all who came before him or her and those who will come after in the generations of Jewish life. The event has great poignancy for the entire family as parents see their son or daughter reaching "maturity" and being able to assume the obligations of a Jewish adult from a heritage where many were exterminated, solely because of their religion.

A celebration always follows the service. In prior times, this meant simple refreshments after the service, or a luncheon. In today's culture, the Bar Mitzvah "event" often takes on a party aspect that many feel is disproportionate to its true religious meaning and significance. The "party" can be celebrated as elaborately as one would celebrate a wedding, with formal dress, lavish food, music, decorations, and activities to amuse the children and many guests.

For a child with disabilities, there are many issues as well as potential problems related to the Bar Mitzvah. To get ready for this event, the child must prepare academically. Most children do this by entering Hebrew school at about age seven or eight and devote many years of after-school and/or weekend class attendance to learning the culture and language of the religion. If a child has a disability, there is concern whether he or she is able to take on and master a new language and tolerate the extra work and stress of Hebrew school classes. Learning to read Hebrew requires attention, focus, and good memory. For nondisabled children, this can be a necessary annoyance, or can cause some minor problems, because Hebrew school attendance deprives children of after-school, recreational time. For the disabled child, Hebrew school can be too great a challenge or can interfere with a very carefully organized life. Some families of children with disabilities do not make Hebrew school attendance a requirement. Instead of spending extra time at Hebrew school, they hire a private tutor to assist the child, or simply do not mark the occasion at all, or do so in the most minimal fashion often with the child's participation only in English and not Hebrew.

Another consideration for the disabled child revolves around the social aspects of the event. Many disabled children are not integrated in the social world of adolescents and may not have a peer group with whom they share recreational time or celebrate events. Thus there are few or no friends to invite to the celebration. Children with behavioral problems are often incapable of conducting themselves appropriately at a public ceremony where all of the attention is focused on them. For Michael, however, attendance in Hebrew school was a really positive experience and it provided another "school" environment where he was acknowledged as successful.

While Michael's family was not very religious, they were observant and mindful of their culture. Having a son who could be a Bar Mitzvah was a most important aspect of their heritage. Because of Michael's autism, the family recognized that there were both academic and social concerns to address. As it turned out, the academic aspect of Michael's religious education was not a problem and Michael did very well in Hebrew school.

I wondered if the Hebrew school personnel were aware of Michael's disability.

> *Shari:* He often arrived at Hebrew school late, and they were told that he didn't go to the school in the area like the other kids. Nobody ever knew where he went to school or why he went to a different school. They didn't ask and I didn't tell them.

Did Michael's behavior in Hebrew school indicate that he was distinctive?

> *Shari:* He kept himself quiet. He did make some unusual faces and some-times he flapped, but mostly he didn't flap in public. He was different and they knew it. But he did his "thing" and they loved him. He actually wanted to be there and learn, which is so different from most kids who are forced to go to Hebrew school and resent it.
>
> In the beginning I left work twice a week in the afternoon, picked him up at school, and brought him to the Hebrew school. I sat in the back of that room and he was humiliated that Mommy was there. But this Mommy let him know that if he was going to go to Hebrew school, I wasn't tolerating any nonsense and he'd better sit there and do what he had to do. And I did that for a month until he begged me not to come anymore and he promised he'd behave.
>
> There were two teachers at Hebrew school that really loved him, and they made it better for him and for me.

I asked Michael how he was treated by the other children in Hebrew school and if they sensed that he was autistic.

> *Michael*: They all knew that I was eccentric and went to a school different from the one they attended. But they thought I was a hard worker and a nerd. Maybe they thought I came from out of town and that's why they didn't know me from the neighborhood.
>
> Also, my mom's friend was the secretary at the school, and she knew quite a bit, but not everything, about me. She didn't tell and she kept the school relationship separate from the personal one. No one else knew much if anything about me.

It's well known that often the behavior of children attending Hebrew school is problematic, because they find the additional hours of schooling more than they want to deal with. I wondered how Michael was able to control his behavior in this after-school environment, when he had so much difficulty in the regular school program.

> *Michael*: I had very few behavior problems at Hebrew school, so I don't know how much they knew about me. It was generally a small class and I guess because the classes were in the synagogue, I thought it was wrong to misbehave there. Maybe I had one or two outbursts, but nothing really ever happened there. Sometimes I got there really late and had a small tantrum at home before school or in the car on the way to school, but not in the class-room. I was always fine once I got started in the class. Also, because I was often late, I was probably only there for about an hour. That was a lot less than the six hours I spent in regular school.

When children approach their 13th birthday, the Hebrew school program is supplemented with extensive and focused preparation on the Bar Mitzvah service. Additional tutoring is usually conducted by a rabbi, cantor (the individual who leads the singing of prayers), or other learned individual. This prepares the child for his or her full participation in the services, as well as teaching him or her to read and chant a lengthy passage in Hebrew.

> *Michael*: I finished my lessons [for the Bar Mitzvah] two months earlier and I went the full eight weeks [before the event] without looking at my stuff. Then we had a dress rehearsal to make sure that I remembered it.

Michael wanted the Bar Mitzvah and if he could manage it, the family wanted to have a celebration after the service. They were unsure of what kind of party to arrange given Michael's difficulty handling social situations, his sensitivity to noise, his dislike of being touched, and his extreme dietary preferences. Michael's behavior in public could be violent and unpredictable and no one wanted the Bar Mitzvah event to be an embarrassment for Michael or his family. Just getting Michael to put on more restrictive "dress" clothes was a challenge for a child who didn't want to get dressed at all and was accustomed to wearing loose-fitting and soft sweat clothes.

Customarily, families can choose many forms of Bar Mitzvah party, from a modest luncheon with a small number of guests to a grand and elaborate party with music, dancing, and amusements for a large number of people. Routine and consistency were the hallmarks of Michael's life and all of his special needs, as well as the potential for his extreme outbursts, had to be considered.

> *Shari*: Every night he practiced his reading, and he rehearsed and rehearsed and did what he had to do. So we started to think about how we were going to celebrate that day. We wanted to celebrate and we discussed it with him. We tried to create a party that would be custom made for him. We didn't think he could tolerate holding himself together twice that day [morning services and evening party], although the tradition is to not have a party on Saturday afternoon, which is still Sabbath. Even something as simple as getting dressed twice that day would be too much for Michael.

(Sabbath observers have many restrictions regarding general behavior and a Saturday afternoon party may not be desirable, because of the prohibitions for Sabbath observance.) The family went ahead and planned to have a Saturday afternoon party that would immediately follow the completion of the morning services at a catering facility a short distance from their temple.

> *Shari*: The services were not the problem for Michael, but the party was. Preparation was everything for him. We were psyching him up and getting him prepared. We talked it and talked it over and over and we prayed. You never knew how Michael was going to be the next day.

I asked how the services went.

> *Shari*: The morning of the service I got to the temple about 20 minutes later than the guys, because of a problem with my schedule that morning. Michael will always say that I came late for his Bar Mitzvah, but it was unavoidable. [Michael remembers his mother being an hour late for services, and hasn't forgotten or forgiven this late arrival.]
> He was so amazing in that temple, because everybody there knew what it took for us to get to that point. It was an extremely emotional day. He

looked at everybody, said the prayers out of his head, and never put his face down to look at the prayer book.

When his father put the prayer shawl around him in the beginning of the service, we cried, my parents cried and everyone else cried. His brother, Scot, was amazing too. He was only seven years old, but he clapped, and so did everybody else, and Scot shouted, "That's my brother. That's my brother." And Michael smiled back at him. You have to remember how Michael could be so cruel and violent to Scot.

We got through the service well and by then although the rabbi knew that Michael had special needs, he and I never talked about how disabled Michael was and had been. When it was over, we had cake in the temple and then we were supposed to go to the party.

I asked Michael about his memory of the service.

Michael: On Friday night, I also had to participate in services and I had a really bad cold that night, but felt well enough for the 15 minutes that I led the service. Somehow on Saturday morning I woke up healthy, but I was nervous about the cold. I had a pile of tissues on the pulpit.

On Saturday I was very focused on the service. It was my day and I felt recognized and the day went very well and my mom was acknowledging me that day and giving me the attention, but she got there very late.

Shari describes the careful planning that went into making Michael's party a success.

Shari: We knew the party could be a problem. We looked at many places to have it. We chose a party menu that was exactly what I knew Michael would eat, because his food was another issue. It was a breakfast in the afternoon. It was omelets and pancakes and French toast and waffles and it was a fabulous brunch. It would all be for him and everybody loved it. It was all dairy foods.

Jake, Michael's father: Over the years when we took him to parties his mother got him ear plugs. At his Bar Mitzvah we didn't know what would be. We made a totally different party with things just for him.

In spite of extensive planning, the unexpected can happen.

Shari: After the service Michael walked outside with some of the children who attended and he was wearing his beautiful Bar Mitzvah suit. He fell into the hedges and ripped his entire pants leg open. He came to me and said, "Ma, I'm sorry, I ripped my pants, what should we do?" I was standing with the doctors I worked for and me, Miss Control Freak, calmed him down and said, "Okay, it's okay, don't worry, we'll go home and change." It's incredible, because I would never buy Michael dress clothes, because he never wore them. But, for some reason I bought him an extra pair of navy dress slacks.

We went home and we changed his pants, and cleaned him up, and then we went off to the party. One of my bosses years later said that he would never forget how in control I seemed and how calm I looked. He should only know how I really felt.

Michael recalls the same event with factual detail:

Michael: We were walking to the car after services and my leg got caught in a bush and I ripped my pants and I had to go home to change. Then we went to the reception. Some people came at 12 and others at 2. My uncle and brother got lost and it took them an hour to get there.

It was all kosher style and all dairy food with all the food that I like, but then they brought out hot dogs and my mom went ballistic. [Kosher rules do not allow dairy foods and meat to be served at the same meal.]

I wondered if Michael had friends attend his party.

Jake: There were very few kids there, just a few cousins and a few kids of our immediate friends. His teachers were there and he got presents from them that you'd laugh about.

I asked Michael who he invited to the party.

Michael: Friends? I didn't invite any of them from my Hebrew school class. I was afraid of rejection, if they wouldn't come. So I didn't invite them. Kids from school? No, I didn't have that kind of relationship, and didn't invite any. We picked out the teachers I wanted to come from my school and they all came.

I asked how Michael handled himself during the party.

Shari: He held himself together. We kept it very calm and cool and he actually had a good time. He knew it was for him, it was all for him, but I was so afraid. He doesn't like hugging and kissing, but he's okay with certain people. He put his best foot forward that day and we watched him have fun. He ate and he even danced.

His teachers were all there. That table of teachers really held him together through many of his childhood years and they were everybody who was important to him. There was one teacher, who remembered that Michael loves White-Out [correction fluid]. He would go through gallons of it, and also he loved Yoo-Hoo, chocolate drinks. And she brought this huge basket of White-Out and Yoo-Hoos. And he just went crazy for that. There was so much support in that room for him. We watched him enjoy it and we all had a really good time.

I asked Michael how he was able to manage himself during the Bar Mitzvah party.

> *Michael*: Noise? Music? It didn't bother me, because I expected it. It was planned and it was about me and they did modify the music. It wasn't the normal, loud music you'd hear at a Bar Mitzvah. I danced with my mother a little bit and the teachers. But I didn't like close dancing—getting close and with some of the dresses some women wore with shoulders showing, it was very disturbing to me and of course, touching people.
>
> I was prepared for the party. There was direct preparation for it and I knew all the people involved.

Transitions had always been a problem for Michael and given all the attention and stress, it was not surprising that the end of the Bar Mitzvah day was unpleasant.

> *Shari*: He was starting a tantrum in the parking lot. I couldn't get him into the car quickly enough. I can't remember what set him off. He was yelling and screaming and he was slamming doors. He was cursing. He was banging and hitting. He was doing everything he could do in a tantrum. So it was all we could do to get him home from this very perfect day.
>
> In the car on the way home, he blew. Immediately. It was just the four of us and everybody else went back to my mother's house. I knew he couldn't handle that. We got back to our house and he had a full tantrum. He was completely off.
>
> We called for a pizza that he demanded and that was just after eating all the other food. It took a really long time for him to calm down when we got back, after this huge day when he had been absolutely perfect. And eventually he went to sleep, which is how he turns off the world.

I asked Michael to recall the same event and his reply indicates how strongly he felt about the role of his mother in his life.

> *Michael*: My mom was relieved when the day was over feeling that she gave me whatever attention I needed. She wasn't so concerned about my existence after leaving there and I had a temper tantrum going home.
>
> We got into an argument on the way home. I think that I wanted pizza for dinner and my mom said we spent so much on this Bar Mitzvah and

there was so much food and now you're asking me about dinner. She said something that rubbed me the wrong way and it was my day and I wasn't going to allow her any room for error and I blew my stack. She could barely drive the car. I leaned forward from the back seat and grabbed her and the car swerved. And when I got home I went to sleep. Between the commotion of the day and that tantrum, I was shot.

The Bar Mitzvah day ended with the bittersweet memory of the triumph of the public performance and the tragedy of the anger and violence that followed within the family. Now, more than ten years later, Michael reflects on the importance of the Bar Mitzvah in his life.

Michael: I really like rules and definiteness. I really took to the technicalities of Judaism for several years and then it wore off. I was pretty religious until the sophomore year of college.

I also wasn't truly aware at that age of not being normal, so the concept of being a "normal Jewish boy" does not specifically come to mind. When I got older and was well aware that I was different, doing normal things, like going to a normal college, became much more important.

It was the first step of the transition from child to adult, the last step of which has still not occurred by my definition. But it did mean that I was expected to take some adult responsibilities, albeit very basic ones like throwing a paper plate in the garbage or putting a plate in the sink after eating. It was also the time that I was told that I shouldn't expect my mother to be in the bathroom with me.

There were many "lessons" learned that day—lessons about becoming an adult, Jewish male; lessons about being the center of attention and publicly celebrating success; lessons about enjoying a happy time with friends and family; and a lesson that is still being learned—how to be just like everyone else.

Author's reflection

Significance for the family

All religions have public aspects to their celebrations with expectations that youngsters will be enfolded into the rituals so that there will be perpetuation of the heritage. This is especially true of Judaism where the Bar Mitzvah is public acknowledgement of the child's role in family life and religion, and a milestone in the transition to adult life and responsibilities. Although the families of disabled children often need to adjust to different goals for their children, each milestone can be a sad reminder that the children cannot meet typical expectations. If a disabled child tries to fulfill obligations beyond his or her ability, it can be publicly humiliating for all.

It's both surprising and wonderful that Michael was an able student in Hebrew school and took to learning a new language and the history of his culture with zeal. He liked all the rituals and precision of the regulated life of a religious person. It is still unclear how he was able to manage his behavior successfully during Hebrew school classes, when many nondisabled students in these after-school hours typically act out. Michael's desire to go to Hebrew school, his success learning, and acknowledgement of his performance all provided positive reinforcement. It is moving to hear Michael say that because the Hebrew school classes were held in the temple, his respect for the sanctuary further encouraged good behavior. This demonstrates Michael's insightful thinking and awareness of the importance of appropriate conduct in some contexts.

The social event

Many people enjoy parties, but social events for disabled children can be especially difficult. Not having peers with whom to celebrate and not showing appropriate conduct certainly mar the fun of celebrating. Michael didn't have young friends to invite to his party, but the event was filled with people who cared deeply for him: family, teachers, and the congregation. There was no emptiness in his world that day!

Michael's fall outside the temple and the damage to his clothes and appearance show how difficult it can be, even with meticulous planning, to ensure that all will go smoothly. This accident was handled with grace and composure and maintaining a calm demeanor is so critical in supervising a complex child such as Michael.

Michael's antagonism about his mother's late arrival at the temple on *his* day reinforces the pre-eminent role of his mother in his life. Her approval and recognition meant all to him. The family's initial refusal to indulge Michael's request for pizza as they drove home and the resulting tantrum show just how fragile Michael's self-control mechanisms were. His comment that he would not allow his mother any margin for error on *his* day provides an insight into his egocentric world and the pattern of demands and capitulation that were so much a part of his family life. Michael, like other autistic individuals, lives in a world of structure and consistency, and when there is deviation from what they want and expect it's not unusual for behavioral outbursts to result. The intense pressure and anxiety that the family experienced on the day of Michael's Bar Mitzvah were more than Michael could understand. As with other adolescents, this day was all about him.

As the family and Michael look at the beautiful pictures in the Bar Mitzvah photo album, much of the sadness over Michael's tantrum gives way to the beauty and joy of most of the day. The Bar Mitzvah was successful in so many ways that it provides wonderful memories for Michael and his family to cherish.

Chapter 7

High School: Things Greatly Improve

I was very nervous the first day in high school. I believe I sat nervous and amazed at my desk even during lunch.

Michael

Michael's high school years forged a new direction in his life. Unlike many other autistic children, Michael's high school experience demonstrated an ability to become part of a peer group, and do very well academically. All of this was accomplished in a school environment where attention to special students was of primary importance.

Changes can and do occur when any teenager enters high school, but when a child is autistic, nothing about adolescence is likely to be easy. During high school teenagers typically develop more independence and place greater emphasis on social relationships. For academically oriented students, high school is also a time of heightened concern about scholastic success as they begin to think about college and career choices. Each one of these concerns is a challenge for an autistic individual.

Adolescents typically have lives that revolve around social experiences, which take precedence over everything else, and they become especially concerned about becoming part of a peer group where they feel comfortable. They also become very interested in developing male–female relationships. Parents of teenagers typically complain that their child's connection to home and family is quickly replaced by an intense involvement with friends, "hanging out," talking on the phone, using e-mail, and dating. Autistic individuals struggle with social connections and the adolescent years can be full of complexity and frustration.

Another challenge for a disabled teenager is finding the appropriate high school and then being accepted into that school. The choice of which school to attend is not only a decision made by the child and family, but is under the authority of the Committee on Special Education (CSE) in the school district where the student resides. The CSE must endorse the family's wishes or attending the school becomes the family's financial responsibility. At times, even finding a high school with the appropriate special education services is frustrating, and as more students are being included in regular schools there are fewer self-contained high school programs for disabled teenagers. Many of the self-contained schools for disabled adolescents have populations of more severely impaired children both in terms of academic potential and behavior.

Special educators know that the transition from lower grades to high school is subject to many considerations. As the student gets older, both the CSE and the family become aware of the need to plan for the child's future with the concern about how the student can be prepared for independent living as an adult. By the time that Michael was ready for high school, there was evidence that his academic ability was very strong and if his behavior and autistic symptoms were "under control," all felt that he could succeed in the right high school setting. The choice of a high school program had to be made by balancing attention to the autism disorder along with a strong academic program.

Michael had always attended a special school with very few students in a class and where individual attention was the norm. Teachers in this setting were totally committed to understanding the needs of the "whole child" so that they could address whatever issues their students were dealing with. Michael had also always been educated with other special needs students, who faced similar behavioral and academic challenges. Would there be a high school program for Michael where both his emotional and academic needs could be successfully met? The challenge was to find the right school.

The move to suburbia

While Michael was in ninth grade and still attending the Center's school, his family moved to suburbia from a more urban area.

> *Shari:* I wanted for us to move out of the apartment. We knew it was going to be tough financially, but we wanted a better life for the boys. We found a house in a good neighborhood. The boys would each have their own bedroom and there was a backyard. Jake and I had grown up in private houses and we wanted the same for the kids.

I also wanted Scot to grow up in a community with good kids and great schools. I expected that Michael would always attend special schools, but that wasn't true for Scot. There were so many problems for Scot having a brother with autism, that I always wanted to make sure that his life would be better.

Any change in routine or schedule was difficult for Michael, and moving into a new home and leaving the security of the apartment and community where he had always lived was of great concern. In fact, when the family moved to the new home, Michael went to live with his grandparents for several weeks so that everything in the new house would be organized before he moved in. This also included getting approval from the new school district for Michael to continue at the Center's school and arranging transportation. Michael always enjoyed staying with his grandparents from time to time during his early years, because they doted on him and lived very close to his childhood home.

> *Shari:* We bought the house, but it needed a lot of work. I was concerned that Michael's brother, Scot, be able to start his school year in the new community when all of the other children did in September. So even though the house wasn't ready to move into I drove Scot back and forth to his new school each day.
>
> Of course I was really worried how Michael would adjust to the new house. He really didn't want to move. He loved his old bedroom and was totally comfortable with everything in that apartment. Michael could never adjust to change and I didn't know how he would do in the new house. I didn't want to create more reasons for Michael's tantrums.
>
> The house we bought was a mess and every day I cleaned and scrubbed it, and finally I thought it was time to move in. We decided to replace the kitchen, because it was a disaster and that took over two months. Can you imagine two months without having a kitchen? We had to eat out every day. It wasn't easy and it wasn't cheap.

Although Michael was old enough to attend high school, Michael's mother felt that with the change in residence it would be too traumatic to simultaneously change schools and she wanted Michael to continue at the Center, which did include students up to age 16.

> *Shari:* I wanted Michael to stay at the Center's school for the extra year in ninth grade so that everything didn't change for him at once. Looking back, after the first year in the new high school where he went the following year, Michael said that he should have changed schools the year before. I told him

that I didn't want so many changes in one year. He said it was a mistake and he blamed me for making that decision. Academically, he belonged in a high school a year sooner. He felt that it was my fault that he lost a year. He's been angry with me about it ever since.

Finding the right high school

After settling into the new home and community Shari knew that they needed to locate a special high school with a strong academic program for Michael's next school year. The choice of high school was also complicated by the family's change in residence. The selection of Michael's prior schools was under the supervision of the urban school district, but the new school district would have to approve a different school setting. In those years many school districts did not have experience dealing with high-functioning autistic children. Most autistic children had severe impairments and required highly specialized programs where the academic program was of lesser concern. Michael was not at all a typical autistic child.

> *Shari*: In the new school district they had a wonderful CSE. They recommended five schools for us to look at when Michael was ready for tenth grade. The Hilltop School [not the actual name of the school] was the only one I liked. One of Michael's teachers from the Center school went with me to visit there, because she knew the Principal. I walked in and I knew that it was the school for Michael and, luckily, he was accepted right away.
>
> When the new school people met Michael, they really seemed to get a kick out of him. It was like an extension of the Center's school, and it wasn't even too far away. Michael would be familiar with the bus route and that should help even though it was a longer bus trip from our new home. There were kids at Hilltop from all over the city, but fewer from the suburban areas near where we were living.
>
> We got him "psyched" about going to Hilltop. He was in tenth grade and he made the change and he seemed okay. Believe it or not, the social worker that was assigned to Michael was someone that I went to school with and she was just wonderful with him!

Shari continued to be an excellent advocate for Michael and her instincts about schools and services was once again "on target."

> *The Director at Hilltop*: Michael's mother is one of the most capable, wonderful mothers we ever met. I truly believe that much of Michael's success is because of his mother's love, dedication, and hard work.

Hilltop, the new school

If the ideal school could be designed for a student like Michael, it would be just like Hilltop School. Hilltop is a private school located in a middle-class urban area. Students' tuition is paid by their residential school districts supplemented by state aid. Almost all classes are held in one building that seems to be just the right size to give an adolescent the feeling of attending a high school, but certainly not as large as the comprehensive high schools in most communities. From the appearance of the building nothing shouts "This is for special kids." It's an ordinary looking structure that fits into the landscape on a street adjacent to a busy parkway. It's not particularly modern or overly impressive, but with an atmosphere of friendliness and welcome, it's easy to enter and find your way around.

On the late spring afternoon of a visit to the school with Michael (who was then finishing college) there was a small crowd of teens outside the building buying lunch from a canteen-truck that made a daily stop there. These students looked no different from the usual assortment of scruffy teens that "hang out" outside any high school in a middle-class community. No doubt the appearance and atmosphere of the school were easily accepted by kids who didn't want to be identified as special or different. A school administrator described the student population as "fragile" special education students, who have good academic ability. An alumnus and friend of Michael's describes the school this way:

> *Gene:* Hilltop is a place that can really focus attention on kids without using those labels and just give that extra individual attention.

I asked Michael how the new school compared with the old one.

> *Michael:* At the old school there were about 6–8 kids in a class and at the new school there were about 12.

Michael didn't comment on how he felt about the school and this required more questioning.

> *Michael:* I was amazed that I was at a real school when I arrived, and I remember the first day. That day was very nerve wracking and I needed time to get used to it. But things that weren't black and white in the beginning started to bother me less after a while. There was less ambiguity for me. I think I also became more flexible.
>
> When I was younger, I had some interesting ideas about school. I thought that every school was just like the ones I went to. You had to get on

a bus and go far away and then you'd be in smaller classes. There's so much that I didn't understand about other kids' school experiences.

An administrator at the school: The first month here Michael was just adjusting and we give the students time for that. We had visited his elementary school before he came here and we knew that we needed to put him in a class where he would succeed. Although he was entering our school in tenth grade, he took both ninth and tenth grade classes, because there were courses he missed at his other school. Not long after, Michael advocated for himself, because he wanted to be more challenged.

The social worker: I think anxiety was a big factor when he first came and time management was also a big thing and he was able to conquer it. This was more in terms of getting an assignment done and not obsessing about will he have the time to do it.

Academic success

The experience at Hilltop proved to Michael, his family, and teachers that he had extremely high academic ability that resulted in overall success from tenth to twelfth grade.

Shari: Academically, he soared. Everything was departmentalized. It's a great high school, a wonderful school and very individual with small classes. Those were great years for him. He did three years there and he took all of his state exams. He was a model student.

When Michael was in college, we paid a visit to Hilltop. Many of Michael's former teachers and several administrators who knew Michael gathered in the conference room during lunch to see Michael, share muffins, talk about Michael's high school experience, and learn about his progress in college. It was apparent that Michael was one of the success stories at this school and that he and his teachers had great fondness for each other.

The Director of the school, Dr. G: Michael was very respected. Knowledge is not put down here and no student is put down for being a nerd. He's very bright and a model student, but he was also well liked by other students. All students respected him and turned to him. He was never isolated in the back of the room and he was part of the group. In fact, he was part of all groups of kids and he could just kind of float from group to group. He got involved with tutoring while he was a student, and he even came back while in college to help others. He was terrific with peer tutoring.

An English teacher. Michael had a sense of humor. He was really funny and he would smile a lot. He was also serious, but not overly serious, and I had a good time with him. We could joke around and it was a pleasure.

A writing teacher. He was an exemplary student, a fantastic writer. He worked on organizing his thoughts. Obviously his work spoke for itself. He was in a very socially "hip" group that year and they were nice kids.

Michael's sincere desire to learn was evident to all:

Michael's home room teacher and an instructor in several classes: There wasn't an arrogance. If he came across that way, he would have had problems. He likes to help other people. He's a nice person and you always feel that you're with a good human being. People who are smart can come across as arrogant and you could be shot down, and this isn't Michael. He's very insightful and breaks stereotypes.

He was a big help to me—a wonderful, very bright young man. His strengths are my weaknesses and at times I can be off in my own world asking "What page are we on? What page are we up to?" I understood quickly that Michael could easily have been an assistant teacher to me and in many ways he was. He's incredibly organized. I'd ask him what we were up to and half the time he'd have the aim up on the board before I got to the class.

An example of his humor: Michael always knew that he could correct me. He said the funniest thing to me at the end of one school year: "This year you handed back 133 papers, but you missed giving back 3. You're one of the better teachers!" I didn't doubt that I had returned 133 papers, and had forgotten to return 3.

Whether this is an example of Michael's sense of humor, his focus on precision and numbers, or more likely a combination of the two, no one can be sure. But it certainly made this teacher laugh.

Because of his physical awkwardness, you wouldn't imagine that physical education classes were a plus for Michael, but this wasn't true.

Michael's physical ed teacher. I remember a happy kid who loved coming to class. He loved running around and enjoyed playing. He got along nicely and wasn't anxious very much. He played whatever we did and he really enjoyed himself.

Michael: I'm a klutz and I have no talent. I have bad feet, flat feet, and it makes everything hard to do.

In special schools, there are many modifications made to meet the needs of the students and maximize their ability to succeed and this was true at this school. The academic program was conducted four days a week and on the fifth day students did a work extension. Michael's work extension included helping at a large community college library and tutoring students in the lower school. The flexibility of this program apparently had a disadvantage for Michael, because when he was in his first year of college, he found that there were gaps in his educational background. He thought that other students seemed better prepared for college than he was. Even though the high school curriculum met state requirements, there was not as much rigor as compared to other high schools. I asked the group of teachers if they were aware of the educational "gaps" and what might have caused them.

> *A social studies teacher:* Each of our academic classes meets four days a week. In general, our philosophy is that you don't continue teaching if there's something that has to be taken care of. With our approach, we cover topics in depth and don't just follow the curriculum if our students are having difficulty.

A shortcoming of this special school is their inability to offer some advanced courses, especially science. Most of the students, however, are not accelerated enough to need the courses, but Michael could profit from an advanced science class. In order to provide Michael with the science class, during his senior year he attended a very large, city high school, just for this one class. The high school was a short distance away and Hilltop provided transportation back and forth every day. This was Michael's first experience in a very different school environment.

> *A teacher at Hilltop:* Michael attended a regular high school for one science subject. Perhaps that made college a little easier. The high school wasn't so student centered and it was good for him to have had that experience before college. Here we try to create a very protective environment where the kids can succeed, but they need to have another kind of experience where they must be independent.

> *Shari:* You know how much I worried about him, especially when I heard that they were sending Michael to that other high school. He took the class at that city high school and he was fine there. Hilltop transported him and he loved it.
> The kids teased him at the new school, but they respected him. They took his books off his desk and he had to go through metal detectors to

enter the school. He was in a class of 35 students, which was totally new for him. But you know Michael, he did "his thing" and he did so well. At the end of the year he got 84 on that state exam for the class.

An administrator at Hilltop: During the semester that Michael attended that other high school, I got a call from them. I feared for the worst. I laugh when I remember that the other administrator told me that she was calling because several of the girls in Michael's science class were concerned about him. The weather was cold and he came to school without a jacket and they wanted someone to know that he was not dressed appropriately for the severe winter weather.

Michael: You know me. I can't keep track of things. I lost four jackets at the new high school. I probably left them somewhere. I decided to just not wear a jacket there. After all the bus was heated and so was the school—so what's the big deal?

The often inappropriate behavior of special education students is an ongoing concern. Even when a student has good academic potential, if they can't conduct themselves appropriately, little learning takes place. When he attended elementary school, a great deal of time was spent dealing with Michael's outbursts and temper tantrums. Would this continue into Michael's teenage years, considering that for any adolescent it's a time characterized by mood swings and emotional turmoil? By the time Michael entered tenth grade, his behavior in the "outside world" was almost always under control. At home problems persisted with tantrums, outbursts, threats of physical violence, and extreme temper.

An administrator at Hilltop: I remember visiting his elementary school and hearing about Michael's outbursts there, but there wasn't one outburst here.

At Hilltop, Michael's teachers were able to challenge his intellect and immerse him in the kind of learning he craved without the need to address disruptive behavior.

His home room teacher and instructor: I kind of forced him to do what the college teachers do, which is not to just give me the literal answers. I made him write in the first person and he'd say "Why are you doing this to me?" He likes to hide. He's wonderful at getting the literal and just giving it back to you, but when he has to talk about himself and show insight and discuss how what he's learning affects him, that's very difficult.

He would hand me four pages of typed written work that he worked on as hard as he could—poured his guts out—but he didn't get the "A" and the kid who gave me one page, who could write succinctly, would get the higher grade. Michael would say to me that there was nothing wrong with his paper. But I wanted him to express himself in a way that other people could understand it without his rambling on and on.

Another Hilltop teacher comments on Michael's intense desire to learn:

> You can be very straightforward and honest with Michael, and while we didn't always agree on everything it left room open for each of us to learn from the other. Michael was very helpful to me in my development as a teacher because teachers can learn from their students—it's a two-way street. His basic reason was to improve the quality of what was going on and he was dedicated towards making the education experience the best possible.
>
> He needed structure and could give constructive ways to improve upon things. A potential problem would be if a teacher has a master plan that can't be varied. If Michael takes a dart and punches a hole through that plan, it could be taken in the wrong way. Michael is very insightful, and he's a truth teller and someone else's ego may not be strong enough to take the truth.

It was clear that disruptive behavior in school was not at all evident during Michael's high school years and it is unclear why this dramatic change occurred.

> *Michael*: I think my time in the hospital at the start of fourth grade made me more conscious of my place in the world, and that my behavior was unacceptable, and that my school was special. Other factors may have been simply growing up or growing out of it and medication.

Friendships

It is especially interesting to learn how Michael related to and was viewed by other students. Before high school Michael never had friends and high school can be a lonely place if you don't fit in. Michael did make friends at Hilltop and became part of a group of four that included Gene. Gene has a lifelong obsession with planes and travel that caused lots of problems in his youth. From time to time, he would disappear from home, get on a plane, and travel. Michael would joke that when he was absent from school Gene would be gone for several days, because he was probably in Paris or London. For some unknown reason, Chicago was Gene's most frequent destination. Gene's parents ultimately made a contract with him that required him to pay for his flights and hotels, tell them when he was going to be away, and that he couldn't miss school. To support his "habit," this high school student became an unofficial travel agent for the Hilltop teachers, who paid him to plan their travel itineraries and make their reservations. Gene's obsession with flying turned into a lucrative career. His wanderlust is now paid for by an international company that sends Gene all over the world to appraise aircraft.

> *Gene:* I never guessed that Michael was autistic, but none of us really knew each other's "labels." He wasn't the type of person that I was initially drawn to, because Michael wasn't outgoing. I would call him a very interesting person, but a "background" person, because he was always in the background. Eventually it became clear how smart he was, and we became friends. We shared the same level of academic excellence and we both were college candidates.

Gene recalls Michael's wry sense of humor even while still in high school. Michael would say that for himself staying "local" meant not leaving his suburban community, but to Gene it meant traveling within the continental United States. Michael also teased Gene that while he visited all over, he never visited sites close to home. Michael would also say to Gene, "Local to you is California. You have to leave the continent for it to be far."

Michael and John: The odd couple

John, who is almost the same age as Michael, also attended Hilltop. The two became friends, even though they were worlds apart in background, appearance, personality, academic ability, and interests. Initially, John saw Michael outside of school by occasionally visiting at Michael's home on weekends. John lived far from Michael, so he began sleeping over at Michael's home. Gradually, John became a semi-permanent member of Michael's family and this arrangement continued into the college years. Michael's mother, Shari, wanted to help John, who she saw as very needy, because he got little emotional and financial support from his parents, who had many problems of their own. Michael and John became the "odd couple" at school and knew each other very well, because John lived with Michael's family part time during and after high school.

> *John:* I met Michael in his first year at high school. He should have been in tenth grade, but was taking both ninth and tenth grade classes to catch up and I was in ninth. I remember the first time we spoke, but I had seen him a lot before that. He always had an extra diet soda with him. I'd come up from sports practice and I asked him for a soda and he gave me one. He'd give

everyone a soda, but he'd spill everything. Then I'd ask him what was the math homework or something.

I asked Michael about bringing soda to school.

> *Michael*: I brought lunch with me every day, but the school sold juice and milk, and I prefer to drink only soda with certain foods.

Michael's food preferences and rigidity about diet appear to be a result of obsessive-compulsive behavior, and, similar to other autistic individuals, he had a strong aversion to many foods. If Michael's favorite foods were not in plentiful supply, or if they were displayed on a plate in an irregular manner, he erupted into a tantrum. This continued throughout his childhood. When he was in college, Michael was willing to try new foods, but he still continued to follow a more restrictive diet than his peers.

I asked John about his first impressions of Michael.

> *John*: He was a nerd. School work was his number one thing and he'd hang out with the select few kids, who were very academic and very different. Michael falls into the category of "don't hit a kid like that, because it's bad luck to hit a kid like that." Lots of normal kids wouldn't even bother with a kid like Michael.
>
> But it was different in our school. Different kids think in different ways. Some kids thought he was a popular guy. He was a tutor and helped them. Michael got along with the academic kids and then there were sports kids and in our school everyone was popular in their own way.
>
> You can look at him and know that something's different. An outside person would know he's not normal—just something simple like knocking over a glass and things always falling down.

> *Michael*: I think that people do notice that something is wrong with me. I wonder what they see.

We discussed that Michael often rocked back and forth and that this behavior abated and stopped by the time he finished college.

> *Michael*: But I rock only when I get nervous and it's very much part of my childhood. I'm not ashamed about being autistic, but I want to know what people know about me. The school was like a family and we never knew each other's diagnosis, but you found out after a while.

John and Michael were a totally mismatched pair; John was a "with it" city kid with street smarts. He was handsome, tall, athletic, independent, a mediocre student, and very "cool." Michael was short, stocky, "nerdy," and pampered, but also excelled at school and was noticeably different from others. What fostered this friendship?

> *John:* The benefit I got from Michael was that he tutored me. He was good at so many things at school and I'm good at so many other things. I'm social and good at sports so I would give him some of that and he would reward me in other ways. I would make him hang out, like go out to the movies.
>
> He's really a good teacher and he can really explain, but dealing with people is something else.
>
> It was a very complementary relationship [John probably heard his friendship with Michael described this way by others, because this is not at all characteristic of his language.] But it was lopsided with more for him. I'd help him day to day like even to help him get dressed. [A significant childhood issue for Michael was his refusal to dress himself and this persisted into adolescence, when he conceded by wearing only loose-fitting pull-on pants and tee shirts that were old and soft. He admits that when he was young he hated the feeling of putting on clothes that were at all restrictive, but also admitted to just being lazy about dressing himself when he got older.]
>
> He's Michael—he'll get on a bus and know the schedule like the back of his hand, but maybe when he gets on he'll hit someone with his backpack and he doesn't know it and I'll just say something to the person, otherwise he'd be dead. He has no street smarts. His books will fall all over. He'll step on someone's foot.

Did you shape Michael up?

> *John:* I'm still trying.

John's background is interesting and provides a profile of another category of student who attended Hilltop. When I met John he was about 20 years old and seemed especially well-mannered, and it was hard to imagine that he had problems so severe that warranted his attending a very special school. I wanted to learn more about him.

> *John:* When I was in elementary school in the city, I had big problems with teachers. Yeah, there was some fighting and I even threw my books out the window one day. But the teachers just couldn't handle me, and they were terrible teachers. One even chained me to my desk and my mother wanted him fired, but he resigned. I was diagnosed with ADD [attention deficit disorder], and people in school called me a bad kid.

I know how to take care of myself, not like Michael. My parents were divorced when I was about five or six, so it didn't affect me much, and I have a younger sister who's pretty messed up with her own kid. My father is an old man and my mother is much younger, but she's become disabled.

My parents didn't understand about me going to a special school, but one summer when I was younger we went to look at special schools. My parents thought Hilltop was the best place. It felt comfortable with only 10–15 kids in a class. There were all kinds of kids there: ADD, hyperactive, emotional troubles, and the school was divided into ability categories.

I wondered how John felt about being in special education.

John: I liked the small class size and personal attention. Today you can't tell that I was in special ed. I'm normal. I've always had normal friends, who went to the regular high school. I used to have a bad temper, but not now. I'm also OCD [obsessive-compulsive disorder], but I don't believe in taking medication. Kids are too pumped up on medication and can be like zombies. I can wash my hands 1000 times a day because I just don't feel clean. My hands get chapped and cracked from all that hand washing.

John uses the word "normal" very often and we discussed what he meant by "being normal."

John: You have to go with the flow in this world to be normal. These days it's okay to live your own way—orange hair, piercings, and you can say this is who I am. I was always mature and I'd tell my friends to cut that stuff out especially at a job interview. At a certain point, it's enough; no one wants to hire a freak.

To tell you the truth, I wasn't supposed to stay at Hilltop for all of high school. During the last three years I was supposed to go to a regular high school, but I wanted to stay at Hilltop. You know I had to travel about two hours each way to get to the school from home. I had to get up at 6 a.m. and I took the train. I also was into sports teams, so sometimes I wouldn't get home until 6 p.m. and then I worked after school. I was a messenger. I had to do things for myself, like I did my own laundry from the time I was ten.

The truth is that I was afraid to join the regular population in the local high school. It's a tough place and I was nervous. The teachers helped me stay at Hilltop and one year I lived with one of the teachers and his family on the weekends. I went lots of places with them.

John continued to be a part of Michael's family even after they graduated from high school. Michael started college, and John talked about going into the navy. For unknown reasons, John didn't enter the navy and kept making excuses that it just wasn't the right time to join up. He was also unwilling to enroll at a local community college as Shari suggested. John went back and forth between Michael's home in the suburbs and his own home in the city for almost two years after high school without much direction. This caused some tension between John and his mother, who felt that she was being replaced.

> *John*: My father was fine but my mom got upset. I can put myself into my mom's shoes and put myself in her position–and tell her that she's my mom. She would worry about me, normal stuff, and I've always been a responsible person. Her life is difficult.

While it might be expected that John was Michael's companion when he lived with the family, he actually became closer to Michael's younger brother, Scot, who sought the attention from this "cool" older brother substitute. Scot had many issues regarding life with an autistic brother and John took on an important role for him. John looked good, drove a car, and had interests similar to Scot's.

Shari insisted that if John wanted to continue living with her family, he had to do something productive. John got a job in a local video store, where he met a girl his age who attended a state college. He eventually enrolled at the same school. Shari was instrumental in getting John to make a decision about going to college and continued to treat him as a full member of the family until she and her husband divorced. Shari takes great pride in helping John during his high school years, and assisting him so that he could enter college. The family visited John during his freshman year at school, but now John only occasionally keeps in touch with the family by e-mail. He says that he is following a criminal justice major in college and hopes to work for the FBI some day.

Girlfriends

Boy–girl relationships are an important part of socialization during most teens' high school years. This can be such a confusing and troubling area for any adolescent, and for Michael it was even more so, as it was very difficult for him to form any meaningful friendships with others. Michael did have a girl-friend in high school.

> *Shari*: He even had a girlfriend in high school, but it wasn't an appropriate girlfriend for him. She was a very troubled girl and I eventually broke it up. It was his first experience with a girl. He was a good boyfriend, because he

was thoughtful and kind. When they broke up, he was sick for a week. He didn't eat. He lost weight. He cried. He felt sorry for himself. He felt sorry for her. He took it really bad, but he got past it. He didn't know how to deal with the whole thing. It was very difficult. And would you believe there was another girl waiting in the wings?

The new relationship lasted even when Michael was in his first year of college, but she wasn't helpful to him either. She got angry when he had to do his school work. John and I talked to him about it, but it took some time for him to see that this was not good for him. He broke up that relationship. He was not sick this time, but the girl couldn't handle it.

Even though they were the same age, she was still a high school student at Hilltop. She would call, write letters, and send pictures and it was almost like she was stalking him. It turned out that she took family photos from our house and destroyed them. I had to talk to her father and after that he talked to her and it got better. Michael was like her therapist and he tried to talk her through the break up and told her that they could still be friends. He didn't want to hurt her, and his trying to help her was so amazing, but she just couldn't let go. She was a really troubled girl.

When it was over he said, "Why did you let it go on?" But I was waiting and watching, and I told him that I couldn't tell him what to do in a relationship, but it was hard not to interfere.

Even through college and after, Michael has had difficulty understanding the "rules" of male–female relationships.

Michael: This continues to be an area in which I have minimal understanding. I will never forget one day in spring of tenth grade in health class when the instructor used the word "masturbation." I was thinking it was simply a difficult vocabulary word, so I raised my hand and asked what it meant. My lack of knowledge of this word seemed disturbing to my classmates. People tend to believe I am either asexual or gay, but I believe my attraction is solely to females.

I continue to have a fear of pursuing boy–girl relationships so perhaps the reason for my being involved with two emotionally disabled girls in high school is explained by the fact that they both pursued me.

High school graduation

Shari summarized Michael's high school experience.

Shari: He did three years at Hilltop and he was a model student. He made friends and because nobody lived where we did, they'd come for the weekend from all over the city. He did very well and that school was a good choice. He had group therapy and individual therapy to deal with social issues.

When he graduated, it was such an emotional day. I wanted to give him a party, so we told him to invite whoever he wanted, and we would take them to a restaurant. There were five boys and five girls including his old girlfriend and his soon-to-be girlfriend.

Graduation was beautiful. He got the President's Education Award. My parents were there and we just cried for the whole graduation. When they called his name, his friends all stood up and clapped for him. It was amazing. He earned everybody's respect.

Michael recalls his high school experience and graduation as well.

Michael: These are the things that I remember most: being nervous the first month or so, advocating for a change in classes the second month, beginning to understand that I went to special schools, and my thoughts about wanting to continue high school in a regular school. I also think that I developed my writing ability and experienced a somewhat more traditional teaching environment. At the Center's school there was not much "in front of room" teaching. Teachers came around and helped you or worked with you in groups or individually. After only going to a conventional high school for one class, I did apply to college as a "regular" student.

Michael does not comment at all on the social aspects of his high school experience, which are often most memorable for teens. External indicators point out that high school was both academically productive and truly enjoyable for Michael, and yet typically for Michael he doesn't respond with emotional feelings about this time in his life.

Author's reflection

Behavior

During high school there were many noticeable changes in Michael. While most of his teachers in elementary school knew that Michael was very intelligent and suspected that he had tremendous academic ability, there were many behavioral problems that prevented him from fulfilling his potential. Anger, tantrums, and outbursts persisted through the elementary grades and helping Michael manage his behavior was a primary focus. By the time Michael entered high school inappropriate behavior in a school setting was no longer an issue.

This positive trend may be attributable to several dynamics: change in medication, physiological development at puberty, greater insight about the importance of controlling behavior, extreme desire to "fit in," years of behavioral therapy, and the nature of autism itself. When Michael was a teenager, he began taking medication that significantly had a more positive result.

> *Dr. B, Michael's psychiatrist:* Before Michael was in the hospital [at age nine], he took an antidepressant. Initially the medication seemed helpful, but then his behavioral outbursts re-emerged. Then he was placed on several other trials, but there was no improvement and by the time he was nine, he was again showing severely disruptive behavior. He was then put on an antipsychotic, and while it seemed to be helpful, he was soon again display-ing disruptive behavior. He was hitting his mother and brother and having similar episodes at school.
>
> The first time he ever used Prozac (or for that matter any other serotonin reuptake inhibitor) was when he was 13. It was from that time that we began to see significant and ongoing improvement. I should emphasize, however, that it was not Prozac alone, but Prozac in combination with a mood stabi-lizer and an antipsychotic.

It can be speculated that the multiple interventions listed above contributed to the improvement in Michael's behavior, but the importance of the right medi-cation cannot be overlooked. As an adult, Michael takes only Prozac (with allergy and cholesterol lowering medication), and his behavior is clearly under his control. Michael has become very self-aware and successfully monitors and regulates his behavior and mood. He knows the importance of staying on medication, knowing when to go to sleep, and keeping very busy, which have all been successful adjustment strategies.

Michael is insightful in describing the positive change in his school behavior and recognizing that his hospitalization at nine years of age was a life altering experience. He's much less able to understand why severe behavior problems persisted at home for many years after his school behavior improved. Michael's view of his behavior at home is in contradiction to that of his family. He denies that he continued to be violent or frightening even during his college years. Instead, Michael feels that his mother and other family members provoked his outbursts by their actions, which might simply have been the sound of his mother's voice or her laugh, especially if she was on the telephone. Michael also thinks that his family exaggerates the severity of his behavior at that time. When asked to recall an incident when the police were called to intervene during an episode, Michael dismisses this as having been an over-reaction on his mother's part. All family members corroborate the seriousness of Michael's aggressive behavior at home even during college years.

Why did the violent behavior persist at home, when Michael was capable of behaving appropriately in school? Many people find that at home and with their immediate family they can let down their guard, and truly be themselves. This is especially true for Michael. He was able to control his behavior in school, where he felt it was most important to be appropriate, but he did "let go" at home. Michael was accustomed to his family catering to him and they indulged him in multiple ways. While the behavior modification plan was strictly followed in his childhood with consequences for inappropriate conduct, this was no longer viable when Michael was older and was physically intimidating. Another explanation might be that the time limits on his "control systems" expired by the time Michael returned from school due to fatigue or medication effects waning.

School achievement

In high school Michael was able to demonstrate excellent academic achieve-ment. He soaked up knowledge and delighted in being recognized for his superior performance. He endeared himself to teachers, because he was so motivated and worked so diligently. As compared to the population of other disabled students in his high school, Michael was a clear front runner academ-ically. Michael was even able to provide academic support to other students by tutoring them. This made Michael feel very good about himself, and it also reinforced the positive feelings that others had about him. Peer tutoring might have been the seed for Michael's desire to become a teacher.

In high school, Michael's brilliance in math became evident to all. Even though his behavior at home was disruptive and embarrassing, his mother and father took great pride in Michael's academic success. Shari was also delighted that her choice of high school worked out so well. The school was sufficiently stimulating, but continued in the tradition of Michael's previous school by being student centered. The experience of going to the large high school for the science class also afforded an opportunity to see how Michael would manage in a very different school environment. Luckily, this also worked out well and it's a credit to the staff at both schools for having arranged and supported Michael in this endeavor. By the end of high school, Michael's promising academic future was evident to all!

Friendships and fitting in

Do most teenagers ever feel confident that they "fit in"? Michael consistently describes himself as an "outsider," but this is not evident in the interviews with his teachers, and his high school friends Gene and John. Michael's appearance and manner were awkward, but he did not seem so different from other academically successful students at his special high school. In a community where all students were quirky and had significant emotional and educational problems, perhaps all being "outsiders," Michael was no trouble to his teachers and school administrators. Michael's superb academic achievement and exemplary behavior at school singled him out for positive recognition.

Michael belonged and contributed in this school in many ways. His service as a tutor brought him recognition and was welcomed assistance. This natural ability to tutor other students was never evident before high school and may have further reinforced Michael's interest in teaching. It's also important to note that even in areas such as physical education, where Michael doesn't have natural ability, he was an eager participant. Again, in an environment where all are different, Michael was not ridiculed for his awkwardness and poor motor skills. While body stature and athletic prowess contribute so strongly to most adolescent males' self-confidence, in the protective school environment this was not an issue for Michael.

Michael also had friends at Hilltop. This is very unusual for autistic individuals who have such difficulty connecting interpersonally. The teachers and administrators all note that Michael was an involved and active participant both in class and other school activities. Michael's mother remembers that he knew several other students well, who lived in various parts of the city, and visited with them outside of school. Gene corroborates that Michael was part of a close-knit group of guys and says that this cohesive clique has remained friends into adulthood. Gene also talks about Michael's great sense of humor with quips such as Michael describing an afternoon at the ballpark this way:

> *Michael*: A $5.00 hot dog at a baseball game equals $0.50 to Gene and $10.00 to me, but we both went to the game to watch the planes flying over the stadium. Gene figured out the aircraft type and its likely destination, while I would quiz him on its schedule.

Michael was also able to succeed in the one class he took at the very large, urban high school, which was a much "tougher" environment. Even in that school, Michael elicited positive responses on the part of others. This was evidenced by the students' concern about his failing to wear a jacket in cold weather. Michael does succeed at endearing himself to others in many different ways.

The relationship between Michael and John and then between John and Michael's family is truly fascinating. This "odd couple" arrangement had benefits for both. What started as a simple give-and-take between two high school students evolved into a strong and deeply personal relationship. This gave John a second family and a view of a world very different from the one he had always known. John profited from his place in this family, and from Shari's attention. Michael profited from a friendship where John was often his social director. John and Michael moved onto different life paths, and no longer regularly keep in touch with each other.

Boy–girl relationships in high school are very deeply felt and complex. Michael had two dating relationships towards the end of high school, but both had unhappy endings. Undoubtedly, when teenagers with long histories of emotional problems and struggles attempt to bond, the relationship is difficult. Is this very different from many teenagers' high school "romances"? Finding and maintaining friends and having meaningful relationships with both males and females are likely to be areas that will challenge Michael throughout his life.

Independence and success

Perhaps the most significant aspect of Michael's high school years is the positive trend towards independence. Again, this is a typical developmental milestone for all adolescents and Michael's high school years depict a success story in many ways. He succeeded very well academically. He was recognized for positive behavior in school by both school personnel and the family. Michael had lots of friendships including two male–female relationships. Michael was also able to navigate in the challenging environment of a tough, urban high school. Another significant change was that Michael became skillful using public transportation which afforded him even greater independence and also gave Michael the ability to move in different circles without his family.

While Michael may not feel that he was "Mr. High School," all objective indicators support his success during those years. The timid, insecure, and lonely young man who began high school in tenth grade became a different person by the time of his graduation three years later. The path to a successful academic career was clearly indicated as a turning point in Michael's development. From Michael's perspective at the end of high school he still lacked an internalized, positive sense of self; others felt he succeeded admirably. Michael exceeded the expectations of his family during the high school years and demonstrated his intelligence, scholastic achievement, and growing interpersonal skills. The high school years definitely gave him the intellectual and social tools to attempt college and move into the mainstream world.

Chapter 8

The World of Work and the Rough Road to Success

Last week I got dressed to go to work and when I got to school I realized that I forgot to put on a shirt that morning. I guess it would be more accurate to say I got dressed from the waist down. I didn't realize this until I went to sign in at school and when I looked down I saw that I was wearing a pajama shirt with holes in it. Fortunately, one of the other teachers lent me a shirt for the day. Hopefully, the memory from this experience will help me remember to get fully dressed in the future and so far this week I'm 6 for 6—6 days of work and 6 days wearing a shirt.

Michael

At age 24, Michael has completed an undergraduate degree and a graduate degree, and is a certified teacher who is working full time. In spite of all of these accomplishments, managing his autism is still a daily concern.

Choosing a career

Michael fully admits that he likes the world of school. It is where he was recognized for high ability, and where he received approval from people he respected. Once Michael entered high school, inappropriate behavior in school was no longer an issue. The disruptive outbursts that had been so much a part of his behavior in the elementary and junior high school grades stopped. Michael was able to shine academically, especially in math. The world of the school became an especially good place for Michael and this impacted his career choice.

Michael: Teachers are primary people that a child is in contact with. It's an important role. Money isn't that important to me. I want to make a difference. I think that I'm making a contribution on most days and I have no regrets about becoming a teacher.

It could be that I'm secure in school—it's familiar.

Michael's desire to become a secondary mathematics teacher was logical given his remarkable ability with math and computers. It took him longer to realize that teaching adolescents involves much more than focusing on math:

Michael: I always thought it was just about math and I could explain it quickly and people seem to understand me. As time goes on I realize there are many other layers to this teaching thing. I expected the job of teaching to be a lot more straightforward. I am surprised at how much "gray area" there is with this job and it requires more time and attention than I anticipated.

I asked what surprises him about teaching:

Michael: There's an incredible amount of work and there's always the unexpected things that happen in a school day. I'm also shocked by the utter lack of motivation for some kids regardless of the school setting: rich, poor, suburban, urban, and I hear these same things from other teachers as well.

Michael's career choice was supported by his family, but with some concerns:

Jake: I do see him being a math teacher. He has the determination. I think that ultimately he wants to teach math to older students and I think he will be most successful if he becomes a college teacher.

Michael's grandmother: Michael looks young and carries himself like a kid. I hope it will be okay.

Shari: I think that teaching was a totally natural choice for him. His heroes and mentors have been teachers. His whole life has been full of teachers that were important to him and his friends were his teachers. He's been happiest when he's in school, because it's the safest, most secure place for him and he loves going to school. He always wanted to teach and math just came without effort.

He can be so successful in the outside world, but he has a disability. He's very needy and he's very fragile, and yet he's accomplished so much. But the outside world is so very different.

Gene is a close friend of Michael's. They met when both were students at the special high school. He and several other friends shared concerns about Michael's career choice given their own feelings about teachers and the enormously difficult job they have.

> *Gene:* Having been in the special education system, our group is aware of the challenges facing teachers. We all had concerns about how Michael would do. To this day we laugh about how hard we were on some of our teachers and we often talk about what traits made us respect a particular teacher. We were worried about how students would respond to Michael. Would they take advantage of his kindness? Would they respond to his style of classroom discipline? We were really not sure.
>
> I was certain that whatever challenges Michael faced he would learn from. Since he is such a fast learner and is passionate about his desire to teach, I was convinced that as long as a school would give Michael a chance, he would learn about his role and grow into the requirements of his profession very quickly. If they all just give him a chance, he will succeed at whatever he puts his mind to.

Student teaching

In the middle of Michael's senior year in college, he decided to switch from the five-year program that combined the undergraduate and master's degree to the traditional four-year undergraduate program. Consequently, Michael unexpectedly was ready to student teach when he was a senior. Student teaching occurs over one full semester and is usually for an entire school day. The assignment may be divided into placements at different grade levels to provide a variety of experience. Student teachers typically need to take one or two additional courses at their college in the evenings after finishing at school. Most find the responsibilities and amount of work needed to prepare for teaching as well as work for their own college classes daunting. Student teachers are assigned one or more "mentor teachers," who are full-time teachers in the school district. The mentor teacher is expected to be a model of good teaching, while providing guidance and feedback to the inexperienced intern. The college also sends a supervisor to observe the student teacher several times during the semester both to evaluate performance and to guide the teaching candidate. A seminar is usually provided by the college supervisor so that student teachers can collectively discuss and learn from their field experiences.

The academic and professional staff at the college were well aware of Michael's strength in mathematics, but were less sure about his ability to work with adolescents. Teaching is a challenging profession that requires interpersonal insights and aptitudes that never came naturally to Michael. Several college staff became involved in locating the "right" placement for Michael's student teaching, where his teaching ability would be fairly evaluated along with sensitivity to his needs. There was legitimate concern about the placement process for a student teacher with a significant disability. While many student teachers struggle when first given teaching responsibilities, there was awareness that Michael might need more mentoring than others. Mr. A, an administrator at the college, was asked to find a student teaching placement for Michael, who was described to him as "difficult to place because of social skills."

Mr. A is a veteran school district administrator, having been an assistant superintendent and principal for over 25 years. He recalled his initial impression of Michael.

> *Mr. A*: He had a disheveled appearance and slightly compulsive behavior that I thought was attributable to nervousness. And during our first meeting he consumed tissues at an alarming rate!

What factors did Mr. A consider regarding Michael's placement?

> *Mr. A*: Academics were never an issue. He got an "A" in almost every class and he could articulate math concepts and he could explain math processes very well. I questioned his ability to be spontaneous and flexible when confronted with unpredictable student behavior and dynamics.

Did Mr. A provide any special help for Michael?

> *Mr. A*: It was obvious that I had to speak to him about his appearance. I suggested proper clothing: shirt, tie, chinos, belt, shoes and socks. He took notes. A few days later, he came into my office wearing a pair of slacks and a white dress shirt. Unfortunately he was also wearing a tee shirt with a bright design that was clearly visible through the shirt. I told him that if he was going to wear a white shirt, he needed to wear a white tee shirt under it.

Michael recalls his preparation for student teaching as well:

> *Michael*: I was a college senior and just got a car and started to drive only a month earlier, but that's another story. At least I had transportation. Before I went out on student teaching interviews, my grandparents took me shopping for clothes, because I realized and was told that I had to look like a

teacher. It took a very long time for me to get the student teaching placement and I wasn't sure why.

Michael interviewed for a student teaching placement at a large secondary school that housed both middle and high school grades. It was located not far from his suburban college campus in a community known to have a diverse student population based on socio-economic factors, as well as race and ethnicity. The college administrators thought this would be a challenging environment for a prospective teacher, but one in which the reality of the career choice could be tried out. A central administrator in this district is a close friend of Mr. A and Mr. A knew that he would be especially sympathetic to Michael, because he has a child with Asperger's syndrome.

Prior to the student teaching placement, it was suggested that Michael observe in this school setting. Two very experienced teachers, Mrs. S and Mrs. T, were asked to supervise him. They were given no information about Michael's background or disability.

> *Mrs. S:* He amazed me even the first day because he looked and acted so different from other college students.

> *Mrs. T:* Something didn't seem right, but he had the most beautiful smile on his face.

Why did Michael seem so different?

> *Mrs. S:* His physical appearance was different and some of the other faculty felt less compassionate and they thought his behavior was strange. We spent a lot of time with him; he was our third partner at lunch. His approach was so different from other observers. He had a black notebook and took notes and asked questions. If we made a suggestion, he followed through. There was always discussion after each lesson. Other college observers don't spend this much time analyzing what they've observed. He took this very seriously.

The two teachers felt that Michael should be given every opportunity to try out his skills as a secondary math teacher and they became his student teaching mentors.

> *Mrs. S:* We arranged a special schedule for him that would give him experience with both junior high school students and seniors. We thought that because the senior class did not have to take the end of year state exams and because they were older, they would be more understanding of him and it worked out beautifully.

Mrs. T: He wore proper clothing every day and I can just picture him during lunch when he would flip his tie over his shoulder to keep food from getting on it. I also remember him sitting cross-legged on a desk and then we'd talk.

He always came into the classroom animated and smiling. He enjoyed what he was doing and he definitely knew his math. He was very receptive to suggestions, but if he didn't agree, we'd have a nice, healthy argument about it and sometimes he'd reluctantly agree and sometimes we let him go ahead with his ideas to see if they worked.

I asked how the teachers learned that Michael is autistic.

Mrs. S: I remember the day that he said to us, "I'm autistic." I could have fallen over. I thought his college would have said something, and truthfully I don't know that much about autism. We were told "zip" and it was probably better, but knowing about his disability would not have made a difference to us. We'd say, "Let's try."

Mrs. T: I remember so vividly the day he told me he was autistic. My view of what autism is, is not Michael, and we asked how he could have gotten this far.

I asked the university administrator about Michael's progress in student teaching.

Mr. A: The majority of problems were about student actions that interfered with his lessons and he was somewhat inflexible. He was obsessed with writing lesson plans. He put too much into them and they were more like a script. There was a lack of understanding about certain group dynamics.

The mentor teachers felt that Michael's attention to lesson planning was a strength:

Mrs. S: He was always very well prepared and just got so into the lessons. It just kept flowing. With math you need to know what comes before and after, and I don't think he was over-prepared.

How did students respond to Michael?

Mr. A: The students' responses were good and few, if any, made fun of him. They recognized his math skills. Kids can be cruel or sympathetic, but this worked out.

Mrs. S: With the seventh graders he did very nicely. The kids looked up to him and they didn't give him a difficult time any more than with any other student teacher. I especially remember one lesson with that group where we were learning about combinations. I gave the class the example of different flavors of ice cream with lots of choices for the toppings. I suggested that we do it in class to see how many combinations we could make. Michael was so thrilled about doing that for the kids and the kids were happy eating ice cream at 9:00 a.m. in the morning.

With another class I thought if he could make it through that group he could make it through anywhere. These were non-academic students in grades 10 and 11 and had all failed math before. Behavior with them and Michael wasn't that much of a problem, but one day a student kind of snickered after he walked out. After that, we had a discussion about being a human being and I told them that I could pick each one of them apart with their problems and I didn't ever want to see that kind of behavior again. And it never happened again in class. Periodically they would try to test him and stump him, but they just couldn't do it.

Mrs. T: I watched him carefully with the seniors. In spite of noticing his different appearance and some unusual mannerisms, they had a tremendous amount of respect for him. They called him "The Human Calculator" and they knew that he really knew his math.

He had good composure with the group. One day a loose chalkboard just fell off the wall onto him, and he and the kids laughed, and he just put it back against the wall and continued with the lesson.

Were there any significant weaknesses that the teachers observed?

Mrs. S: He had to learn teacher behavior. An example was the morning that I found him sitting on the floor outside the classroom before it was opened and then we had a talk about appropriate professional behavior.

He always took suggestions willingly and had a good sense of humor about himself. One day he was wearing a very dark shirt and when he leaned against the blackboard the entire lesson appeared on the back of his shirt. When he turned around, the class was hysterical and told him. He thought it was funny too, and said "Okay, let's get over it and get back to math."

The mentor teachers agreed that Michael probably thought of them as surrogate mothers and were especially touched when he brought them little books of quotations about teaching for Mother's Day presents.

I asked Mr. A to comment on Michael's potential as a teacher.

Mr. A: He is the kind of person who made me feel useful and I will never forget him. After more than 25 years of experience with teachers, Michael is a breath of fresh air. He has candor, spirit; he's bright and interesting, and has a sense of humor. He doesn't take himself seriously. Michael exhibits a strong desire to succeed. He carefully weighs every word of advice given and tries to follow the prescription to the letter. A diamond in the rough.

At the conclusion of the student teaching experience, the university supervisor gave Michael a fine rating.

> *From the report of Mr. F, the university supervisor:* Michael continues to demonstrate a level of expertise that is outstanding. His lesson planning demonstrates the care and effort he places into all of his professional responsibilities. The actual lesson presented demonstrates creative motivational approaches that led into a sequential and logical development of his educational objectives.

As with all new teachers, Mr. F gave Michael suggestions to aid his effectiveness in classroom management, and also gave him high praise.

> *Mr. F:* Throughout your student teaching experience, you have demonstrated a degree of professionalism that is outstanding. Every task you have undertaken is more than successfully completed. Keep up the good work.

Mrs. S summarized Michael's performance.

> *Mrs. S:* I've had lots of student teachers over many years and I'd rate him in the top 5 percent of all student teachers I've had. So what if his social skills weren't the same? But he has the personality to do well, and he's like a sponge and all that he observed became part of him. There are teachers who teach because it's a job, and others for whom it's a calling, and for Michael it's a calling.

Michael has fond memories of his student teaching experience.

> *Michael:* Student teaching was a very controlled and enjoyable experience. The mentor teachers kept the kids motivated and I could focus on the mathematics and the explanations. The teaching was very good there. Whatever weaknesses I had, the mentor teachers could make up for as compared to when I'm on my own in teaching. But they didn't make it easy for me. They would give me guidance, but expected me to experiment and do things my way.

Michael graduated with an undergraduate degree at the end of that semester and was ready to begin a job search. (College graduation is described in Chapter 2.) That summer Michael enrolled in a master's degree program in math education at a very competitive branch of the state university. He finished that graduate degree during the following summer with superb grades. Aside from being an inexperienced teacher, Michael did not seem very different from the other math education graduate students. Michael's graduate course load each semester, the demands of the advanced math courses he was taking, his employment as a secondary teacher in demanding roles, and tutoring for an agency presented an enormous workload that he managed successfully. The simple logistics of traveling over 50 miles each way from home to work and to the university were successfully accomplished. The engine on Michael's old car burnt out, but he didn't!

Interviewing and the first teaching job

Beginning teachers know that there's keen competition for getting the first job, but in math education, there's considerably more opportunities than in other teaching areas. A successful interview is key to getting to the next step, which is usually a demonstration lesson, and many students practice their interview skills to prepare themselves. Because of Michael's sometimes halting use of language, as well as an awkward and blunt manner, there was reason to wonder how his interviews would go.

> *Michael*: After the first couple of job interviews, I didn't have very much of a response. The interviews were quick and dry and weren't successful and then I practiced the interviewing. It was hard for me, because I don't always portray feeling when I talk and I can speak in a monotone and be very matter of fact. I had ideas about teaching, but I really hadn't formulated them into words and I didn't have much to say in an interview setting.

Did any of the educators who interviewed Michael recognize that he was different?

> *Michael*: Only in one school district did they realize that I had a relationship with a special school. I had indicated on my resume that I tutored at my old high school and they knew that it was a special education school. That interview was over quickly.

Michael asked several experienced math teachers to suggest sample questions he'd likely be asked during interviews and then he practiced his responses to typical questions with a seasoned professional. What did Michael learn from the interviewing process?

> *Michael*: I interviewed for five weeks before I got a job offer and as the interviews went on I got better and had some second interviews. Even the first

interviews were taking longer so I could tell that I was getting better. I could see what turned [the school people] off and what mistakes I made. You have to say things in a politically correct way. For example, there was a question about how I would handle a parent who complained about his child not making the honor roll, because of the grade in math. I realized that there were two ways to handle that question: I could say that "the grade is the grade," or I could say that "it warrants review." [School administrators] want something that pleases both sides, but to me that's an ambiguous response. It's part of my issue that I believe when you compromise, you are vague or indecisive.

Evidently, Michael became better at interviews, because references were checked regarding his suitability for a junior high school math position in a fairly affluent and educationally oriented community. One recommendation focused on Michael's extraordinary math aptitude, his commitment to education, and included the suggestion that the school administrator seek feedback from others who had observed Michael during student teaching. It was particularly interesting to hear the school administrator comment that when Michael interviewed there were long pauses between questions posed and Michael's answers, and Michael was less talkative than other candidates. The administrator attributed this to a thoughtful and introspective style without suspecting the underlying disability. Michael was offered a part-time position teaching afternoon math classes, but was terminated from the position only three months into the school year.

> *Michael:* The person who hired me left the district before I started and the new administrator was older and more traditional. He was a "Do as I say or else" kind of person and I'm a fairly opinionated person and like to express my ideas and understand the framework. This administrator just wanted me to follow him blind. I'm more into discussing examples and explaining and he wanted me to just put lots of work on the board and keep the kids busy.
>
> Discipline was an issue. The school admitted that I had some of the more difficult kids in the grade and I was scheduled to teach them at the end of the day. There were a few parents who didn't take a liking to me over what I considered small incidents—like giving lunch detention. I think that the administrator was looking to get rid of me, because he didn't like me. I don't think it was an "autism thing," but probably a non-autistic person would have handled it differently.

Michael recalled memorable incidents in this assignment and discussed what he had learned about himself and teaching.

Michael: Other teachers have a persona or a way of communicating what is unacceptable regarding students' behavior. For some reason, kids find it acceptable to act out in my classroom. Being a new teacher could be a factor, but there's a gap—something I don't know about. Some things can slip under my radar until they get to the next level and that's the missing piece for me.

There was an incident of one student who literally crawled up the wall and crept behind a TV monitor that was mounted on a post. I turned around and there he was. Another teacher might have noticed him get out of his seat, or realized that he was antsy that day, but me, I didn't tune into whatever was happening and it was pretty extreme.

One day in the third month of teaching, they called me to a meeting just before dismissal and told me not to come back the next day. It was especially confusing, because just the week before they had me go on a three-day trip upstate with the students and I wondered how could they trust me with the students in that situation and then fire me.

I asked how he handled being fired.

Michael: I was very upset and depressed. I was very sad driving home that day and I just took a nap and cancelled my tutoring appointments. Over the next few days, I started to feel better and realized that I wasn't totally surprised that I was fired, because I had known that there were "issues" for a while.

I wondered if this made Michael rethink his career choice.

Michael: I had questions about looking for another job and continuing in teaching, but I thought I'd take a week or two to mellow out before deciding and I thought that the only way I would know if I should be a teacher was to try again.

Michael's father and others in the family wondered if teaching was the appropriate profession for Michael given the termination. They recommended that he consider another career where his math strengths would be utilized without the pressure of having to work with teenagers. Other professions could be more lucrative. Michael, however, refused to reconsider his career choice and began the search for another teaching position.

The next job: Another disappointment

Shortly after Thanksgiving Michael began applying for new teaching positions.

> *Michael*: There were fewer interviews because of the time of year and it took me ten weeks for this job search. I was not getting offers from the interviews I went out on. My interviewing skills went down at first and there were fewer jobs. I definitely felt that I was close to a couple of positions, but I realized that I had to get used to interviewing again.
>
> I was a nervous guy in his first year.

Michael had an interview for a position in a middle school math "lab" to provide instructional support to students who were failing. The role didn't require him to be the primary teacher for these students, and perhaps this secondary role would be more appropriate for Michael's teaching ability, especially in this middle school setting, when students are at an age where classroom management and motivation can be challenging for any inexperienced teacher. The district is also identified as having "high needs" with many families at the poverty level. Excellent classroom management would be an essential aspect of effective teaching in this district known for having many difficult as well as non-English speaking students. Michael stayed in this district throughout the spring semester and it was unclear if he would be asked to return the next year.

> *Michael*: One time a girl walked up in front of the class and just pulled her pants down, but fortunately she had on a long shirt that covered her. Another time, there was a big fight in the hall and no one else was around, so I dove in and wound up flying into a closet.
>
> The first month it went reasonably well, and I would go through the various stages of discipline: calling parents, and then going up the chain of command in the school. Ultimately I was judged by the number of kids that I referred to an administrator and said there were problems with. The administration didn't want to handle the problems.
>
> The shoe incident—one afternoon, I leaned my knee on a chair. It was the end of the day and my feet were tired. One of the students noticed my foot up in the air and covertly came behind me and pulled my shoe off. Then I lost my balance and another kid came and took the other shoe. I spent the rest of the period in my socks and I just went on with the lesson. Fortunately at the end of the period they gave the shoes back. It's probably one of those things that only happens to me and I probably didn't notice the warning signs.

Some would say it was another teaching failure given extreme incidents with disruptive students, but Michael didn't.

> *Michael*: It wasn't a failure and it wasn't a successful experience; but it wasn't worth perpetuating [the next year]. I think it was a purposeful experience.

How did this experience with very disruptive students impact on Michael's idealism about children and teaching?

> *Michael*: I was aware that there was little sense of appropriate manner or morals for a lot of the kids [in this school]. It was a school with disadvantaged kids to start with, but I didn't see any attempt to mitigate the problems by the administration. The kids act how they are raised and these kids weren't raised in the right type of way—it's a fact for some kids. Many were not raised by two parents in a stable setting so how can you blame them? I don't hold the kids responsible. I had no way of knowing what to do with them. Some didn't even speak English. Plenty of teachers struggled and I wasn't the only one let go.

What next?

Michael was keenly aware of the financial demands and responsibilities of maintaining an adult life. He's frugal by nature and didn't want to get into debt. Michael answered an ad for a math position for a summer school program in a private, urban school.

> *Michael*: They gave me a two-minute interview and a math test. I got 50 out of 50 correct and they gave me a job for the summer. I also continued my job search for a fall position.

Michael described the new school and the position.

> *Michael*: By and large, these were all Asian students who wanted math enrichment. The school was located in a middle-class community in the city. Many of the kids wanted to go to a specialized high school and some were from underperforming schools. Some of their parents couldn't afford full time private school, but they could send them to this supplemental program. They thought this would keep the kids on track for the competitive exams for the better high schools and for college entrance exams. Compared to the previous teaching jobs, these kids were much brighter and they were well behaved.

With no significant student behavior problems to attend to, there was optimism about Michael's likelihood of success.

Michael: [In this position] I felt that I was doing what I intended to do—explaining and clarifying math. There was not much of that in the other schools. Here, there was only one complaint about me that I wrote too small on the chalkboard. Obviously I started writing bigger. Oh, and another time I was told that I talked too loud, but the same day another group said I talked too low. My voice can be uncontrollable—too loud or too soft and sometimes I even nod when I'm on the phone instead of talking.

The last week I asked how I did and they said that everything was fine. It's a family run school and a small, informal setting. They asked me to return during the school year to teach in their Saturday program.

This school reminded me that while I want to help kids and mold them and get them ready for work, my priority is explaining mathematics, and this was the first time I was able to do this since student teaching.

Michael was becoming more sophisticated about his job search, but he faced a dilemma. He did not know if it was helpful to include the two unsuccessful teaching experiences on his resume. Having experience is always a plus when seeking a job, but having been terminated was certainly a problem. Michael weighed the advantages and disadvantages of listing his prior teaching experience.

Michael: I decided to list my two other jobs on my resume as temporary leave replacements [not really expected to last beyond the year]. It was better than having no job at all. I guess the school where I taught in the summer never called any references, because my previous problems were never mentioned.

In August, Michael responded to another newspaper ad for a math teacher in a parochial school located not far from the private school where he was working. The school was located in an urban, ethnically diverse, lower-middle-class community that Michael was familiar with, because his uncle is an optometrist close by.

Michael: I went for the interview and they offered me the job immediately. Being able to teach math and computers were both important and they liked that I had taught at two middle schools. They were in need. It's a parochial school with low pay.

Michael described the new school setting:

Michael: It's a small school that has both elementary and secondary grades. The kids are one notch down [in ability and behavior] from the children I taught in the summer. They can be rowdy, but really the worst thing about their behavior is that they are very chatty. They aren't dangerous or anything like the kids in the middle school in the poverty community. Sometimes there are small scuffles, and I think that these students are very immature for their age. Their parents are very involved in their education and make sure that the kids keep their ethnic and religious identity.

This school really doesn't pay well. Many of the other teachers are also young. Other teachers are older and speak with a heavy accent. There's also a leisurely attitude about being on time. Most of the kids come from various parts of the city and therefore the buses can be late. And many of the teachers aren't punctual either, so when I'm late it's not a problem. I get there late some mornings and the kids just wait for me.

At the end of his first year, I asked how Michael was doing in this school.

Michael: If I have a problem, I can tell the Principal or the Assistant Principal and they support me. I don't have to keep quiet if there's an issue, and I couldn't do that in other schools. I know everybody, because it's a small school and I feel comfortable there. I am the only non-Catholic teaching in the school now and this has never been a negative to either the faculty or most of the students. Everyone is treated well.

I think that the kids like me because the other math teachers are very hard on them both in terms of discipline and academics. Two other teachers have heavy accents, are hard to understand, and are very old-fashioned. The principal must have heard that the students like me, because they also asked me to teach night school for the high school kids who have to repeat a course.

What are your plans for next year?

Michael: I plan to stay there. I have a positive feeling about this school and I still have much self-improvement to work on and I can do this in this atmosphere which is not stressful. I want to become a better teacher and I need to work on my teaching skills, to help the kids get better test scores, and get further in the math curriculum.

How does Michael think he compares to other teachers?

Michael: I think that I'm more relaxed about some things as compared to other teachers. When the principal says something, I don't take it is as literally as some of the others, but on the flip side some things bother me that don't bother others: disruptions, changes in routines, kids disturbing the class in the middle of work, and especially loud voices from the kids do get to me. I try to get them to stop misbehaving or just wait a few minutes and let them burn out. They're young.

The faculty and administration in this school do not know that Michael is autistic, or that he attended special schools. I asked Michael how other teachers view him and whether any note traits in him related to autism.

> *Michael*: Other teachers don't think I have a disability beyond the typical proclivities of a math person. Math people are generally strange.

What about future goals?

> *Michael*: Eventually I plan to move up to teaching at the college level and that should rectify some of the issues that I struggle with in teaching younger students.

Does Michael acknowledge aspects of his teaching and demeanor that reflect autism?

> *Michael*: I'm in control of myself, but sometimes I don't know what to do. I guess I don't always feel totally in control of the situation. Trying to come up with a way to motivate the kids or explain something, when they don't get it, can frustrate me. These are two areas that I struggle with. And then there are just those days when everyone is making so much noise that I just don't know what to do.
>
> One day I fell off a chair, and I'm klutzy, but math teachers are klutzy and the kids didn't make much of it. Another time, I was leaning back in my chair and it caught on the chalk ledge and the kids wanted to help me. We all laughed about it.
>
> Being on time is always an issue. I don't have the sense of time running out each period and I tend to stay late in the evening. I'm on another planet. I can say something and it seems like my words are just in the air. I'm obsessive about getting things done. Also, because I was never a student in a "regular secondary school" I do not have that intuitive sense of how things are supposed to work.

I wondered if Michael thinks that there are aspects of autism that contribute to his success.

> *Michael*: Because of my background, I think that I am more aware of individual and group strengths and weaknesses. Also, my attention to detail is helpful in preparing my lessons beforehand and analyzing them afterward in order to make improvements so that students understand and get the appropriate curriculum coverage.

By both objective and subjective measures, it appears that after two very unsuccessful teaching experiences, Michael has found career satisfaction. In this private school environment, where disciplining students is not a major necessity, he is able to truly teach mathematics. Although he complains that too often the students seem unmotivated and just don't "get" math, he's full of optimism and has good will towards the students in his classes, the colleagues with whom he works, and administrators who both supervise and support him. What lies ahead is anyone's guess, but few who know Michael would be surprised to see him teaching at the college level in the not too distant future. Who could have predicted this outcome when they saw a very disabled, young autistic child many years ago?

Author's reflection

If you met Michael today, you would see a stocky young man, usually dressed appropriately, and who seems friendly and approachable. Most would agree that he fits well into the world of computer people and math teachers, who are stereotypically odd and often lack social competence. But Michael is not a perfect picture: he can forget a shirt or a belt, doesn't easily pick up social cues, is more rigid than most, and doesn't always know social conventions. Conversely, in a school where he is unlike all others because of religion and ethnicity, Michael has found acceptance and has settled into the beginning of a productive and fulfilling career.

The same deficits that Michael has always demonstrated initially caused major problems in employment. Michael had difficulty supervising adolescent students, which required awareness and insight about their behavior. He did not have sufficient physical presence to command the students' respect and focused more on math content rather than on the dynamics of overseeing a classroom of active teenagers. He did not have the "political" acumen to develop a good relationship with school administrators, and his bluntness caused problems with parents. Michael did not intuitively sense the appropriate way of handling difficult students and sought assistance from administrators, who then became aware of problems in his classes. It's critical to recognize that Michael was not appropriately mentored in his first two positions and this would have created problems for any novice teacher. Because Michael attended a very special secondary school, he was also unaccustomed to the "normal" routine, behavior, and expectations for both students and teachers in a "regular" school. Michael needed someone "to show him the ropes" and this was lacking.

Michael also possesses strengths that assisted him when he began teaching in a more disciplined and supportive environment including: a sincere desire to succeed in teaching, an ability to profit from experience and change behavior accordingly, accepting constructive feedback, and simply working hard. When balancing Michael's vocational strengths and weaknesses, the scale tips to the positive side. He is now recognized as a genuinely caring and dedicated teacher.

Challenges in teaching and getting the first job

Anyone who has been a teacher at any level knows how difficult it can be. Effective teachers do not only share knowledge of subject matter, they must relate to their students in meaningful ways. This was something that Michael had to learn, because he originally thought that teaching math was only about math, and certainly it isn't. His desire to work with adolescents was an added challenge, because the age group is notorious for emotional issues and volatile behavior.

Through hard effort and willingness to learn from others Michael succeeded in student teaching. His math brilliance aided him, but problems with insight, flexibility, and maintaining a professional presence that others feared would be barriers, were either corrected or didn't present over-whelming problems. Mentoring for any inexperienced teacher is necessary, and this was an aspect of the very supportive student teaching placement, but wasn't present in Michael's two unsuccessful teaching situations. While all professionals acknowledge the importance of guiding new teachers, this is still absent in too many school environments. As a result many new teachers flounder, become disillusioned, or leave the profession. Michael's determination did not allow this to happen and he's to be commended for maintaining an optimistic view of children and teaching even after the two negative experiences, where he was not sufficiently mentored.

Getting the first job is never easy and when you're autistic there are particular challenges. Michael was not a natural at interviewing, but did realize that he had to improve his skills. An important aspect of Michael's ability to succeed is his ability to learn from others and his willingness to seek advice. Michael also has traits that endear him to others, who then want to help him. It's most fortunate that Michael now works in two schools that acknowledge his positive traits and where he is accepted by his peers. Oddly, in both environments Michael is very different from the others, because his religion and ethnicity make him a true minority in these settings. This has not been a barrier to Michael's sense of belonging and acceptance in these two schools. Obviously, not having to deal with very disruptive students and having the confidence of the administrators are essential to Michael's success.

Personal characteristics, autism and teaching

When Michael first indicated to his college professors that he wanted to become a secondary math teacher, most were skeptical about the career choice. All acknowledged Michael's high intelligence, brilliance in math and computer science, and work ethic, but felt that he lacked essential personal traits needed to be an effective teacher. Michael always lacked insight about others, could not be spontaneous, showed rigidity, and struggled with interpersonal skills. Michael's development as a teacher has been remarkable. In Michael's first two teaching positions, he met with failure. However, in his present positions he is doing very well and shows remarkable growth in insight and adaptive behavior.

Many other autistic individuals share Michael's genius with math, but few others can explain math processes as well as he does. Michael sometimes gets discouraged when the adolescent students he teaches are less interested in his explanations than they are in just getting a correct answer. He truly does not understand why they don't love math the way that he does. In spite of this, as well as his occasional lapses in verbal facility, Michael has become a sought after teacher and tutor.

Michael is very focused on career goals, extremely hard-working, and optimistically wants to make the world aware of the importance of math in all aspects of life. His determination gives him the motivation to continue when others, faced with disappointment, might easily give up. Michael is hopeful about children and has not become disillusioned after two unsuccessful experiences in the past.

Michael hates ambiguity and the daily, repeating pattern of school life meets his need for orderliness and structure. Michael is a curious mix. While he is still rigid in many ways, he has also demonstrated flexibility with an ability to learn from others and profit from experience. He has been willing to modify his behavior, and he's also willing to listen to reasoned arguments of others, and modify his views.

Having been in special education himself enables Michael to view students' strengths, instead of focusing on their weaknesses. He knows first hand what it's like to be different and to struggle. While compassion does not come naturally to an autistic person, Michael has developed the intellectual skills that allow him to recognize the emotional needs of the children he teaches. For example, Michael knows how important motivation is to learning and attempts to find stimulating ways to interest his students. He also knows that praise contributes to self-esteem. While many social conventions are not part of Michael's behavioral repertoire, he has learned to adapt his manner and appearance to conventional expectations. Unlike some others, Michael is very honest about himself in many ways. When he doesn't meet with success, Michael is extremely analytic and tries hard to determine what was at fault and wants to learn how to improve. Michael also takes criticism easily as long as it comes from a respected source.

Many have commented about the perpetual smile on Michael's face and at times, its appropriateness can be questioned. The friendly demeanor does attract people to Michael, which is helpful because he has difficulty initiating relationships. Most importantly, Michael's optimism and pervasive idealism reflect his sincerity and a desire to help others. He wants to "fix" the injustices in the world of schools and give every child a fine opportunity to learn math. Some might think that Michael goes through life "tilting at windmills," but most admire his perseverance and genuine concern. One of Michael's mentor teachers aptly said, "What if his social skills are different, because his value far outweighs superficial deficits." Another professional refers to Michael as "a diamond in the rough," and these days the gem that he is has become more and more polished in important ways.

Chapter 9

Adult Life

He has a life that I could have only dreamed of for him. He's doing what he loves and he's good at it. He has a wonderful and a full life. He has friends. He goes places and travels. He goes to ballgames, bowling, movies, and other places too. He's very involved in his teaching and he just loves both of the schools where he works.

He's a miracle and I'm very proud of him, and I love him.

Shari

At age 24 Michael is very much in charge of his own life and is doing extremely well. His daily routine is structured around the activities that most adults have: work, recreation, and lots of doing what Michael calls "errands." Michael has made a conscious effort to look and act more like everyone else. Being independent and self-supporting are essential parts of his adult life.

Living arrangements and everyday life

Michael's parents divorced shortly after he finished his undergraduate degree. His younger brother, Scot, lives with their mother, and Michael and his father moved into a home in a neighboring community. Michael continues to have a great deal of anger toward his mother and everyone in the family agreed that it would be better for him to live with his father.

> *Michael*: I live with my dad and his girlfriend on the ground floor of his townhouse. I take responsibility for these activities: getting myself up in the morning, paying rent, cleaning up, doing laundry, and most meals. Dad is basically with his girlfriend so there's not much contact and she takes care of his social needs. My mother? We don't talk too often, because she can be very preoccupied with her fiancé. She's available when she wants to be available.

Are there times that you still need help with daily life?

Michael: Nothing manifest, but sometimes I get stuck, or I can't find out something, or I get into a situation and then I'll ask for help—my mom or dad or another relative. Last year I had to buy a car and I needed help with that.

Uncle Joe: The last two to three years have been the greatest growing years for Michael—from the time he went to college, to working, the divorce between his parents and now doing things for himself.

Although Michael claims that he has little to do with his mother at this time in his life, it is obvious that when he needs her assistance he calls her, and she willingly helps out. The problematic relationship between Michael and his mother has continued into adult life. The violent behavior towards Shari in prior years has ceased, because of Michael's maturity and their living apart. However, Michael can be very critical of his mother and lets her know his feelings without regard for its effect on her.

Shari: When he was ten, he wrote an article about me and he said I was wonderful. I gave him everything I had and then I wanted him to be independent. When he went to live in the college dorms, he said I was throwing him out of the house. The more I've tried to make him independent, the more he resents it.
   I call him a couple of times a week and leave a message on his cell phone. It can go a week or two and I don't hear from him. And then if he needs something, I can hear from him every day. Here's an example. He calls me when he runs out of medication and tells me to call the doctor for a renewal. I tell him that he can do this for himself. He says that if he doesn't call and tell me to do things, then I'll forget that I have a son.

When Michael lived with both parents, his life had been closely monitored, and his mother catered to his every need and provided all of the necessities. Michael always demanded that even the most simple activities be done for him by other members of his family and until Michael lived in the college dorm he did not take responsibility for the practical aspects of daily life. Michael's current independence did not occur without conflict. The change in living arrangements required that Michael assume more responsibility for himself and this did not come easily.

Uncle Joe: He had to be pushed into maturing and there's still resentment for his mother as she tried to wean him off depending on her. Michael was always very lazy. His mother was very much into "it's easier just to do things for him" than to push him to the next stage.

Recently I went to his house and there were clothes all over the place. I said "Okay, we'll do your closet for you" and we put in shelves. He was very happy with it and it's an example of some things being meaningless to him that he has learned to take care of. Some people look at him and just write everything off to his condition, but lots of things that he neglects are really part of his personality.

Michael's father comments on his son's new level of independence:

Jake: When he was with his mother, he expected her to do everything for him and she did. Now he's living with me and I have several jobs and I can't do everything, so he has to help out. He takes care of his own room and if he was living with his mother, he wouldn't do that. Actually, the best thing for him was the divorce.

I asked Michael about handling this new independence.

Michael: I try to self-regulate—time to wake up, time to get dressed, dent in my car, should I see a doctor, etc. All of these things I have to do myself and I would still prefer that my mother do all these things for me. I wouldn't have a lot of the gaps that I do if my mother was still regulating my life. I'm 24 not 54 and still need someone to watch over me until I learn to do things myself. I've been let go of and have to learn to do things myself, but I was forced to do things before I was ready to some extent. It's a benefit, but there are a lot of struggles.

Michael's grandmother: I now see in him a maturity that we are so proud of.

Food choice and meal preparation were always important aspects of Michael's life and I wondered how he was managing meals. In childhood he had strong aversions and preferences for food that could result in tantrums. Gaining weight was also an issue.

Michael: My diet isn't regulated. For example, I had pizza twice today. I don't have that intuitive sense about planning meals. When I'm hungry, I eat. Typically, I'm just on my own going out to eat or something. Out of 21 meals a week, I eat 15 out, and 3 I make, and sometimes someone else cooks. It's expensive to eat out and I want to work on that. I can make pasta and cereal, but I can't really cook.

It was humorous that Michael described putting cereal in a bowl and adding milk as one of his "cooking" skills. He defended himself by saying that cereal preparation is a "process." Diversity in Michael's diet has increased as Michael's autistic traits have diminished through the years. His family finds his new diet preferences extraordinary, given the rigidity of his childhood years.

> *Shari*: As a child he only ate the blandest things—always a bagel and cream cheese and pancakes and we had to create his Bar Mitzvah party around his diet of eating only breakfast foods. Now he orders Cajun chicken!

Michael needs to address his future living arrangements, because his father is now planning to sell his townhouse and move into his girlfriend's home. Michael will not be going with him and expects to live with another relative on a short term basis, and then find his own apartment.

> *Shari*: At some point he will have to find his own apartment. He can manage very nicely on his own and he can do everything for himself so well.

Managing money

As a child, Michael had no regard for money. When he was a teenager, he began working part time in a local drug store as a stock boy, and spent most of his salary on fast food. During those years, Michael had a history of being careless with money and often lost and sometimes found significant amounts of cash in his room or in his pockets. When Michael began college, he was fortunate to have gotten a scholarship that paid for almost his entire undergraduate education. Although frugal by nature and being a person who doesn't care about buying new things, during college Michael did enjoy having money to spend at restaurants near the campus. The first couple of years of college, Michael's scholarship was supplemented by his part time work at the drugstore, and in his junior and senior years with money earned as a college tutor. After he finished his undergraduate degree, Michael assumed the cost of his graduate tuition, and his decision to go to a branch of the state university was dictated by his concern for tuition costs. Michael paid for graduate school from savings accumulated through gifts and from his teaching positions.

Michael is most fortunate to come from a family that is generous in terms of their time and devotion as well as with financial support. His grandparents have been extremely helpful throughout his life by taking him shopping for clothes as well as buying him other things. Both of Michael's uncles and their families have also provided assistance. Michael's first car came from one of his uncles, who acquired the used car from a friend of his. However, as an adult

Michael is very concerned about managing his money. His is aware that his parents had stress in their marriage that resulted from financial burdens. After college paying for his car and other expenses became adult responsibilities that Michael had to assume. Michael's teaching positions, although they had modest salaries, provided fairly steady income, but there were many new expenses. Michael describes how he manages his money.

> *Michael:* Even though I'm a numbers person, I don't have that intuitive sense of money. I'm not a spender and I don't indulge myself. I do like to gamble but not a lot. You know that I'm good at figuring out odds and I always think that I can win when I play cards.

> *Shari:* I can't ask too many questions about this, but his Uncle Joe tells me that he's doing fine.

Michael's friend, Gene, discusses the quirky nature of the way he and Michael think about money.

> *Gene:* I remember that in high school Michael was working a minimum wage job at a chain drugstore while I was working as a doorman at a posh hotel in the city. We would joke about how many hours of work it cost us to go to a ballgame and that the food at the game cost him three or four hours of work! When Michael wants something, he really doesn't care about cost, but he's not impulsive.

Figuring out his budget, managing his living expenses, and deciding where and how he lives next year will be ongoing challenges for Michael.

Driving a car

For all adolescents learning to drive is a milestone. Driving provides mobility and independence and is a clear sign of maturity. It also signals to the rest of the world that a young person can do what adults do. When an individual is handicapped, learning to drive and being entrusted with a car can be daunting challenges. Few people who are autistic or who have obsessive-compulsive disorders can manage driving a car. Michael is an exception, although there are many tales of woe about his driving ability.

Michael has always been "klutzy," but he did learn to ride a bicycle when he was older than most children. He had many bike accidents, because he didn't pay attention to things around him, was not agile, and seemed to suffer from poor peripheral vision. Michael's mother always worried about him when he was on his bike, because he just didn't seem to be sufficiently aware and had many bad falls. Because Michael enjoyed bicycle riding and it gave him mobility, she felt that she couldn't stop this activity.

Michael was always fascinated by cars and transportation and throughout his childhood he especially loved the fantasy world of being a "bus driver" on a route to pick up and deliver children to and from school. Michael enjoyed "pretend driving" while sitting on his uncle's lap behind the wheel of his car, and first expressed an interest in learning to drive when he was in college. Getting to and from the college by public transportation was very time consuming and inconvenient and Michael would definitely need better transportation when he began student teaching. Although very concerned about Michael's ability to drive, his mother told him that she would find a driving school that would work with special needs individuals.

> *Shari*: I didn't know what to expect. He falls off his bike. I worry a lot, and I didn't know what he'd do in a car.

> *Michael*: In the summer I took eight driving lessons. I didn't tell my instructor anything out of the ordinary about me. He always made a big deal of it when I hit a curb, but I treated it as no big deal. To me he was very obsessed with perfection and he would be critical of anyone's driving.
>
> As with any other activity, my method of focusing is different from others. I probably don't have the same driving method as most people for monitoring and perceiving surroundings on the road. I don't know if I'm better, the same or worse than others.
>
> I tend to stay away from other cars and don't like it when they get close to me—back or sides. When traveling with speed, I'm very safe. However, when I am going very slow I am more likely to bump into things: fences, parked cars, curbs, etc.
>
> My compulsiveness is, perhaps, helpful. For example, I always go through the four steps of checking mirrors whenever changing lanes: rear view, over the shoulder, and side mirrors. Also, riding buses for over 12 years, and just the kind of mind I have, gave me a good sense of direction. I always think in terms of north, south, east, west, when I drive and don't do what most people do which is turn here or there at landmarks.

How did the driving instructor evaluate Michael's skills?

> *Michael*: My driving instructor thought I would fail the road test. He thought I was too casual with curbs and wide turns, etc.

Michael finished his lessons and practiced driving with his parents. He felt ready for the road test and was given an appointment for Sept 11, 2001. No one could have imagined what a tragic day that would be and all regular business was curtailed.

> *Michael*: That afternoon I got a message that my 5:00 p.m. appointment was cancelled due to obvious reasons. The test was rescheduled and I passed it on my first try on Thursday, Oct 18, 2001.
>
> I couldn't parallel park very well and didn't do it at all on the road test. I was also marked down for the way I approached an intersection, either because I went too far before looking, or was too hesitant. But I passed. The examiner did tell me to practice parallel parking more before driving alone.

Michael's uncle arranged for him to get a used car from a friend and Michael began driving a Toyota with over 200,000 miles on the clock. Michael did not seem at all afraid to drive and over the next two years he added nearly 40,000 miles (and many parts and dents) to that car before it completely deteriorated. After that, Michael purchased a better used car so that he'd have reliable transportation for work. During Michael's very first week of driving, there was an "incident" with a gas pump.

> *Michael*: A few days after getting the car and not being the world's most observant person, never having driven into a gas station before, and the gas pumps not being raised on concrete or having a curb around them, I missed pulling up to a gas pump by a few inches. I didn't even notice anything wrong until I looked for the guy to come over to fill the car and then saw four people running toward me. My right door brushed against the front panel of the pump destroying the nozzle and perhaps a dent to the pump also. But fortunately, there was no actual damage to the gas pump.
>
> I called Mom. She came to meet me at the gas station and we waited for the police to make an accident report, then we drove home. The next week my dad and I went to pay for the repairs to the gas tank which was a great deal of money. When I returned to that station and was turning in from the street, the gas attendant stopped me, and he drove the car up to the pump for me. I paid him the money for the damage, got gas, drove back onto the street and I never went to that gas station again.
>
> Learning to steer close to a gas pump was not something the instructor ever showed me. Maybe he figured that I wouldn't pass the test and would never drive. He did tell my mother that I needed lessons for highway driving, but I learned that on my own.

Michael's driving record continues to be marred by bumps, dents, and scrapes, but having this independence provides the mobility he needs. Driving enables Michael to be truly independent and accomplish all of the things that are required in a busy, adult life.

Social life

Perhaps the greatest challenge for an autistic young adult is filling leisure time and developing a social life. Making friends and maintaining relationships are especially difficult.

> *Michael*: I don't have much free time and when I have it, it's sort of weird. I ask myself, "What should I be doing?" I wind up doing those nagging things that other people just leave nagging, but free time is always a problem. Teaching requires more time and attention than I anticipated, so I spend less time in other areas of life than I would have previously expected.

What does Michael enjoy doing in his free time?

> *Michael*: I go to the movies and bowling. I like to read, because there are interesting things to find out about. If I'm not doing something, I feel guilty that I should be doing something purposeful. TV? I watch it, when I go to sleep, and I seldom watch TV for entertainment. There was a program about a high school and I used to watch that, because it related to my life as a teacher.
>
> I have some interest in sports, but I'm less obsessive about it as compared to when I was young. For an obsessive person you're either totally involved or not in sports—watching the statistics for example. And it can become obsessive, because there's no middle ground of just enjoyment for me. So I'm careful about sports.

I inquired about whether Michael has maintained friendships and if he's made new friends. According to Michael's mother, she thinks that he's busier with friends now than he has ever been before.

> *Shari*: He really, really has a life. Who could have thought this would happen from where we started and I think it will only get better and better and better for him. He loves to travel and meet more new people.

Michael and Gene have been good friends since they met in high school and became part of the more academically minded students in that special school. Their friendship is based not only on history and similar interests, but on a deep personal connection. (Gene is Michael's friend who has the obsessive interest in planes and travel.)

> *Gene*: It's as if we have our own language. We can talk about distances, time, or money and translate them into our own language. Whenever we meet, we immediately ask each other if the other person has eaten. Whether we spend the whole day together or just the afternoon, we have a tradition to always

eat three meals (and sometimes a snack). Now we joke about how old we've become, because we no longer have the appetites we used to and we find it difficult to fit all three meals into a six-hour time frame.

I also just laugh because of the way Michael says things. He says that although I am 28, I'm really 40, and the first day I came into his high school classroom, everyone thought I was a substitute teacher. All of the group from high school love Michael, just because he's Michael. Every time we joke around about how fast he drives or how tardy he can be, we always end up laughing, shrugging our shoulders and saying to each other, "That's Michael."

Gene also described the level of deep friendship and trust he and Michael share.

> *Gene:* I've shared things with Michael that I would never have thought others could appreciate and understand. It is almost as if we support each other through absolute acceptance. We know each other well enough to trust each other's character and we share a unique level of confidence knowing that we have the same moral values. We have an underlying confidence that regardless of what we reveal to each other, Michael will be Michael and Gene will be Gene. We accept each other and all the peculiarities that make us who we are. The fear of being ridiculed because we are self-conscious has been replaced by the strength of our friendship knowing that we always respect and accept each other for who we are.

I asked Michael to talk about relationships with others, especially females.

> *Michael:* I keep in touch with a male friend from high school and a friend from a previous teaching situation, who is female. We're pals and eat dinner together, or go to a movie, or have a mutual errand, because we're teachers. One friend is 28 and the other is 39. We have a lot in common, but there are a lot of differences as well.

I wondered how much these friends know about Michael's history and asked him what he's told them about himself.

> *Michael:* Yes, I told them I'm autistic several months after I met them. They knew I had something about me that's different and telling them helped to explain things.

What did they notice?

> *Michael:* They were aware of personal things about me: my need for certainty or something I would say "out of the blue," or I would talk when

someone else was talking, or I just change topics from what is being talked about. Sometimes they'll ask me a question and 45 minutes later I'll answer the question after I finally processed what I was asked.

Are these male–female relationships or friendships?

Michael: They are friendships. I don't understand the dating thing at all and I can't pursue girls. If they like me, that's something else.

I have a lack of feeling, knowledge, and experience about some things. Dating—haven't done much of that, and the little bit was with two female classmates in high school of similar background to me. Presently, I'm not dating, but I am interested. I'm not one to pursue a new thing especially when there is a fear of rejection. Things don't reject you, but a person may. I don't like making demands on other people, because I can be too demanding and the same is true with friendships in general.

I would like to continue to find friends who complement my interests and help me understand the world, and perhaps meet a member of the opposite gender to date or just spend time together to start with.

Michael's friend, Gene, discusses the complexity of male–female relationships for people like Michael and himself.

Gene: We talk about girlfriends and try to understand if it's possible to meet someone who is interested in another person as a human being. We can't stand the concern for superficiality and appearances. We're both not touchy/feely people. Girls also want a well-defined relationship early on and we don't relate to that. We ask each other, "What's a date?" If we eat out—is that a date? What are the meanings and definitions of relationships?

We didn't have the traditional teenage social experiences, because we didn't have the time and we were so consumed by struggling with our own difficulties.

We need to be fascinated and intrigued by a person and solid friendships are hard to find.

Shari: I hope that he'll have a woman in his life, but I don't know if this will ever work for him. He needs someone who accepts him for who he is. He still doesn't like to be touched. Even now I can hardly hug him and it's not really touching.

I asked Michael about other friends that he made several years ago, when he became part of an Asperger's group.

Michael: I found them on-line and they're adults with Asperger's. They're from 18 to 38 and there are six of them—all male. I'm the most mainstream in the group and the one with the least PDD [pervasive developmental disorder]. Others have more visible disability than I do. They get stuck even in those situations that I can manage. For example, they can't figure out where to meet, how to order in a restaurant, or how to spend time. Their social skills are poorer than mine. One of them is married, but his wife never goes out with us and I've been told that she's very heavy. They look more disabled than I do, where with me on the right day you wouldn't know I'm disabled.

It's a regular routine with the group. Friday nights we eat and then go to the movies. If we change and meet on a Saturday night, we call it a special event and it takes weeks of planning in advance—lots of pomp and circumstance with that group. We usually eat at a fast-food restaurant, but in general I don't sense too many issues with food in the group. Almost all of them travel independently, but they don't all have the coordination to drive. Only a couple of us have a car.

What's Michael's attitude about disability and his awareness of others' needs, especially given his ongoing involvement with the Asperger's group? He is aware of the difficulties encountered by the members of the group. This is especially interesting, because autistic individuals are typically unable to perceive what others are feeling.

> Michael: I don't have much feeling toward disability. I have it too to a certain extent and there are parts of me that other people have to accept. Am I embarrassed to be with them [the Asperger's group]? No. I don't usually create social situations that involve them with other friends, because it wouldn't be interesting to them and they are two different kinds of people. It's two different sides of me and I find both sides interesting. If someone asks [about my other friends], then I just introduce them to each other. It's no secrecy thing.

It's apparent that Michael doesn't readily disclose his disability and, in fact, wants to maintain his anonymity in this book, choosing to be identified by his middle name. While he says that this decision is based on his concern about people prejudging him, especially at work, not many in his present life know that he's autistic and the difficulties that this caused him throughout his childhood. Michael strongly feels that he shouldn't be given special consideration or accommodations because of his disability.

> *Michael:* I don't tell people because it's irrelevant or I don't want to be judged. In a personal situation I don't care if I'm judged, but in a professional situation I want to make it on my own without special consideration

or accommodation from others. People might be afraid of the potential that something could happen. Sometimes I can notice things about people that might be a touch of them being autistic—math people can be peculiar and kind of PDD, but I can usually differentiate between just being odd and having autistic tendencies. I always thought that one of my college professors was somewhat autistic and then I found out that he has an autistic son, so I was right.

Michael has frequently said that all of his life he's felt like an outsider, and I wondered if this is still true.

> *Michael*: I feel less like an outsider especially in my current school where I teach. It's a school where more people have a genuine interest in teaching.
>
> My socialization has gotten a lot better. I'm still not sure about some things—when to interrupt a conversation. My timing can be lacking with people—talking into thin air because no one notices that I'm talking.
>
> I think that others are more aware of what to expect and how to handle situations without first having to think out their response. With the stress of my job and my condition, I have to keep my mood stable and not let students know what mood I am in. I am still working on this.
>
> Also, being overweight and on medication, I do not have the same stamina as others do. But perhaps this is an effect of teaching six days as well as several nights a week.

What lies ahead is anyone's guess, but few who know Michael would be surprised to see him teaching at the college level in the not too distant future.

> *Michael*: I would like to continue my education, either with another master's or a doctorate, but perhaps not right away—perhaps in one to three years. I would like to focus my time now on becoming a better and more efficient teacher and making less mistakes.
>
> I'm different so that everything I do is different, but I'm much more comfortable with people than I used to be.

Author's Reflection

All parents hope that their children will develop into responsible adults, who are independent and enjoy a good life. For the parent of a disabled child, this dream can be illusory, with the recognition that some handicaps create life long challenges and dependency. The diagnosis of autism occurs in early childhood and the condition continues forever, although autistic traits may change and be managed better by some than others.

Parents also hope to have a mutually satisfying relationship with their adult children, but for some this never happens. Advice columns in newspapers are replete with complaints from adult children as well as their parents about misunderstandings, hurt feelings, and disappointment. Michael and his mother presently do not enjoy a positive connection. This may not be so different from the problems other families face. This relationship will mend as Michael's mother cares deeply about her son, takes tremendous pride in his accomplishments, and wishes him continued future success. Adult children can profit from their parents' life experience as well as their emotional support. However, even adult children can have a difficult time adjusting to new patterns of family life after their parents divorce.

Michael has fulfilled his parents' wish that he be independent and have a good life. The journey has been difficult and heart wrenching, because there were many years when Michael had extreme problems regulating himself and his autistic traits. Today, it is evident that Michael has a good self-awareness and has developed strategies to manage adult life. When Michael appeared inappropriately dressed for work, or accidentally got his clothes dirty during the afternoon before a parent conference night, he realized that he needed help. In one instance Michael borrowed a shirt from another teacher, and in the other he went shopping with his uncle at a local store to quickly find a replacement wardrobe. Michael has learned to ask for help from others, and to learn from these experiences to be like the proverbial "boy scout" who is always fully prepared for the unexpected.

Time management is still an issue for Michael, who seems to operate perpetually behind. Michael is aware of this and has learned to be on time when it's essential, and to accept this quirk within himself, by finding environments where being late is not considered to be a significant problem.

Some young men take to domestic life more easily than others. It is truly remarkable that Michael has learned to perform daily living tasks that he had to assume because of the changes in his life after his parents' divorce. This is still a sore point for Michael, who claims to be "unfinished" and therefore unready. Because of his intelligence and out of necessity, Michael has been able to take care of his daily needs: job, wardrobe, diet, money, medical care, and transportation. It's a well-known stereotype that autistic people can be brilliant with mathematical calculation, but don't have practical sense about money. This is somewhat true for Michael who admitted he doesn't get money management intuitively, but is deliberate and conscientious about paying his bills and making appropriate financial decisions. Everyone in the family finds

Michael's new independence both surprising and delightful and feels that he could live alone and do well.

In childhood, Michael was very rigid and this was a tremendous problem, especially when it was accompanied by compulsive thoughts and obsessive behavior. Today, Michael recognizes that he needs a great deal of structure and he has created a life where he can usually depend on the orderliness of events and actions. When the unexpected occurs, Michael no longer panics or tantrums and he can successfully problem solve, especially by enlisting help from others.

Michael has also learned to fill his life with many activities so that "down time" doesn't plague him as it used to. His world is full of keeping busy in productive ways as a result of working very hard (usually having two jobs at the same time), looking for opportunities to learn more, and being socially involved with others.

Michael has also learned the importance of good medical care, both to monitor his autistic traits as well as to provide for general good health. Michael has located good medical care for his allergies and follows through independently. While Michael feels that he doesn't have the time or motivation to pursue psychological therapy, he knows that his childhood psychiatrist, Dr. B, is always ready and willing to assist him.

For an autistic individual, Michael's socialization is incredible. While he still has difficulty initiating new relationships, Michael is interested in making new acquaintances. Michael's ability to maintain friendships from both high school and college, and his loyalty to his Asperger's group indicate his fine qualities. Many friends comment about the help and concern that Michael exhibits and enjoy his friendship. Whether or not Michael can find the appropriate mate some day is conjecture, but certainly can't be discounted.

Michael has a tremendous sense of humor, which can be self-deprecating, but is useful for describing his own traits and daily trials in a light tone. Michael likes to tell jokes and when he's "on," he can make everyone laugh and enjoy his company. His uncle calls this the "juice" Michael got from the family, and both his wry manner and quirky view of life are engaging. While Michael can certainly appear preoccupied at times, this does not reach the level of isolation and disengagement from the world that had been a part of his early years.

There's no question that Michael is still "a work in progress," but all evidence indicates continuing success managing adult life. This is truly not very different from other young adults in the early stages of career and independent living. Michael lives a life of success with autism, instead of succeeding despite autism.

Chapter 10

Being Michael: Multiple Perspectives

The two extremes of him were incredible. When he was "on," he was an amazing boy, and a fun boy. But when he wasn't, it could be terrible and frightening.

Today it is like watching a movie and waiting for next week's episode. He's a charming guy and you can never tell what's just ahead.

Uncle Joe

We have learned a great deal about autism, but there is still a great deal more to know. While scientific research provides interesting information about the condition, it is the personal accounts of those who are intimately familiar with autism that provide genuine and helpful insight. Michael, his family, and the professionals who have known him for many years offer information that helps us begin to unravel the interior world of what it means to be Michael. They help to "break the silence" about autism.

Being Michael: A psychiatric perspective

Michael first met Dr. B when he was seven years old and has remained a patient of his ever since. Dr. B is a psychiatrist who specializes in work with children, and has a great deal of experience with autism. He recently reviewed all of his records about Michael, which describe Michael's full history. Dr. B also shared his thoughts about autism in general.

Review of Michael's records documented that Michael had a full range of classic autistic features in early childhood and was diagnosed autistic during the preschool years by well-respected medical doctors. The original, early childhood diagnosis of autism was confirmed when Michael was seven years old by a pediatric neurologist, who noted classic autistic symptoms in the child including: tantrums, hand flapping, rigid and concrete thinking, difficulty adjusting to new routines, unusual diet, and living "by the clock." This doctor also believed that Michael was suffering from a "reaction to childhood," which may have been a description of Michael's severe emotional problems and behavioral deterioration at the time his brother was born.

At seven years old Michael was given a full Wechsler intelligence test with this result: overall IQ 112, performance IQ 95, and verbal IQ 124. Dr. B noted the very high verbal score and commented that it was unusual for an autistic profile. This information confirms the comments from Michael's elementary school teachers, who believed that he was an intelligent child who could succeed if his behavior was more appropriate. Dr. B also commented that while children with Asperger's syndrome, a disorder related to autism, also have verbal facility, their language characteristics are very different from Michael's. Therefore, while Michael is truly high functioning, he does not appear to meet the criteria used to diagnose Asperger's syndrome. Thus there is no doubt that Michael has an autism spectrum disorder and was diagnosed as having infantile autism in childhood.

Dr. B shared his thoughts about Michael and autism.

> *Dr. B*: At this point, within the spectrum, Michael is in the milder range. When he was younger, he looked like he was in the more severe range. I've definitely seen other children who appeared to be very severe when they are younger and have grown up to be quite successful.
>
> Autism is not something that you do or don't have. You can have variants of it, and people in the milder spectrum can do okay in the world. Autism may not be one disorder, which is why the term "pervasive developmental disorders" is more accurate. People with PDD are very different from one another, although there are certain symptoms that are usually present, e.g. perseverative behaviors, difficulty relating to others, and difficulty reading social cues. Asperger's syndrome is in that group, where language is better preserved, but the language is usually stilted and pedantic.
>
> Psychiatric diagnoses are made on the basis of clusters of symptoms. At this time we do not know what the underlying pathophysiology is and this makes it difficult to know whether each diagnosis is a discrete entity. As we are able to learn more about the function of the brain, for example with PET scans, we are able to delineate which areas are involved in causing certain symptoms. In the future psychiatric diagnoses will probably be made on the basis of what the malfunctioning in the brain is, rather than relying only on symptoms. Using symptoms is akin to making a diagnosis of "fever" without differentiating what the cause of the fever is.
>
> Psychiatry in general has broadened its definitions. We've chosen to treat certain things that are more obviously severe, but as we learn more, we

treat milder cases and we don't restrict treatment to people who are severely ill.

I asked Dr. B about his treatment of Michael through many years.

> *Dr. B*: I treated certain symptoms, but the core symptoms of autism cannot be specifically treated with medication. There were some seemingly promising treatments in the past that didn't prove effective and caused significant problems with some people. Most of the treatment was geared towards Michael's symptoms of attention deficit disorder, obsessive-compulsive behavior, and depression.

Dr. B reports that many medications were tried throughout Michael's childhood. Some were initially useful in managing Michael's behavior, but then behavioral outbursts re-emerged, and the medications were changed. When Michael was 13, he began taking a new antidepressant and an antipsychotic. According to Dr. B, at the same time there was significant and ongoing improvement.

As discussed in Chapter 4, when Michael was hospitalized at nine years of age, he reported hearing multiple voices. This appears to be unusual in the personal histories of autistic individuals.

> *Dr. B*: [Hearing voices] is not typically associated with autism, but more often with psychotic depression, bipolar disorder, schizophrenia and dissociative disorder.

Michael identified several different personalities with distinct voices that spoke to him throughout his childhood and this continued into his adolescent years. Research about autism indicates that often those who are diagnosed with autism or PDD may have additional clinical disorders and this is referred to as "co-morbidity." Mood and anxiety disorders and especially depression are often seen in people with autism, but there doesn't appear to be professional literature that documents the prevalence of auditory hallucinations or hearing multiple voices. I questioned Dr. B about the issue of Michael's voices.

> *Dr. B*: Michael does not have schizophrenia and the diagnosis of schizophrenia in childhood is rare. He did not have a dissociative disorder, formerly termed "multiple personality disorder." Regarding the issue of co-morbidity, people who have one diagnosis may have another. Actually in psychiatry this is the rule rather than the exception. Co-morbidity is very common.

No diagnosis in psychiatry is well understood, because we know little about what is happening in the brain. It's not unusual to see reports of "voices" with many types of severe psychopathology and auditory hallucinations are most common in children with bipolar disorder. Hallucinations in children do not have as serious prognostic significance as when they occur in adults. No one knows why there are hallucinations.

A psychologist who treats many autistic children and who worked with Michael in the later childhood years, reports awareness that other autistic children also hear voices. He further speculates that this may be more common than reported, because unlike Michael, many autistic children do not have the ability to articulate and share their inner world. Most striking is that Michael says that hearing "voices" became less frequent as his autistic symptoms abated during adolescence.

Michael: The voices decreased as problems decreased. Nowadays it's more like I ask myself a question. The voices may have been the different thoughts or perspectives in my mind. The voices acted on their own, and perhaps I could ask them a question, but they had their own opinions. I used the voices to help me reason what to do next. I was never aware voices were abnormal until I was much older and they had subsided about age 16.

Another psychologist, who knows Michael as an adult, speculates about the cause of the voices in Michael's childhood. He feels that the "voices" may have represented Michael's different childhood aspects and thoughts, and would indicate poor personality integration. As Michael matured and was better able to regulate his autistic tendencies, Michael began to develop a sense of "self" and the "voices" became integrated into the multi-faceted person that Michael is today.

Perhaps the most crucial question to answer about Michael is why he has been so successful managing his autism, when others haven't been as fortunate.

Dr. B: There is a combination of factors at work here: intelligence, mother's advocacy, motivation to learn, and the ability to learn. Of course the fact that he was given special services in a school that understood this disorder and a social worker at that school who was very dedicated to Michael and his family, helped greatly.

Michael is a very intelligent individual. He also has a very dedicated mother, who was always active; pushing and following up to get whatever best treatment was available. Some people get better treatment because of someone being very active. Having an advocate makes the world of difference to anyone, especially a child with an illness, who cannot speak up for him or herself.

Michael wants to learn and he wants to succeed. He especially did well academically in school. He really profits from learning and this changes him.

I discussed Michael's career choice with Dr. B.

> *Dr. B*: He wants to teach children mathematics, but not necessarily interact with them. Clearly, autistic individuals do better in the world of facts and figures. They have a very hard time reading emotions—it's like a learning disability of emotions.

Dr. B has a tremendous satisfaction knowing Michael today, because Michael is a charming and insightful young man. He has come so far in his journey with autism.

Being Michael: A perspective from a clinical psychologist

During Michael's senior year in college, he saw a therapist at the university's psychological services center. At that time, Michael was experiencing difficulty getting along with his mother, and was feeling isolated, confused, and depressed. At the therapist's recommendation, Michael was given a full psychological assessment to determine his level of cognitive and emotional functioning. The evaluator was familiar with Michael's full history, but did not have experience with autism. She assessed him using the same battery of diagnostic tools that she would use for any adult. The results of this assessment confirm many of the insights Michael has about himself as well as the impressions of others.

During the testing sessions, Michael was cooperative and friendly and even joked with the examiner. His mood was good and he appeared clear and focused, but he was very intense and sought reinforcement that he was doing well. It was no surprise that Michael approached any task that required math calculation with confidence, but he had significant problems with tasks that required physical manipulation and coordination, which he performed in a random and mechanical fashion. Unstructured parts of the testing caused him more anxiety.

The results of the intelligence test administered documents Michael's very high intellectual ability: full scale IQ 131 (very superior), verbal IQ 138 (very superior), and performance IQ 116 (high average). In addition to obtaining superior scores in math, Michael did extremely well with tasks requiring short-term memory and mental operations as well as showing good abstract reasoning and verbal judgment. While his performance scores were relatively high, he had extreme difficulty with attention to detail and an inability to recognize essential from inessential details.

Michael presented attributes that seem especially unique for an individual with autism. For example, the evaluator commented that Michael showed good judgment and an ability to make use of practical information based on past experiences. More typical of an autistic profile was Michael's difficulty paying attention to visual detail and difficulty anticipating consequences in social situations. While Michael's strong academic ability was evident in this testing, his oral language skills were poorer than peers of his age at this level of intelligence. The evaluator commented that Michael's difficulties with inter-personal skills may be increased by his weakness in oral language.

This evaluator's conclusions about Michael's emotional functioning are especially interesting, because they echo many of the concerns that Michael has expressed about himself. During the evaluation, Michael had difficulty showing adequate interpersonal judgment and seemed to rely on trial and error solutions to solve his problems. He also revealed problems dealing with stress and an inability to regulate strong emotions. This apparently causes Michael to feel overwhelmed and results in impulsive behavior. Michael also demonstrates difficulty handling ambiguous social situations and this makes him feel inadequate. It was also evident that Michael recognizes many of his shortcomings and this helps him change and grow. Michael frequently describes himself as an "outsider" and this may enable him to look at and monitor himself in a manner that is far more objective than that used by most.

In spite of Michael's many strengths, the examiner noted that while he has experienced success dealing with the world, Michael lacks the necessary coping skills to make him feel comfortable and fully at ease. This can cause him to feel isolated. Michael also tends to deny emotional distress, which results in an elevated level of depression. Michael also focuses on his shortcomings and discussed himself and others in an overly intellectualized manner, which could lead to more difficulty relating to people in a natural fashion.

In summary, this examiner accurately depicted the world of a high-functioning autistic adult in this manner:

Michael appears to have several personal strengths. He is very ambitious and focused on a future career in the area of mathematics, in which he is very capable of succeeding. Despite some difficulties in interpersonal communications, he is able to interact with others. He also has a good sense of humor, which is an asset that will help him better relate with others.

Michael needs help to deal with underlying negative emotions, which may be associated with his difficulties in interpersonal relationships…and his concern about performance. It appears that at times he may be too self-deprecating and is often unable to see partial progress and he views success as an all-or-nothing outcome.

Michael also needs assistance exploring emotional factors which may be interfering with his ability to construct complex exchanges with people as well as learning to take perspective of the thoughts and emotions of others.

This examiner and Michael's therapist recommended that continuation in psychotherapy would be very helpful to address his emotional needs. Simultaneously with this evaluation, Michael saw his psychiatrist and resumed taking medication that he had independently stopped. Michael's depression gradually improved, and once he felt better, he became focused on school activities and terminated therapy. Today, Michael's emotional adjustment is more consistent and stable. He actively seeks out the companionship of others with whom he enjoys recreational time, and he has a very busy and productive professional life. Michael also expresses a desire to begin a dating relationship, if he can find the right person.

Being Michael: Perspective from the family

While "it takes a village to raise a child" the need for expanded resources is multiplied when the child has special needs. Michael's immediate and extended family were all enlisted to provide assistance at every stage of his life. Initially, Michael's mother and maternal grandmother were the most involved family members. Together, they sought medical advice to learn why Michael seemed so delayed and different from other children. They also searched to locate resources for Michael to get the help he needed. The women would not abandon their belief that progress could be made with Michael, if only the appropriate experts were found to provide treatment in an emotionally supportive environment.

Shari: I went from person to person on gut instinct, and if it worked for a while that was good, and then we moved on. He was also lucky that he had so many people in the family who helped him in so many ways. When Michael started at the Center, everyone including grandparents, aunts, and uncles went there to learn how to help him. And everyone visited Michael when he was at the hospital.

While his father was less active in this process of seeking medical and psychological help for his son, he was also very concerned and involved.

Shari: Jake did as much as he could. He was a "hands on" dad, and he could sit with Michael for hours and play board games. He was his playmate, but it dwindled when he got older. He couldn't handle Michael's outbursts in any logical and rational way.

Shari and Jake had different ideas about how to handle Michael's aggressive behavior, which caused tension between them. Ultimately Shari didn't want Jake to be the disciplinarian.

Shari: I kind of pushed Jake to the side with discipline.

Jake: Most of his anger was directed towards Shari—physical and verbal. And I would step in, but I'd get the worst of it, because his mother didn't think I handled it right. It was a lose-lose situation for me, but there were times that were so scary I had to step in between them and hold him back.

Michael also had a strong emotional attachment to his father's parents. His paternal grandfather died when Michael was very young, but Michael truly loved his grandmother. Shari remembers that when the family made annual visits to the cemetery, Michael would lay on the ground or over his grandmother's headstone, because he just wanted to be near her and talk to her.

Michael has both maternal and paternal aunts and uncles, who have also provided emotional support, financial assistance, and helpful advice. Michael knows that there is always a place for him with his uncles and their families and seeks them out whenever he needs aid.

Michael's maternal great-grandmother was his first baby sitter and she lavished love on this first great-grandchild for many years. She always thought Michael was extraordinary, because he was beautiful and was fascinated by some toys. This great-grandmother could not accept that there was any reason to be concerned about the child, when the rest of the family became aware of Michael's unusual behavior and language delay. When she took ill and was bed-ridden, Michael would spend a great deal of time lying next to his great-grandmother in her bed. Many in the family remarked that while autistic children do not easily show affection, Michael was sensitive and demonstrative with his great-grandma.

Michael's maternal grandparents have been especially important in his life. They've provided respite care, when he was too great a burden for his mother, and give him their time, attention, praise, financial help, and unconditional love. They are so devoted to Michael that at times, Michael's younger brother feels slighted.

> *Shari:* He lived with my parents several times throughout the years. When he was 12, he lived with them for 6 months, and then again while he was in college, when we weren't able to get along at all. My mother's a tough grandma, but my father's a mush. They both have a place for Michael in their hearts and do everything for him. For example Michael would say to me, "I need a menu of all my meals 72 hours in advance, because I want to know what the food will be for every meal." Then he'd say, "Grandma will do that for me." Grandma and Grandpa would do anything for Michael whenever!

Throughout his childhood, when Michael disagreed with his mother's actions, he would call his grandmother on the phone to enlist her support against his mother. He thought that his mother would have to follow her own mother's directives. While Michael still loves his grandparents today, as his social world has expanded, he sees them less often. Similar to most grandparents, they lament that Michael seldom calls.

Michael's disruptive behavior outside the home dramatically changed to more appropriate conduct when he entered his adolescent years. In comparison, his behavior at home was still unpredictable and, at times, truly terrifying.

Michael's friend, Gene, identifies with Michael's difficult relationship with his immediate family, and especially with his mother.

> *Gene:* Our mothers wanted us to be "normal." They probably would have preferred if we got into trouble and did usual teenage stuff—go out to clubs, get drunk, instead of talking about airline and train schedules.
>
> Michael always felt emotionally removed from his family, and I couldn't tell who put the distance between them. When I visited, I thought here was a family and here was Michael. I compared him to a movie in which a family adopted a child that they simply could not understand or relate to, but not in a bad way. Of course, these opinions came from conversations with Michael so I heard only his side of the story. I never knew Michael's family well

enough to really understand the dynamics of their relationship, but Michael's point of view was one of a misunderstood child, and hence a gap that there was the family and then there was Michael.

What people outside the family did not know was that at home Michael was demanding, difficult, threatening, and intolerant. According to Dr. B, the most common cause for Michael's childhood tantrums was simply hearing his mother talk on the phone. The worst aspect of Michael's behavior at home was physical aggression, usually directed at his mother. Michael's father was subjected to the abuse when he intervened to protect Michael's mother and brother. There were times that Shari was forced to call the police to restrain Michael, when things truly got out of control.

> *Shari*: The police came to the house three times and it was one of the lowest points in my life to have to call the police on my own child. I grew up believing that no one outside your house should know what goes on inside. All those years with tantruming, and his yelling, and hitting, and breaking things. I closed the window and put the stereo on loud so people wouldn't hear him. I was afraid that if people knew what went on inside our house, then they would take him away.

Scot, Michael's younger brother, remembers the incidents well.

> *Scot*: There were countless times when Michael would attack our mother. He'd hit her and she'd be black and blue and my dad would throw himself on top of him and he'd start punching my dad and it would be a whole big mayhem. When I got bigger, I punched him back and he'd stop attacking me.

Michael has consistently felt that his family exaggerates his violence.

> *Shari*: He denies the violence today. Now, he's embarrassed.

Michael used intimidation to control his family.

> *Shari*: He would threaten, "I'm calling." He would make a mean face and say that he was dialing [the police emergency number] to report that I was an abusive mother.

One time as an overweight teenager, Michael dialed the police emergency number to report that his mother was starving him, because there was none of his favorite pizza in the freezer. He didn't complete the call and hung up the phone, but he was embarrassed that the emergency operator actually returned the call to see if there was a problem.

In his adult years, Michael does not have violent outbursts. He has learned that medication keeps his moods more stable, he no longer lives with his mother and brother, whose presence could trigger rages, and he has learned to close his eyes and rest when he feels overwhelmed.

Michael and his mother

The relationship between Shari and Michael has been complex throughout the years, ranging from Michael's total dependency on her and affection for her in the early years to his extreme anger and violence towards her in later years. Shari and other family members say that she was literally bruised and battered by Michael, when even the sound of her voice could cause him to have uncontrollable outbursts. Michael denies that this is true and feels it's an exaggeration of his conduct. Shari was the one individual in the family who was the primary target of most of Michael's rages even though Michael can dispassionately describe the importance of her role in his early years. Their relationship was especially bitter when Michael was in college, and his mother describes the strain in those years.

> *Shari*: He'd tell me what a piece of garbage I am and that I'm useless and I do nothing. He's called me every name in the book. I used to be a good mother, but I'm not a good mother anymore. I don't even have good armor up anymore—my armor is off. It didn't used to hurt me as much as it hurts me now. I used to be tough and strong and I took it and it bounced off me and I knew he was sick. He's so successful in the outside world, but I can't take his behavior any more. It's an emotional thing and I try to separate the rational and intellectual from the emotional, but it's hard. That's why I'm at the point I am now.

I asked Shari why she thinks she has been the target for most of Michael's violence.

> *Shari*: First of all, he'll never forgive me for bringing Scot home. And I'm safe. He knows that whatever he did to me, I would forgive. And he knows that I love him.
>
> He's been so horrible to me, but I remember one night when he came into the bedroom at 2:30 in the morning and said to me that he was shutting the window so that I wouldn't be cold in the morning and then he said, "Thanks, Ma, I love you." I said, "I love you too." Another time he said, "You have a child. You gave up your life. You are not allowed to go out at night.

You're not allowed to go on vacation. You gave up that right when you had a child."

Michael couldn't stand the sound of my voice and he couldn't tolerate me being on the telephone. He would slam doors. Just before his father and I moved apart, he still wouldn't let me be on the phone. I could be in my own bedroom with the door closed, and he would come in and scream at me because I was on the phone.

I was so well trained in trying to keep the peace, in trying to avoid the explosions, but it stopped working.

As discussed in Chapter 9, Michael and his mother have less contact at this time, and he harbors very strong resentment towards her and her current life.

Michael and his brother

All sibling relationships can be complicated by competition and rivalry, but Michael's relationship with his brother has been extremely problematic. Scot was born when Michael was six years old, and Michael was still a very needy child. The parental attention that was required to care for the infant resulted in time taken away from catering to Michael and Michael could not tolerate this. Resentment for Scot increased through the childhood years. As Scot grew older and became more of a physical presence in Michael's life, Michael became aggressive towards his brother. The family had to protect the younger child and Shari was especially concerned about the effect of having an autistic brother on Scot. She freely admits that she spoiled Scot to compensate for Michael's behavior towards him. Even while he was in college, Michael remained jealous about the attention and possessions Shari gave Scot. Michael even resorted to measuring the square footage of each of the boys' bedrooms to prove that Scot got the bigger room, which meant preferential treatment.

> *Shari*: Michael has to deal with my relationship with his brother and it still brings out jealousy. He wants to weigh and measure everything to prove that he's treated unfairly. He wants to know in dollars and cents how much money comes out of my pocket for his brother's college education, because he wants to know if I spend one more penny on his brother's education than I spent for him.

Shari freely admits that Scot's life was negatively affected by having an autistic brother, and she tried to compensate for this.

Shari: I make a lot of allowances for Scot, because of how he had to grow up and it's total over-compensation. I brought Scot into this difficult situation, which I didn't fully realize, because when he was born Michael was doing well. But then it became a nightmare for me and Scot. Scot never knew what it was like to have me alone and to have a peaceful house. Michael would have a tantrum and I would pick up Scot and put him in his crib so that he wouldn't see what was going on. Michael was so cruel to him.

Scot feels that his brother ruined important parts of his life and has been very critical of Michael's behavior and demands on the family.

Michael and Scot are as different as two brothers can be. Michael disdains superficiality and appearance, while Scot is a typical teenager, who is most concerned about the approval of his peers. At times, it seems that for Scot there is nothing more important than the way he looks.

Scot: I really believe that one day I will be famous and when you're in the public eye everyone has their eyes on you and they are looking at you. So, I like to groom myself especially well to be confident. The clothes that I throw out Michael will use. He wears flip-flops and shirts that are ripped and faded. I like brand new clothes. My career goal is to be a pro wrestler or be in sports or business management and I have a good head for business.

Throughout Scot's life he was embarrassed by Michael's behavior and appearance.

Shari: Scot's gotten numerous awards from the school district. We'd go to the Board of Education meetings where they'd give out the awards. Michael came with us once and his hair was a mess. Scot said that he should sit somewhere else, because he didn't want his friends to see that Michael is his brother. He was so embarrassed and he's humiliated by his brother. Scot said "I don't want anybody to know that he belongs to us."

Having an autistic brother has meant changes in Scot's life.

Shari: Scot loves his friends and is very popular. Michael has fits in the house when there are other people around and it has been extremely embarrassing. I'd try to muffle his outbursts and put him into a separate room. Scot wasn't comfortable about bringing kids home. Scot was completely humiliated by him and sometimes he would try to help his brother saying "Tuck in your shirt, straighten yourself out." Michael couldn't care less. He's oblivious.

Scot: It was harder for the folks than on me, but there were days when he locked me out of the bedroom and I'd have to sleep on the couch until our parents got the door unlocked. He always had a lot of tantrums and anger and would attack me and my mom and grab us and throw us against the wall. When my friends would come over, he would try to scare them and it was the worst.

Scot freely admits the effect his brother had on his life including their ongoing rivalry and mutual jealousy.

Scot: When we were out in public it was embarrassing—his appearance and his behavior and his temper. He just stood out or he would go crazy.

We are two brothers and two siblings should get equal attention, but it was always more him even though he would say it was more me. He's in denial about that. Both of our parents feel that I'm spoiled, but I don't agree, but my mother does buy me clothes and other things to make up for the way things were at home.

My grandparents are always on Michael's side and they believe anything he says. They keep him as the center of attention and they've taken him all over the country on trips and they will do anything for him. They don't care about me in the same way. They still think that he is extremely challenged the way he once was and he takes 100 percent advantage of them. To this day, my grandparents still baby him and he gets away with murder. If I throw a temper tantrum, I won't get my way, but he will.

Scot was diagnosed with attention deficit disorder (ADD) in childhood, for which he occasionally took medication, and he was also in therapy. Scot realizes that he may not be as calm or quiet as other students, but doesn't think that this impacts on his academic achievement, and he has done well in high school without special services. Scot is extremely social and fully participates in his high school's extra-curricular programs, works part time and has started several small businesses supplying bagels at sports events and distributing advertising flyers. Scot looks forward to starting college away from home this year.

While Scot has always been highly critical of his brother, he does acknowledge Michael's academic ability.

Scot: Michael was one of the smartest kids in his high school and at college he spent most of his time on academics so we didn't argue as much. He's smart and sometimes he helps me with school work, because he can think like a teacher.

At age 18, Scot can also see that his life with an autistic sibling provides him with greater understanding about others.

Scot: Because of Michael's disability, I can deal with people with problems easier. I had a kid in my camp group this summer with Tourettes, OCD, ADHD, and every other initial you could have. I'm more understanding of people with problems and people who live with others who have problems.

When Michael got his driver's license, Scot took full advantage of this and had Michael drive him around town, if his mother was unavailable. At that time the brothers had a better relationship than ever before. After their parents separated, Michael became more interested in his brother's welfare. Michael thought that their mother was neglecting Scot, because she was too occupied with her own needs and her new life. Michael thought that as the older brother he should provide supervision for Scot. This was a very new aspect of their relationship.

Shari: Now Michael feels sorry for his brother, because he thinks that I'm not mothering him enough. When his brother graduated from high school, he sat next to me and he said, "Well, you did it. He graduated. You're finished. You go off and have your life."

Scot is skeptical about Michael's behavior problems, which persisted even when he was in college.

Scot: When he was in college, I think he knew exactly what he was doing and he did things purposefully and used his behavior to his advantage. To me it's like he was performing, because when he walked out the front door, it was like he's a totally different person.

It seems that the brothers have a better relationship because they no longer live together due to their parents' divorce. They have also gotten older and somewhat more insightful about each other.

Shari: Michael's relationship with his brother is much better. They can talk and do things together and have things in common to joke about, especially when they laugh at me and their father.

Scot: My view of my brother has changed to a point. I see him more as a normal guy now, except when he's around our grandparents. Our relationship has changed. We don't really have anything to fight over as we no longer live together. Our relationship consists of a phone call to discuss using our e-mail account, or maybe to see if we want to go to a baseball game or to dinner.

I don't really know how Michael is. Nothing has really changed lately. He gets along well with everyone in the family, as long as he gets what he wants. He still yells and gets mad at our mother, when she doesn't do *exactly* what he *wants*. The problem of friction with Mother exists because of Michael. Michael needs things done his way, and if this doesn't happen, he's had it with Mom.

In spite of their problems with each other and her tense relationship with Michael, Shari takes great pride in both her sons.

> *Shari:* I have two good children in the outside world. They have an incredible work ethic. They are good natured and would give you the shirts off their backs.
>
> My life was my kids and I took care of my kids. And now the kids are fine without me. I did make them independent men. I pushed them to be independent of me.

It will be interesting to see if these two brothers are capable of forming a closer relationship in the future, because they are truly very different from each other in so many important ways.

The parents divorce

Shari dramatically changed the dynamics of Michael's family life when she sought a divorce from his father. She attributes this decision to long-standing problems with the marital relationship and differing expectations. As Michael grew in independence during the college years and seeing her younger son enter high school, Shari decided that she wanted a different kind of life and future. She was both physically worn out and emotionally exhausted from her role as the care-giver/manager of her family's world.

> *Michael's maternal grandmother:* Her life was devoted to the kids and she hadn't been ready to make a change and get a divorce. Friends aren't surprised that they're divorced and it wasn't a happy home. We've celebrated our fiftieth anniversary and everyone is getting divorced: cousins, sisters, brothers, my children. Only we're not divorced. We shared quite a bit with being caretakers and it wears you out, but you need to do it.
>
> *Uncle Joe:* Shari was burnt out after the first 15 years of Michael's life and I don't know how she lasted. She did everything for him, because she was very much into it's easier just to do it for him than to get him to that next stage. He has to be pushed into maturing and his resentment for his mother is from her trying to wean him off and she was still doing things for his younger brother and not for him.

Michael's father did not initiate the divorce and has a different perspective on its cause.

> *Jake*: Experts told us that most parents who have children like Michael get divorced. They made suggestions that we find time to have a relationship as husband and wife and to keep the marriage together. Once the kids were born, it was always the kids, and the only reason we were together was because of the kids and then it wasn't any good any more.
>
> There were always tensions in our marriage because of Michael. At a point in time, I was probably jealous that I wasn't getting the attention I had been getting in the years before the children. In later years I was angry all the time, because of what she did or didn't do with Michael. We had very different ideas about Michael.
>
> According to Shari our relationship wasn't working for many years. What I had before is gone and now I have something new. What's over is over, and you move on.

An area of contention in Michael's adult adjustment is his anger towards his mother. While this anger was often a prominent problem for Michael when he was younger, it increased as a result of the divorce. While Michael does not have a great deal of involvement with his father and can be critical of him, he forgives Jake without disapproval. He says that his father is doing the best he can. This is not true of Michael's relationship with his mother and he has become increasingly cynical and antagonistic about the role of his mother in his present life. He also views her current life with disdain. Michael literally feels abandoned by Shari and says that she's stopped being the mother that he still needs.

> *Michael*: I don't have my mother. She can be very preoccupied with her fiancé. She wants to be available, when she's available, and she wants to be appreciated for all the good that she's done regardless of when she's done it. But she's not dependable. She wants everything to be hunky dory without effort and I resent that.

Shari presently lives with her fiancé and her younger son, Scot, and has formed a close relationship with her fiancé's extended family. Michael resents his mother's involvement with "the new family" and thinks that her affection for them is disproportionate to the time she has known them. He feels that he has been replaced by others.

> *Michael*: It upsets me because she doesn't place a greater priority on me and my brother and those other people step in one day and they are our equals.

Twenty years of raising us and one day these people step in and they are our equals, or are a higher priority for her. My brother doesn't feel the dependency that I do. I feel a lack and he doesn't. He feels that he's done growing up and I don't. I don't deny the possibility that she was burnt out, but I don't forgive her.

Shari enjoys her new life and has a great optimism about her future, but she is sad that her relationship with Michael has suffered.

> *Shari:* He has a wonderful world and then a separate world about me. I have to stand in the background now. Somehow the more I tried to get Michael to stand on his own and cut the apron strings, to make him grow up, the more he got angry at me. He always resented when I did things for his brother. I gave my boys everything I had and I wanted them to be independent.
>
> It's too much for Michael that his father and I got divorced. There's a lot for him to deal with—another man in my life, and other people in my life that I love and he can't share me. He thinks that I don't have the right to a life, because I didn't since the minute I gave birth to him. He thinks that my purpose in life is to take care of him and there should be nothing else—ever.
>
> Our relationship is minimal. I call him all the time, but he says that everything is always my fault. Whenever I'm involved with him, he's like five years old and he needs his mommy.
>
> I have to be in the background now. A lot of people can't understand this, but in some ways it's self-preservation for me. I can live with the fact that Michael may never want to have anything to do with me for the rest of his life, because I know that what I had to do was necessary to get him to where he is today. The sacrifice is that I can't have a relationship with him now. But he can have a life in this world, and I can deal with the reality that right now we cannot have a relationship.

Michael says that the parent of an autistic child needs to be a mother or father forever to continually fulfill parenting responsibilities. He truly feels that his mother is no longer functioning as his mother, but isn't critical that his father doesn't do more for him. It is sheer conjecture to speculate about the nature of Michael's relationship with his parents in the future, but it is evident that all children, regardless of their age, feel a tremendous impact when their parents divorce or do not live together. Michael counted on the support system of his parents that abruptly ceased before he was ready to be independent.

Author's reflection

The term "autism," and prognosis

There is more awareness that children with "autism" can exhibit a wide and diverse range of symptoms and have different levels of ability. Today, professionals often use the concept of an "autism spectrum disorder" as an umbrella for many of the autism related diagnoses, including: pervasive developmental disorder (PDD), pervasive developmental disorder–not otherwise specified (PDD-NOS), autism, childhood disintegrative disorder (CDD), Asperger's syndrome, and high-functioning autism. The Diagnostic and Statistical Manual IV of the American Psychiatric Association describes autism as one of several related disorders within the larger category of pervasive developmental disorders.

As a toddler Michael presented all of the classic features of autism, and was diagnosed at two years and nine months of age with infantile autism. While Michael did develop language and appeared to be highly intelligent in his school-aged years, the prognosis was poor given the severity of behavioral problems. No one who knew Michael as a child could have predicted his life today as a responsible and productive adult, and consequently some observers even question the accuracy of the original diagnosis.

The underlying causes of autism as well as the best treatments are still illusory, although much more is known today than when Michael was a child. Michael's very high intellectual potential, his ability to profit from learning, his mother's good instincts and hard work in locating helpful professionals, and early intervention and appropriate schooling, all could have predicted an optimistic prognosis. However, because the troubled childhood years were long and so difficult, it was hard for the family to be hopeful and continue to be energetic. It took well into Michael's adolescence for significant progress to be realized, and even then behavior at home was still a problem. It is very difficult for a family to be optimistic and stay fully engaged in the care of an autistic child through many long and trying years, but the lesson from Michael's history is clear. Continued efforts and maturity can produce remarkable results, but it takes time and dedication—a great deal of time! and a great deal of dedication!

Michael verbalizes his continuing desire to "fit in" and be just like everyone else. He continually works at modifying his behavior as he profits from experience. He has also lived in an environment that adored, nurtured, and protected him, and also one that provided many enriching opportunities.

Michael's innate superior intelligence and his drive to succeed are critically important factors that cannot be overlooked. We may never know why Michael was able to leave the world of silence, isolation, and dependency, and unlock his true ability. Michael's success in adult life is an enormously positive outcome for an individual with autism. His history should remind all families with an autistic child and the professionals who work with these children, that it is very difficult to accurately predict future development from childhood behavior. Michael's story is so important, because it validates the possibility of a positive future for any child who is diagnosed within the autism spectrum.

Treatments: Medication and therapy

At various times in Michael's life he exhibited debilitating behavioral symptoms and episodic depression. Dr. B says that there is no medication that addresses the "core disorder," but medication was prescribed to ameliorate behavioral problems. A strict regimen of behavior modification was begun after Michael's hospitalization at age nine and this appears to have had a desired effect of reducing the worst behavior in school. Michael thinks that the childhood "talk" therapy was pleasant, because he received individual attention and did enjoyable activities with a sensitive professional, although he does not think that this had much impact on his behavior. Until the college years, Michael feels that he was not able to be truly insightful about himself.

Michael's episodic depression can be attributed to his condition, but from adolescence on it was exacerbated by his non-compliance with medication. The pattern is familiar. Often when individuals take mood altering medications to good effect, they feel so well that they think medication is no longer needed and consequently stop taking their pills. Without the necessary medication, depression and agitation often return. This was true for Michael during his junior year in college. When the residual medication left his system, Michael became more and more depressed and did not recognize this until he was in crisis. Today, Michael fully acknowledges that he must continually be on his antidepressants to keep his mood stable.

It is interesting that even in college Michael viewed talk therapy as non-productive, because he felt that it did not aid him. Michael lives in a world where he seeks to avoid ambiguity and he values clear cut definitions and a specific plan of action. He did not put much faith in a discussion and reflection process that often resulted in more questions than answers. Michael did follow his therapist's recommendation that he join an appropriate social group to reduce his feeling of isolation. Michael located a local Asperger's group of adults and has enjoyed his relationship with the members for several years. With greater self-awareness and the ability to be reflective, psychotherapy can be helpful for an autistic adult's continuing growth. It can provide support for dealing with ongoing concerns, and be an additional resource whenever problems arise.

Behavior and aggression

In the later childhood years Michael began to exhibit appropriate behavior in the world outside his home, but could not maintain self-discipline at home. This might be explained in several ways. Michael expected and was accustomed to his family complying with all his wishes and he could manipulate their conduct with his rages. He also knew that inappropriate behavior outside the home had very negative public consequences, whereas although there were consequences at home, he was "safe" there. Michael says that he has always felt that at home he could allow himself really to be himself with all of his problems without fear of drastic retaliation or embarrassment. Michael was not understanding of his family's needs and he was unwilling to tolerate any of their actions that didn't comport with his demands, even into his college years.

During his adolescent and college years, whether Michael isolated himself from his family because of his behavior and intolerance or whether, as Michael feels, the family rejected him, is really a moot point. No doubt this was a cycle. As Michael continued to show threatening behavior, the family pulled away from him and this, in turn, caused more feelings of rejection. Many times, the family could not understand Michael, and he could not understand them. Michael's autism truly resulted in his being different from the other members of his family, and in that sense he was always separated from them and the world in which they lived. The family also anticipated that with Michael's maturity and school achievement, his behavior at home should match the better behavior exhibited in the outside world. When this did not always occur, there must have been tremendous frustration. Additionally, new dynamics occurring in the home because of the growing estrangement between Michael's parents, as well as the parents' need to attend to a demanding and younger adolescent son, created competition for time to devote to Michael.

As children mature they learn that to be part of a family means to be able to compromise and this ability did not come until much later in Michael's life, and occurred outside the immediate family. The aggression and anger towards Michael's mother appears to be closely related to his dependency on her. The more Michael depended and needed his mother, the less able she was to meet his requirements, and in her own words she could never fulfill all of Michael's wishes. Because she was smaller than both Michael's father and brother, and truly did not fight back, Shari was an easy victim.

The divorce

All children's lives change when their parents divorce and their adjustment to new living arrangements can vary based on their age and other circumstances. Michael interprets the divorce between his parents as his mother abandoning him and this caused both a physical and an emotional separation between them. He describes himself as a fledgling pushed out of the nest before he was ready. All of Michael's family, however, think that it is unlikely that Michael could have ever easily separated from the extreme dependency he had on his mother. Learning to be self-sufficient did not come easily to Michael, and the divorce abruptly imposed new responsibilities on him. Fortunately, Michael was able to learn and grow when these challenges arose and consequently he is a much more self-reliant person.

While Shari continues to maintain phone contact with Michael, and sees him occasionally, it's clear that Michael is embittered about his mother's new life and what he still views as her abandonment of him. When Shari reaches out to her son to assist him or to include him in her life, Michael views this with skepticism and says that she's only interested in sharing good times. Michael related that one time he drove to his mother's new home and saw that the house was filled with adults, children, and noisy pets. He said that he couldn't bring himself to go inside. It's not clear if this was a result of Michael's inability to cope with the tumult or because of jealousy and an inability to share his mother. He called his mother on a cell phone from the curb outside her house and said that he wasn't able to visit. One more time Michael and his mother failed to connect and this reinforced Michael's feelings of separation.

In spite of Michael's ability to lead an independent and full life, he still has many issues about his mother. This is undoubtedly a reflection of Michael's history of making his mother a target of his anger and a result of her decision to divorce his father, which dramatically altered Michael's life. While most young men his age seek emancipation from their parents, this has not been true for Michael. All members of Michael's family agree that the divorce and physical separation from his mother required Michael to tackle new responsibilities and mature, but it has been an extremely difficult transition.

Family and social relations

Michael has exhibited the capacity to be a good friend and is especially caring to some members of his extended family, especially his grandparents. He evidences concern for others, but the compassion often does not extend to those closest to him. According to his good friend, Gene, Michael is capable of understanding situations about others, and giving good advice and support. In some ways, Michael acknowledges that he is behind in his social adjustment. It's clear that his world has expanded far outside his family and that socialization with others is a priority. It will be fascinating to see how Michael continues to change in the years ahead and whether he will be able to have a fulfilling relationship with those who care the most about him.

Chapter 11

Being Michael: From Michael

My Autobiography
My name is Michael. I am 14 years of age. I was born on 4–21–80. I have eyes that vary in color. Sometimes hazel, sometimes blue, or even sometimes gray. My hair is a dark brown. My favorite hobby is studying astronomy. I like to be with my family the most. I am shy near people I don't know, but talkative when I'm with my family. I like my intelligence the best about myself.

Judith: Michael, what is it like to be autistic?
Michael: I don't know. I've always been autistic.

There are no data about the prevalence of autistic individuals who are as high functioning as Michael, and only a few cases are well known. Consequently, we cannot be sure just how remarkable he and others like him are. Regardless of the degree of Michael's uniqueness, his perspectives about autism are fascinating, because so little is known about this very different world. Michael is both articulate and intelligent and can describe what it means to be autistic from a truly personal perspective.

Being Michael: Perspectives from Michael (at ages 21 and 24)

The following is a dialogue between Michael and the author that occurred when he was 21. At that time he was moderately depressed and especially introspective about what autism meant to him. Approximately three years later Michael reviewed his original comments to consider whether his earlier thoughts were still accurate or were more reflective of a particularly difficult period in his life. (Comments that Michael made at age 24 are so noted.)

Being in your own world

One of the most important issues with autism is that the individual seems to be in his or her own world and not communicating with others. Several behaviors seem to be very common with autism, for example: self-stimulation, staring at objects, and not making eye contact. Do you remember any of this in your life?

> *Michael*: I think that I still go through that kind of thing. I'll always shy away from a group and it will take a conscious, not normal effort to re-enter the normal world. It's more than shyness, though, it's a real fear, not of the initial speaking, but of the long-term results of entering a conversation. It involves fear of something happening and weeks and weeks of retrospection having to follow that event.
>
> The main thing about autism is you're not a person in the world. You're a viewer of the world.

From time to time it's not uncommon for everyone to feel that he or she is not part of others' lives.

> *Michael*: But there's time to time and then there's always. I think I can make an intellectual effort to think of myself in other ways for a short time, but I feel that way always. Always.

Self-image

When you think about your self today, what do you think your strengths are?

> *Michael*: My strengths? There is no "my" so it's kind of hard to answer this in itself. I'm a viewer, so there is no "my."

Don't you think that you are Michael? Who do you think you are?

> *Michael*: No, I don't think I'll ever think I'm Michael. The whole world is a show and I'm a viewer. Maybe I have a role in the show—Shari's son, or whatever.

When you look at yourself in a mirror, who looks back at you?

> *Michael*: No one looks back at me. I see my face.

Let's talk about the person who is Michael. What things do you do well?

> *Michael*: I remember things. I don't do anything well.

If you were a guidance counselor writing a letter of recommendation for Michael, who is applying to college, what would you say?

> *Michael:* I'm a good student. I'm a friendly person. I try to be helpful. I don't think that's anything special. I think that all has to do with being autistic. Being helpful is part of being a viewer, seeing something that bothers you and taking the appropriate action. Being friendly is a similar thing. Being a good student, you're just doing it.

Do you think that people who aren't autistic may also lack self-confidence?

> *Michael:* Yeah, but that's only part of it. Other people may not have self-confidence, but they don't have all these other symptoms. This overall image of the self or lack thereof is very different. I'm not an outsider; Michael is not a person. He's a non-person. He could be like a dolphin. I don't know what being a person is.

Are there aspects of being autistic that provide benefits that others don't have?

> *Michael:* Being autistic allows one to make sure that something they're responsible for is taken care of. An autistic person, by their nature, can't shirk responsibility. An autistic person views the world and feels bad if something goes wrong. Something is going wrong, because they are not doing their share and not doing what they're supposed to do. You don't want to view a world with faults.

My impression is that you often really don't care about others' opinions of you, because you do and say what you feel is right.

> *Michael:* A lot of teenagers would say that I'm not wearing the right clothes and kids are going to make fun of me. That's nothing to do with autism. I have my personal beliefs—opinions that I have. I guess if you have autism and you don't overcome it, you aren't able to form opinions. I did care more about others' opinions when I was younger.
>
> When I was younger I thought that you can never recover from autism, but you can recover. Intellectually, I know that there's a self, even if I don't feel there's a self. Therefore, if I know there's a self, I can form some opinions. One of these opinions is that there's a problem with superficialism in the world, like dressing or petty arguments. In the past I felt that my own arguments were never petty, but today I realize that some are petty.

You are extraordinarily intelligent.

> *Michael:* I don't think so.

How would you rate your intelligence on a scale of 1 to 10?

> *Michael [at age 21]:* "5": Average. Nothing takes me off the average. I believe that I'm a self with intellectual aspects. I just don't feel that I'm intelligent.

> *[at age 24]:* I guess I would now rate it higher. There are so many dumb people in the world, dumber than me. I thought people were smarter. Even teachers disappoint me. Last week a teacher I work with said she didn't know what to teach after finals for the last week of school. I suggested a topic and it is disturbing that she couldn't think of that, and she found my idea so novel.

There are many things that make you the person you are composed of: ability, personality, a physical body, etc.

> *Michael:* I know they exist, but I don't feel they exist. I feel that they're lacking, although I know of them.

What things about yourself are you aware of?

> *Michael:* I'm not tall. I'm fat, ugly, annoying, inadequate. I could give you a lot of weaknesses. Autistic people always look in on the world and always want to make sure everything is right, so they're always going to look at weaknesses. Don't ask autistic people for strengths, because you're not going to get an answer, because we only look at weakness.
> My sole focus is the reduction of weakness.

What would you want to change about yourself? Managing autism can't be easy.

> *Michael:* That might be, but that's who I am. I guess I'd want to be less lazy, more motivated to get things done. I don't like getting up in the morning. I love getting into bed at night. I like to sleep.

From what you're saying, it appears that you're constantly battling your weaknesses.

> *Michael:* I guess you can infer that. I'm always evaluating weaknesses, not just to prove myself as a person, but in everyday life.

I've been told that you are always honest and sometimes this honesty can be hurtful to others.

> *Michael:* To me compliments are superficial. I've tried to be diplomatic now that I'm in college, but I take misunderstandings very personally.

Language and communication

Many people associate autism with the lack of language ability which is necessary to express yourself and to be able to connect with others. You have a tremendous command of language.

> *Michael*: You equate autism with the lack of language ability. I equate autism not with language ability, but with the fear of using it. I had the language ability, but I was afraid of its use. That's why it had to be broken down with colorful magnets and different things. You had to present language in a form that quelled my fear.

How does a child overcome the disability or fear so that he or she starts to communicate?

> *Michael*: You never overcome the fear. You have to deal with the fear. Take the fear for what it is, be aware that it's something inside of you—and adjust so you can manage to live life with this fear.
>
> I think that this is a gradual process. Some competence has to be built. Somehow you have to get this person to do something despite the fear once or twice and then it works. Though you always have the fear, you can start to live with it and despite the fear do certain things that the fear would normally not allow you to do. You always fear something's going to happen, but you push yourself to defy that fear each and every time. Possibly, that's just an intellectual effort. The person dealing with the fear, adjusting with it, maybe it's just luck. Everyone doesn't overcome autism so I don't know if it's any more than luck.
>
> My intellectual ability was never a problem. I think I always had the ability to demonstrate language, I just had the fear of rejection in communicating, so I had to be given a medium because my voice was no good. It had to be a medium I was comfortable with, so it was never an intellectual problem.

What was the medium that worked for you?

> *Michael*: The magnet letters. I used them to spell. I wrote sentences, not really whole sentences and it was when I was two or three years old. I mostly wrote my thoughts.

[Michael's mother relates that he used the magnet letters the way a child uses toys. He did spell words at an early age, "mommy," "daddy," "car," but it seemed like playing and not really communicating. He was totally absorbed in this play and would not attend to his surroundings. This behavior caused Michael's parents to wonder if he could hear, but it also proved to them that something was going on inside of him. He was spelling words that he couldn't or wouldn't say.]

Managing life

You have succeeded far better than most autistic individuals do.

> *Michael*: I don't know many autistic individuals. I know I went to school with a lot of people with various problems, and I'm probably in the top quarter. I never thought I wouldn't function in the world. For as long as I can remember, I always thought I'd be an adult, drive a car and have a job.

What do you think has helped you manage your autism?

> *Michael*: I think autistic people have, at least very generally at the beginning, the same ability to learn and to become intellectual. All of them do. The difference between the low ones and high ones, despite fear and the inability to communicate, is how much do they actually learn throughout the course of life, the environment they are raised in, and the stimuli they respond to. That's where the separation occurs.
>
> I think the hospital stay was when I made a final change. If one says that a total cure of autism is being normal—maybe I'm 85 or 90 percent. When I was at the hospital I think I crossed the 50 percent mark and I think I became more normal because of the hospital stay.
>
> I guess I realized that actions have consequences; things that other people would realize younger. Also, I think the hospital woke me up to the severity of punishment for particular actions. Maybe I just became used to functioning in society as it is, as opposed to my own little world, which I still live in. Maybe I just found out about expectations of the world during the hospital stay.

[Michael was nine years old when he was in the hospital; this is described in Chapter 4.]

There were terrible problems with your behavior that required the hospital stay. Do you remember thoughts of self-destruction?

> *Michael*: There are still thoughts of self-destruction. I think it is a consequence of being a viewer and not having a self image—the frustration of being viewed. I think there's always thought of self-destruction.

Did you ever discuss these thoughts with other people, your doctors and family?

> *Michael:* The doctors and psychologists never spoke about autism. They discussed behavior problems going on at home, how to deal with Mom, behavior in the classroom, etc. I was too young to look at it this way until fairly recently. I don't think I could have had this discussion even when I was in high school.

Obsessive behavior

You've struggled with being obsessive.

> *Michael:* Yes. If you obsess too much on one thing you never get on to anything else. It becomes boring. You obsess. You obsess. You obsess.
>
> I obsess more in thoughts, but there are other physical things. Socks pulled up. Shoes tied. My books in my book bag had to be in a certain order. When I was young, I would spend the entire 45-minute class session making sure everything on and in my desk was in the right place and I never did any work. I was always late for the school bus, because I wouldn't leave the classroom until everything was lined up in my bag.

When did that stop?

> *Michael:* One obsession ended and another started. I seemed to have some months of one thing and then it would end. Don't remind me of the things I used to do, because they'll start again. Now closed doors have to be closed all the way. If I see a little space in the doorway, it bothers me. Sometimes you can't get rid of the space. But there are certain things that I ignore and certain things that I can't.

How does this impact on your school work?

> *Michael:* When I read, I often go back and start over. I can't check my work, because if I check it once, I'll check it a million times. I can't move on from there.

Besides compulsive behavior, what would you like to change about yourself?

> *Michael:* All autistic people are outsiders. If there's one thing about the autism that I'd like to get rid of, it would be that. Or even to just be normal; be an insider. I'm not even peripheral; I'm outside.

What's an "insider"?

> *Michael [at age 21]*: The inside of a conversation. The inside of a group. People on the outside always try to get in, but cannot because they are non-existent.

> *[at age 24]*: Over the last few years, I think I have taken further steps in more normal thinking, so I don't think this extremely anymore. However, these comments were my thoughts for many, many years up to that age, and not just due to my short-term thinking as a result of that depression.

Author's reflection

Michael redefines what many think of as being "autistic." He is smart, accomplished, independent, and social. He has a sense of humor, and he cares about others. Michael has been successful regulating his problematic autistic tendencies and every day he consciously makes the decision to be "engaged" with the world around him; and he has succeeded. Yet, Michael reveals many self-doubts and struggles and his self-reflection is both poignant and compelling. Michael describes himself not as a person with strengths, but as an observer, who continually attempts to reduce his weaknesses. There are many challenges that still surround his adult adjustment including: a sense of isolation, poor self-esteem, problems communicating, understanding others, learning social behavior, managing daily life, behaving obsessively and rigidly, and managing episodic depression.

Ironically, Michael finds that as some of his more problematic "autistic" traits have reduced through the years, he has also lost some of the special abilities that he remembers having had. For example, Michael recently bought a compass for his car, when he discovered that his innate "map" for directions is not as perfect as it once was. Also, his rote memory and ability to stay focused are less keen.

The dialogue with Michael reminds us that although Michael experiences success as a young adult, he also struggles with the "ups and downs" that are a perpetual part of autism. But all adults face challenges resulting from many individual factors: personality, ability, environmental circumstances beyond their control, and those that arise from the complexity of adult life in a stressful world. Today, Michael is not so different from everyone else.

Chapter 12

Reviewing my Life for this Book: An Essay from Michael

The process of interviewing for and then editing the different chapters of this book have given me the opportunity to revisit my childhood and also to interpret my past experiences from a more mature perspective. Reading the chapters took me several steps back and made me recall some things that I didn't remember at all. A great deal of the childhood memory has become visual, similar to when you watch a movie and the story moves you. Here the fascinating thing is that you are the story, and you're drawn to it because it's all about you. Looking at my life through the chapters in this book really has given me a frame of reference to reflect on. Intellectually, it also enables me to compare my younger years to the lives of the children I teach and helps me to understand the world of my students.

The process of reviewing my life wasn't always easy or pleasant. Two different kinds of emotional reactions have resulted. The first is disappointment and sadness about my younger years. The second important feeling is anger.

From an adult perspective I have great disappointment in my childhood years and sadness about my struggle. When I was young, I didn't have the knowledge or capacities to put things together. Sometimes I ask myself, "Why me?" Now it all seems so simple, but it wasn't then. I'm surprised at the difficulty I had coming out of my shell. I don't understand why I didn't do things differently then and why things didn't click into place for me sooner.

With autism you can be smart, but you just don't understand the simplest things. Sometimes you have to explain things ten times before an autistic person will understand. Whether this is due to a problem with processing information or perception, I'm not sure. Autistic people need a great deal of positive recognition as well as interaction with others. I believe that they think all the time even though they may not have the words to describe their thoughts.

I'm also sad because there were things in my life that I missed. Other people talk about the positive experiences in their childhood and my social development was so different. I didn't have friends. I wasn't ready to have friends for so long and I just didn't have any knowledge about what friendship means. I didn't participate in the kind of experiences kids have in school every day. I'm not embarrassed about having been in special education, but I realize that today some would judge me, if they knew my history. I know that I was a rowdy kid, and it's okay with me that I was in special education.

There's another part of me that I don't want people to know about and that has to do with the violence and the issues at home. I acknowledge that when I was a young child I was sometimes violent, but I deny that my family's perception of my aggression in later years is accurate. I truly think that they have exaggerated my behavior in the years after the hospitalization. Now I have a far better appreciation for how my family views me, especially my mother and brother. The fact that they all remember me as being so violent is truly hurtful.

For my whole life I rejected contact with others. As I got older and after the hospitalization, I wanted to make the effort to become more normal, to become someone the family would be proud of, but I felt that the family started to ignore me. They could not be bothered with me anymore and I feel that my attempts at complying and growing up were completely rejected. It seems to me that they have blown minor altercations so out of proportion. This shows me that all the good I did was not considered. They wanted me to be perfect and comply and not be heard. They were thinking "We are done working on this. How dare he scream or say something?" Were they thinking that they just wanted to get rid of me totally and no longer have me as even a minor consideration in their day or their lives? I believe that at times there was no effort to listen to or accommodate me and all this occurred at just the time I was beginning to communicate. An autistic person needs to be recognized and guided. My family (particularly my mother) provided much less of this in the adolescent years, inhibiting and, perhaps, almost compromising all the progress that I was making.

The other important emotion from reviewing my life is my anger. I did my fair share of things to other people, but I also think of myself as a victim. Now that I have a better understanding of other people, when there is a disagreement, I can at least view their perspective and understand that there is a reason they feel the way they do. Today, while I might feel disappointed or upset, I rarely have angry feelings, for anger arises out of hopelessness and non-understanding. Unfortunately the exception is my mother. I cannot understand or forgive her severe lack of interest in me and the life I lead since she has assimilated into her "new" family.

I still think of myself not in the same way that others see themselves. My concern is always having to reduce and manage weakness and this is a very important part of me. Today, I do realize that I'm intelligent and I've made some progress toward thinking of myself as "me." Years ago, I talked about myself in the third person, because there really wasn't a "me." I don't do that anymore and now I can refer to myself as "me" and there's a cognitive acknowledgement of my "self" now. I don't think that other people struggle with this lack of a sense of self. I still think of myself as an outsider, who typically observes rather than participates.

I also realize the impact I have had on my family. For example, my parents didn't interact with other families and didn't have the kind of relationships that other families have. We kept everything within our family, including my grandparents, who were like another set of parents, and my aunts and uncles. Regarding my brother, even if I wasn't autistic I know that we are very different kinds of people. My behavior when he was younger had a direct impact on him. I know that I embarrassed him, especially because he always wanted to be conventional and to fit in and be accepted. I've never been like everyone else and today my brother has begun to accept my quirkiness. Now that my brother is growing up and my life has changed, we are no longer from two totally different planets and there are things that we share. There are certainly more parallels in our lives now.

I don't necessarily think that I am the cause of my parents' divorce. My parents stalled their lives while caring for me. It is quite possible the experiences they missed would have provided the positive moments that they needed to stay together. It is also possible that Mom would have divorced my dad sooner except she delayed the progression of her life while caring for me and my brother.

Even today, I feel that at times it would be easier to just retreat from the world. It used to take great determination to just get out of bed each day and decide to be part of the world. This has changed. Now in my job the circumstances are fairly predictable and at least I know the structure of every school day. Unfamiliar circumstances are the worst for me and at one time even being able to say "good morning" to people was a struggle. A lot of that has passed, but I don't cope well with things that are unpredictable and I still don't know how to handle many common social situations.

The families of autistic children are critically important to the child's future. They have to provide as much help as possible. Being autistic is not like having a broken leg that will heal with time. It goes on forever and ever and parents of autistic children have a key role in the child's life throughout the lifespan. But parents should take care of themselves, even if it means denying themselves to their child at times, because they have to preserve their sense of self so that their parental role can be sustained. A parent should not become so immersed with a child that they lose knowledge of society. But vice versa, a parent should not be so immersed with the world at large, that he or she loses basic awareness of the child, as my mom has done over the last several years.

I now realize that my mother burnt out from her life with me. Perhaps if she didn't push herself so far when I was young, she would be different at this point. My mom was extraordinary and put in triple efforts and even that wasn't enough, because I also needed my grandparents and I appreciate the role that all the school people had in my life.

In recent years I've come to recognize the improvements in my life. I truly don't remember the intensity of autism in my childhood, but I do remember being too afraid to say or do something for fear of being rejected, not acknowledged, or told I was wrong. Something got me over much of my fear, but some of it is still apparent today. The hospitalization was a turning point, because before that I assumed that all kids were like me. Being in the hospital changed my thinking and I realized the consequences of my behavior. I changed so drastically at that point. Now I can read about other people like me and this helps me to understand myself and autism better.

My family, especially my mother, gave me the determination to be normal, whatever that means. I haven't met that expectation yet. I thought that when I reached my present age (24) I'd be 110 percent normal. Now I know that I don't want to get to that point, because there are things about me that I really don't want to change and I've modified the idea of who I want to be. I'm a math person, so I would say that I'd like to be approximately 90 percent normal, and the rest would be the quirkiness that I want to keep. I've established friendships, but still feel uncomfortable and don't know what to do in some social situations compared with the average person. I don't like to function in a world without predictability and structure.

People who shared their reflections for this book are all people who have had a positive interest in me. They all wanted the best for me. They balanced many negative things about me with the positives and it seems that for most of them the scales tipped towards the positive side. If you are high functioning and have intellectual ability, it gives you something to compensate for other attributes that you lack.

I know that there is joy in life. I have resources when something goes wrong. There are people I care about and who care about me and there are real friendships. I'm optimistic about my future.

Author's reflection

Michael has come far in his ability to think about his life and candidly discuss and share his emotional reactions. The process of reviewing a tumultuous life had to be difficult for him and, I hope, it has promoted new self-understanding. Arriving at this final essay was complicated. It took interviews, written drafts, editing, and revision to arrive at this "finished" piece composed by both Michael and myself.

There are several issues that Michael raises with which others in the family disagree. Michael continues to discount his aggression in the years after the hospital, while all family members relate that violent behavior continued long after the hospitalization. With his growing size and strength they were truly afraid of the damage an enraged Michael could inflict on himself and others. Michael either cannot come to terms with this aspect of himself, or like other autistic individuals he truly cannot conceive of others' thoughts and reactions.

Contrary to Michael's view, the family feels that he remained the central focus of their lives up until he graduated from college. They acknowledge that Michael's brother was given an abundance of material things to help compensate for the disruption in his life and the incredible amount of attention that Michael was given. However, all family members believe that their lives continued to revolve around their devotion to Michael and especially their need to comply with his demands in order to pacify him to prevent his tantrums. They are saddened that Michael doesn't feel that this is true.

While Michael can intellectually acknowledge the important role his mother had in his early years, he still harbors tremendous anger towards her for now having "abandoned" him for a different life. The change in the family circumstances did not come about until Michael finished college but, even today, he sorely feels the absence of his mother's care. He says that he still needs her and her physical absence from his home indicates that she must no longer be interested in him. Michael acknowledges that his mother was emotionally and physically depleted at the point of deciding to divorce and he recognizes that the marriage was unfulfilling for her. Regardless, Michael cannot forgive the disruption that resulted from the divorce as well as his mother starting a new "chapter" in her life with others. How ironic that Michael advises parents not to devote all of themselves, and all of their time to their children. He understands that this is detrimental to their own well-being and would limit their ability to fulfill continuing parental obligations. Michael advises parents to spread attention to the child across the lifespan so that parents do not become depleted. This is an intellectual understanding, but emotionally it seems that Michael always needed and continues to need a great deal of attention at his request.

Michael's mother does not agree that she has "abandoned" him. Although she is deeply hurt by Michael's anger and distance from her, she is compensated by knowing that in other respects Michael has a life that is full and rewarding. Michael's mother also finds that Michael rebuffs her attempts to include him in her life, because he is unwilling to share her with others about whom he is highly critical. Conversely, Michael feels that his mother feels "entitled" to his joining the new, extended family and this has not occurred. The members of the new family do not have a history with Michael and haven't seen his progress through the years. They also have difficulty truly understanding the nature of autism and recognizing that Michael is autistic in spite of his outward success.

The strength of Michael's personality, his determination and strong-mindedness all contribute to his success. However, autistic individuals often lack flexibility and don't understand others' perspectives and these are lifelong challenges. Perhaps in the future Michael will be able to establish a better relationship with his mother and members of her new family. Family should continue to be an important resource for Michael and his success today is both a reflection of his own ability and of the determination and advocacy of his family, especially his mother.

Michael has come far in developing into a "whole" person who finds meaning in his life. While he still struggles with some things, he realizes that much in his world is continually getting better and this provides him with comfort. Michael has become a very successful person—professionally and socially—especially in view of his disability and compared to the lives of others who are autistic. How wonderful that he is optimistic about his future and finds joy in life!

Knowing Michael has changed my personal and professional life in many deep and rewarding ways. He is a part of me and my family and I cherish our relationship. Most of all, I love, value, and enjoy Michael for the person he is. He makes me laugh and helps me put the important things in life into perspective.

Index